THE PRICE

OF PERFECT

JUSTICE

THE PRICE
OF PERFECT
JUSTICE

*The Adverse Consequences
of Current Legal Doctrine
on the American Courtroom*

MACKLIN FLEMING

Basic Books, Inc. PUBLISHERS

NEW YORK

© 1974 by Basic Books, Inc.
Library of Congress Catalog Card Number: 73–78892
SBN: 465–06314–4
Manufactured in the United States of America
DESIGNED BY VINCENT TORRE
74 75 76 77   10 9 8 7 6 5 4 3 2 1

If we disregard due proportion by
giving anything what is too much for it,
too much canvas to a boat, too much nutriment to a body,
too much authority to a soul,
the consequence is always shipwreck . . .
Plato, *Laws* III, 691.

PREFACE

THE Goddess of Justice is traditionally depicted holding in one hand the scales of justice, with which she weighs the Right, and in the other the sword, with which she executes it. As Jhering has told us, the sword without the scales is brute force, and the scales without the sword are the impotence of law.[1] The sword and the scales belong together, and the law is in phase only when the power with which the Goddess wields the sword is equaled by the skill with which she balances the scales.

In ultimate analysis the law requires compulsion—intelligent, reasoned, measured, and tempered, but compulsion nonetheless. Legal analysts describe the three basic elements in law as the norm, the delict, and the sanction; or in today's terms in civil law: the rule, the violation, and the liability; and in criminal law: the prohibition, the offense, and the punishment. If we remove the element of compulsion from law, what remains may be a perfectly devised system of ethics and morals, but it will not be a working system of law.

This book argues that, in our perpetual adjustment and tinkering with the Goddess's scales in order to strike a perfect balance, we have allowed her sword to rust and her right arm to atrophy; that, as a consequence of this neglect of the compulsive element, the legal system as a whole has been thrown out of kilter and into disarray. In criminal law judges and legislators are hard put to devise suitable sanctions: capital punishment is attacked as cruel and unusual, hard labor is proscribed as involuntary servitude, confinement with loss of privileges is challenged as an infringement of personal right, and money fines are suspect as a denial of equality under the law. Moreover the sanctions that are adopted may never be put into execution because the judicial process finds itself incapable, more or less, of reaching final judgment in its endless preoccupation with minute adjustments of the scales and new combinations of weights in the balance pans.

The present incapacity of the Goddess to dispense justice lies partly in our existing system of courts, partly in the way we use the system, partly in the relationship of the courts to other branches of government, but most particularly in the theoretical view taken by the courts of their own functions. And here we find a striking paradox. For the same courts that refuse to recognize their own capacity to achieve final judgment in a particular cause show little hesitancy in creating new general law by means of judicial decree. And the judges most reluctant to act with authority in the disposition of a particular cause are often those the most eager to function as legislators in the creation of new general law. The chapters that follow describe some of the currently fashionable legal theories that have led to these results, among them theories of perfectibility, retroactivity, parallel review, multiple review, due process of law, and equal protection of the laws. The practical consequences to the judicial process of an unrestrained and untempered application of these theories are examined in particular cases, and suggestions for basic changes in our present judicial system are put forth in the final chapters.

References to judicial opinions are drawn principally from the opinions of the United States Supreme Court, because those opinions are the most important, and from the opinions of state and federal courts in California, because those are the ones with which the author is best acquainted. In referring to specific judicial opinions the author in no way intends to reflect on the abilities of the authors of those opinions, but rather to illustrate the trend of current legal theory and develop the thought expressed by Cardozo that the blunders of courts have their origins in false conceptions of the limits of judicial power.[2] Cardozo in 1924 thought the courts too timid, whereas the author in 1973 finds them bold to the point of recklessness. Somehow, the golden mean continues to elude our grasp.

These chapters focus on those parts of the body of the law that are malfunctioning and sickly, and that need diagnosis and therapy—principally the judicial process. Those parts in good health and good working order —and these include the great bulk of private civil law—have no comparable need for critical analysis and are not discussed.

Los Angeles, 1973   MACKLIN FLEMING

CONTENTS

I

Perfect Justice

II

The Mechanics of Perfect Justice

III

Perfect Justice in Operation

IV

The Price of Perfect Justice

I

Perfect Justice

1

THE IDEAL OF
PERFECTIBILITY

T HE fuel that powers the modern theoretical legal engine is the ideal of perfectibility—the concept that with the expenditure of sufficient time, patience, energy, and money it is possible eventually to achieve perfect justice in all legal process. For the past twenty years this ideal has dominated legal thought, and the ideal has been widely translated into legal action. Yet a look at almost any specific area of the judicial process will disclose that the noble ideal has consistently spawned results that can only be described as pandemoniac. For example, in criminal prosecutions we find as long as five months spent in the selection of a jury; the same murder charge tried five different times; the same issues of search and seizure reviewed over and over again, conceivably as many as twenty-six different times; prosecutions pending a decade or more; accusations routinely sidestepped by an accused who makes the legal machinery the target instead of his own conduct.

Why, we ask ourselves, have such diligent attempts to create a perfect legal order fared so poorly in practice? If a physicist or engineer or musician or cabinetmaker seeks perfection in his work, he may not achieve it, but in making the effort he will elevate his standards and improve the quality of his performance. Should not the same hold true in the operation of a legal order?

The answer, perhaps, may be found in the reason given by Macaulay for the failure of ambitious governments: the government that attempts more than it ought ends up doing less that it should.[1] The contradiction of more producing less in the quest for perfection derives from the nature of

3

perfection as complete conformity to an absolute standard of excellence. Perfection itself carries little meaning until we ask the question—perfection for what? And in pondering the answer we come to realize that perfection implies limitation and selectivity, that the ideal of perfection implies movement in a limited and selective direction. The law cannot be both infinitely just and infinitely merciful; nor can it achieve both perfect form and perfect substance. These limitations were well understood in the past. But today's dominant legal theorists, impatient with selective goals, with limited objectives, and with human fallibility, have embarked on a quest for perfection in all aspects of the social order, and, in particular, perfection in legal procedure.

There is nothing esoteric or mystical about legal procedure. Essentially, it amounts to nothing more than a compilation of means and techniques that have proved effective over the years in handling legal business. Why then, the reader may ask, cannot the subject of legal procedure be left to the lawyers to set to rights at their leisure? A short answer is that more is involved than legal mechanics, for the ubiquitous and expansive nature of modern legal procedure makes it a serviceable vehicle with which to achieve continuing and effective control over modern social policy.

Today's use of legal procedure is no longer limited to adjudication of private controversies and interpretation of traditional legal rights, but extends to the resolution of almost all public issues of the day, which can be brought to life as legal causes and then made to run the gantlet of legal procedure. The process is not only feasible for issues traditionally considered juridical, such as abortion and capital punishment, but it can be brought to bear on issues of general government policy, such as operation of welfare laws, development of natural resources, use of public property, expenditure of public money, management of the armed forces—indeed almost any public policy a partisan desires to challenge. If the legal perfectionists find themselves unable to persuade a majority of voters or legislators of the verity of their particular cause, they may seek to paralyze traffic by an accusation of imperfect procedure. Once in control of a system or function by means of the device of legal procedure, they can then direct the course of subsequent events by imposing impossible procedural demands, in much the same fashion that the king in *Rumpelstiltskin* directed the miller's daughter to spin straw into gold. Since the accordionlike nature of legal procedure can be expanded to cover practically any matter of substance, the perfectionists have acquired a powerful weapon to shape policy and effect change in society along lines of their desire.

Current manifestations of this perfectionist technique are found in every sphere of social activity. In most areas we can muddle along with the consequences of legal perfectionism—welfare moneys can be wasted, construction of new power plants indefinitely delayed, issuance of franchises and licenses postponed, construction of highways and drainage of swamps halted, service in the armed forces avoided—and catastrophe will not engulf the activity involved. But in the field of criminal law, where the impact of this phenomenon has been greatest and where the concept of effective procedure has been almost completely displaced by the ideal of perfect procedure, the consequences have been disastrous.

What happens to criminal procedure when we begin to think in terms of absolutes, in terms of perfect procedure? Perfect procedure requires a perfect tribunal, which in turn demands perfection in court and counsel. Therefore, every criminal cause must be prosecuted by a Thomas Dewey, defended by a James Otis, and tried before a John Marshall. The jury must never have heard of the cause, the parties, the witnesses, and the issues, and must be wholly free from opinions or preconceptions about any proposition of law or fact likely to arise in the trial. The parties must be free to present their contentions to the fullest extent and to best advantage. Each legal and factual contention of possible relevancy must be explored in depth, both exhaustively and repetitively, in order to eliminate the possibility of error from the proceeding. If the trial does not satisfy each of these requirements, then the cause must be tried again.

Yet the elements of effective procedure are interrelated, and perfection in one aspect of procedure can only be achieved at the expense of other elements that go into procedure:

> Ideally, perfect procedure encompasses the right to be heard to best advantage by a tribunal wholly indifferent to every aspect of the cause; practically, an unlimited insistence on a perfectly impartial tribunal, unaffected by any preconception on any aspect of the cause, amounts to a denial of the competency of any tribunal whatever to sit on the cause.

> Ideally, a party should be given an unlimited right to develop his side of the cause; practically, an unlimited opportunity to be heard may foreclose the tribunal from rendering a timely decision.

> Ideally, all evidence and witnesses presented to the tribunal should be of unimpeachable integrity as to content, source, and impartiality; practically, society must often rely on disreputable informers, for the strongest protection against organized thievery lies in the fact that thieves sell each other out.

5

Ideally, the correctness of the tribunal's result should be demonstrable; practically, demonstration of the correctness of any human activity always remains subject to the limitations of human frailty.

The quest for perfection in procedure is comparable to the experience of a man who blows up an inner tube and tries to stuff it into a tire too small for the tube. Just as he gets one side in place, out pops the other. In our pursuit of the will-o'-the-wisp of perfectibility, we necessarily neglect other elements of an effective procedure, notably the resolution of controversies within a reasonable time, at a reasonable cost, with reasonable uniformity, and under settled rules of law.

And here we confirm Macaulay's observation that a system which attempts too much achieves too little. For when we aim at perfect procedure, we impair the capacity of the legal order to achieve the basic values for which it was created, that is, to settle disputes promptly and peaceably, to restrain the strong, to protect the weak, and to conform the conduct of all to settled rules of law. If criminal procedure is unable promptly to convict the guilty and promptly to acquit the innocent of the specific accusations against them, and to do it in a manner that retains public confidence in the accuracy of its results, the deterrent effect of swift and certain punishment is lost, the feeling of just retribution disappears, and belief in the efficacy of the system of justice declines. An overload of court machinery with retrials, rehearings, and collateral proceedings gives us an unworkable system unable to function, like the ostrich that has wings but can't fly, or like the beautiful mockup of the SST that never got off the ground.

The ideal of perfectibility denies the existence of price and cost, and, at least in criminal procedure, relies heavily on the argument that no sacrifice is too great when human life or liberty is involved. Better that a hundred guilty men should go free than that one innocent man be convicted, is the rallying cry of the perfectionists. But this slogan gets us no further than does its obverse—better that one life should be sacrificed that a hundred others may be saved. The plain fact of the matter is that in human affairs we balance the cost of human life against other considerations in almost everything we do, and it is incorrect to say that the sacrifice of human life to attain particular ends is never justified. The real question is one of relative values—is the end in view worth the price it is likely to cost?

This balancing of relative values and weighing of the cost of alternatives takes place in all human activity. Consider a few examples. If we build Golden Gate Bridge across San Francisco Bay, we know that lives will be lost in its construction, and actuarially we can calculate it will cost, say, twenty lives to build the bridge. If we followed the principle that no sacri-

6

fice is too great to save human life, we would cancel plans to construct the bridge and do nothing. But with what consequences? Ferry boats would continue to collide in the fog of San Francisco Bay, and a certain number of passengers would be drowned. Medical patients in Sausalito would lack ready access to the more extensive hospital facilities in San Francisco, and some would die who might otherwise have lived through the use of the bridge. Undoubtedly, after weighing these and other factors we would conclude that the lives it was going to cost to build the bridge would be a worthwhile sacrifice for the common good.

The use of the automobile costs 55,000 lives a year.[2] How many lives would it cost not to use it? Could doctors, hospitals, and fire departments perform their duties with horses? The cost of human life *with* the automobile must necessarily be calculated in relation to its cost *without* the automobile.

DDT has a deleterious effect on wildlife. But in malaria-prone countries such as Ceylon and Thailand, DDT has been the greatest boon of the century and has substantially lengthened the span of human life. To what extent do we ban the manufacture and use of DDT?

Strip mining of coal desolates the countryside and is an abomination, but strip mining is four times safer for the miner than shaft mining; hence its direct cost in human life is only one quarter that of shaft mining.[3] Do we outlaw strip mining at the cost of the extra expenditure of human life that shaft mining entails?

Sometimes the balance of relative values is very direct, as in war, but more often the balance is either concealed or so obscured that we can avoid thinking about it. One example is that of drunk driving. In the 5,000 yearly accident fatalities in California, alcohol is involved in well over half, and half of this alcoholic half involve concentrations above .15 percent blood alcohol, a concentration universally considered intoxicating. It seems demonstrable that the price we pay in California for our tolerance of drunk driving approaches 1,000 lives a year.[4,5] Part of this price is attributable to the procedures we follow to combat drunk driving. Essentially, we take procedures of investigation, inspection, temporary detention, and arrest, procedures designed to cope with the dangers of an intoxicated pedestrian walking on the sidewalk at three miles an hour, and apply them to the driver of a two-ton vehicle traveling on the highway at sixty miles an hour.

Legislative attempts to solve the problem of drunk driving have been hamstrung by rules of procedure geared to meet the problems of another era. One such attempt is the law in California which declares that a driver lawfully arrested for drunkenness who fails to submit to a chemical test for intoxication will have his driver's license suspended for six months (Vehicle Code, § 13353). The obvious purpose of the law is to promptly remove drunk drivers from the highway. This law, however, has been interpreted in such technical fashion that it is easily possible for a driver who has refused to submit to the test to litigate the matter in the courts for a period up to two years, meanwhile retaining his driving privileges and continuing to drive. For example, the driver who *has not* been instructed by the police at the time of his arrest in the exact words of the suspension statute may succeed in avoiding suspension of his driver's license even though he did not submit to the test, while, conversely, the driver who *has* been instructed in the exact words of the statute may argue that the instruction was so technically worded he did not understand it.[6,7] As long as plausible contentions are outstanding and unresolved by the highest courts—a period of roughly two years—the courts consider it unfair to put a six-month driving suspension into effect. In this instance our preoccupation with perfect procedure has largely frustrated the purpose of the statute, which is to promptly remove drunk drivers from the public highway.

Solutions to the problem of drunk driving are available. One solution in effect in Norway and Sweden for many years is to use strict sanctions, including compulsory chemical tests for drivers and mandatory jail sentences for drivers with blood alcohol levels above .05 percent.[8] But to date we have been unwilling in California to adopt strict sanctions, and so we continue to pay a price of approximately 1,000 lives a year for the privilege of driving on the highway with minimum let or hindrance. In this instance the cost in human life appears grossly disproportionate to the value of the procedural benefits obtained.

In comparable fashion it would be possible to compile a rough price list of the cost in human life of various items of procedure. For example, how many narcotic deaths could be prevented by searches on hearsay warrants, how many prevented by wiretapping of suspected narcotic dealers, how many prevented by interrogation of addicts about sources of supply? Would the saving in human life brought about by a particular change in procedure be worth more than the freedom we were giving up? Through such a cost analysis of each item in our procedure we could determine whether a particular item was worth its cost and whether we desired to continue to pay its price. Some items, such as the right to be secure at home against police invasion without warrant at night, would undoubtedly be valued at high worth, and for them we would be willing to pay a high price. Others, such as the right to loiter in the vicinity of public toilets at night without being questioned by the police, would probably be valued at a low worth, and for them we would be willing to pay no more than a low price. By the use of this process of evaluation it would be possible to strike a rough balance between the present worth of a particular procedure and its present cost and then decide whether we wished to continue to pay its price. Human life, obviously, is one of the elements that enter into the equation of price, value, cost, and worth.

But, the perfectionists argue, no sacrifice is too great to assure that in a given case perfect justice will be done. Ignored is the sacrifice of the legal order itself and of the life, liberty, and property of those that the legal order is designated to protect. Ignored also is the necessity that the procedure we follow lend substance to the moral and ethical idea that those who take up the sword shall perish by the sword.

Each time the criminal process is thwarted by a technicality that does not bear on the innocence or guilt of the accused, we trumpet abroad the notion of injustice; and each time a patently guilty person is released, some damage is done to the general sense of justice. Most unfortunate, the perfectionists reply, but we must strive for perfect procedure no matter what the consequences. Repeated enough times the slogan gains currency and becomes dogma. In this way the ideal of justice is transformed into an ideal of correct procedure.

What has occurred during the past twenty years is that the legal theorists in their zeal for perfection in procedure have become prisoners of their own concepts, and in their preoccupation with techniques they have lost sight of the ultimate objectives of a legal system. This Holy Grail of perfectibility has been sought before, and with equally disastrous results. Gibbon tells us that under Roman law at the time of Justinian the expense of the pursuit of law sometimes exceeded the value of the prize, and the fairest rights were abandoned by the poverty or prudence of the claimants.[9] Holdsworth tells us that in nineteenth century England the equity rules aimed at doing complete justice regardless of any other consideration.[10] In describing the collapse of the system he said: "But we have seen that the delays need not have been so great if the ideal of completeness had not been so high. By aiming at perfection the equity procedure precluded itself from attaining the more possible, if more mundane, ideal of substantial justice."

Contemporary legal theorists usually link the theme of perfectibility to a companion theme that courts and the judicial process are the chosen instruments with which to achieve perfectibility. The operation in practice of these twin theories is examined in the chapters that follow.

II

*The Mechanics
of Perfect Justice*

2

PERFECTIBILITY—
THE MOVING FINGER
REWRITES THE PAST

BECAUSE the ideal of perfectibility presupposes conformity to an absolute standard of excellence, it implies universality and uniformity, for if the perfection of one particular standard is assumed, the necessary imperfection of others follows. Since this premise ordains that there is only one correct way of doing things, diversity and heterogeneity of method become suspect. When applied to legal procedure, these theoretical assumptions bring about important consequences, among them the doctrine of retroactivity: the notion that improvements in the law can be applied backward in time as well as forward and an imperfect past thereby restructured to fit the views of the present. But how far do we dip into the past and to what extent do we restructure? Let us examine the operation of retroactivity in specific cases.

In criminal law and criminal procedure the issue of retroactivity arises whenever a court adopts a new criminal rule in a particular case. The new rule will, of course, be applied to all such cases in the future. What the new rule amounts to is the discovery of a better way of handling matters, an improvement in the existing state of the legal art, an adaptation to changed conditions, or an adjustment brought about by obsolescence of former conditions. Yet adoption of the new rule carries the theoretical implication that cases decided under the old rule had been decided under a rule which was only second-best, that is to say a rule less than perfect. If

13

the current litigant receives, and future litigants are entitled to receive, the benefit of the new rule, is it just to deprive past litigants of the benefit of the same rule? From this question arises the tendency to restructure the past.

The tendency to restructure is accelerated when the new rule is based on constitutional doctrine, as almost invariably happens when the new rule has been created by federal courts for mandatory use in state court proceedings. Since almost invariably no change in the text of the Constitution occurs at the time of the creation of the new rule, it can logically be argued that if the new rule is constitutionally compelled today, it was equally compelled yesterday by the same language of the same Constitution. Under the pressure of this argument courts have drifted into the habit of condemning former criminal rules as unconstitutional whenever new improvements in the rules have evolved. Naturally, defendants convicted under the old rules promptly seek redress for convictions under laws and procedures that have been pronounced unconstitutional.

Driven by this logic courts have overturned existing judgments in wholesale fashion. Yet practical necessity eventually brings to a halt the process of perpetual change that is the consequence of an unlimited retroactivity. The resulting compromises have led to a crazy quilt of rules of retroactivity in specific situations under which logical distinctions have all but disappeared. Some new rules are fully retroactive; some are not retroactive at all; some are retroactive in all cases whose judgments are not final; and some are retroactive to specific dates, selected almost at random. The bewildering complexity of the current rules of retroactivity provides criminal lawyers and judges with much of their current business.

The consequences of retroactivity in practice may be seen in *Gideon* v. *Wainwright,* a Florida case in which the United States Supreme Court ruled in 1963 that as a matter of federal constitutional law every indigent felony defendant in the state courts is entitled to the assistance of counsel for his defense. In so ruling the Supreme Court directly overruled its earlier decision to the contrary handed down in 1942.[1] The decision in *Gideon* to extend the right of free counsel to indigent felony defendants makes good sense and is part of a developing progression under which the constitutional right of indigents to free counsel, first applied in capital cases, then extended to felony cases, then to misdemeanor cases,[2] is in the process of extension to certain types of civil cases, among them civil confinement for juveniles, civil confinement of persons for addiction or for mental illness, and child custody disputes.[3] It is not difficult to visualize further extensions of the right of indigents to free counsel in all civil and criminal litigation. This evolution not only reflects the growing wealth and resources of the country and its increased ability to furnish specialized services free of charge but also mirrors the current socializing trend to provide free services in areas heretofore considered within the sphere of private responsibility. Quite obviously, this change represents an adjustment to present-day conditions, a realization that private and volunteer legal services are no longer capable of meeting today's legal needs but must give way to professional state-supported legal aid, just as the nineteenth-century volunteer firefighting associations were replaced by municipal fire departments employing full-time firemen.

But the adoption of a better system of legal aid geared to the needs of the present does not mean that the older system must be anathematized, nor does it require the retrospective holding that those persons whose cases had been finally determined under prior procedures had been unconstitutionally dealt with. Retroactive application of the new procedure in *Gideon,* summarily put into effect by the Supreme Court at the end of 1963,[4] is wrong for at least two reasons. First, the state involved, Florida, had been operating under constitutional law as interpreted up to that time by the ultimate authority on constitutional law—the Supreme Court itself. The characterization of a criminal proceeding as retroactively unconstitutional and void seriously reflects on the integrity and honesty of the law and suggests to those previously convicted that the law is a fraud and they are its innocent victims. Such insinuations ought not to arise each time the Supreme Court changes its view on what is appropriate procedure in the handling of a criminal case. And if the thunder and lightning of retroactive unconstitutionality is routinely called out for each change in criminal procedure, it may not have its full terrorizing effect on occasions when it is genuinely needed.

But the retroactive application of *Gideon* is wrong for a more compelling reason. As a consequence of the decision all inmates of Florida prisons who had been convicted or who had pleaded guilty without counsel became entitled to new trials or to release from prison. Over 6,000 Florida prisoners filed postconviction motions, which led to either new trials or the prisoners' release.[5] In this process much happenstance was bound to occur, for in some instances witnesses would still be available for retrial while in others they would not. At this point the vice of the retroactive application of *Gideon* becomes glaringly apparent. Release from prison has become related to the feasibility of new procedure and been divorced from the merits of the individual case. Release from prison is no longer determined by such rational factors as degree of culpability, amount of rehabilitation, and potential for adjustment to the outside world, but instead has evolved into a process of random selection dependent on wholly fortuitous factors

15

having little connection with the crimes for which the prisoners were committed. Release from prison, instead of being governed by the crime itself and the degree of blameworthiness involved, has been tied to chance factors of procedure. In short, release has become dependent on form and not substance, and the moral lesson of causal relationship between crime and punishment has been displaced by one that suggests the dominance of chance. For those confined in Florida prisons the causal connection between degree of crime and degree of punishment was largely severed.

A few specific examples of the operation of retroactivity will illustrate its irrational and capricious nature. A typical case is that of *Woods,*[6] adjudged a habitual criminal in California in 1959 by reason of his plea of guilty to robbery and his admission of four prior felony convictions. In 1966 Woods sought by petition in the California courts to attack the validity of his prior conviction for auto theft in Nebraska in 1932, on the claim that he had not been furnished counsel in 1932 when he pleaded guilty to the Nebraska charge, and therefore his present status as a habitual criminal should be redetermined in the light of the retroactive application of the rule in *Gideon* that an indigent felony defendant has a constitutional right to court-appointed counsel. Court records of the 1932 Nebraska conviction were ambiguous as to whether Woods had been furnished the counsel to which he was entitled under Nebraska law, but the California Attorney General argued that since Woods had admitted the prior Nebraska conviction at the time he pleaded guilty to the California robbery in 1959, he had waived his right to question the validity of the Nebraska procedure. To this argument the California Supreme Court replied that since *Gideon* had not been decided until 1963, " [n]either petitioner nor his then counsel can be held accountable for failing to raise objections which could only be sustained by reference to cases yet to be determined." The Attorney General urged that the rule of accountability should work both ways, that 1932 court records should not be called upon to set forth matters with greater precision than had been required under the then state of the law, that to do so would be to hold those courts accountable for failing to maintain records of their proceedings in conformity with decisions not yet rendered. "The truth of this observation cannot be denied," the court replied.

> "But neither can it be denied that retrospective application of constitutionally-grounded procedural rules necessarily entails this result. . . . The circumstance that records of long-past convictions are inadequate to accurately determine questions of advice and waiver, while lamentable, is quite irrelevant to the fact that the determination must be made, and made upon the basis of whatever materials are avail-

16

able in the particular case, in light of guidelines heretofore enunci-
ated by the United States Supreme Court." (64 Cal. 2d at p. 8)

The superior court in California was then directed to hold a hearing in
1966 to determine whether Woods in Nebraska in 1932 had been advised
of and had intelligently waived his right to counsel.

Nor is the operation of the principle of retroactivity restricted to a single determination in each case. Once a final judgment has been vacated on
one ground, the case is normally reclassified as one currently pending, and
other rules of retroactivity applicable to judgments not yet final may come
into play. Consider *People* v. *Boyden,*[7] where a 1960 affirmance by the
appellate court of a judgment of conviction for a 1959 armed robbery was
set aside in 1964 because of the retroactive application of the 1963 decision of the United States Supreme Court in *Douglas* v. *California* that free
counsel must be furnished on appeal.[8] Justice Roy L. Herndon of the California Court of Appeal had this to say:

> "It is with almost melancholy nostalgia that we recall how only five
> years ago it was possible to sustain a judgment of conviction entered
> in such a clear case of unquestionable guilt and to accomplish it with-
> out undue strain. Today, however, the situation is vastly changed. Al-
> though appellant's conviction was effected by police and judicial pro-
> cedures which conformed in every respect with the requirements of
> then established law, he presently argues that he was deprived of sev-
> eral fundamental constitutional rights that demand reversal of the
> judgment herein." (237 Cal. App. 2d at pp. 696–97)

Boyden's judgment of conviction was again affirmed in 1965. However,
another new rule promulgated in 1967, the requirement of the United
States Supreme Court in *Chapman* v. *California* [9] that error be nonprejudicial *beyond a reasonable doubt,* brought a third appellate review of the
judgment, and for the third time the judgment of conviction was affirmed.

There is no limit to the number of years retroactivity can travel backward. In *People* v. *Brunson,*[10] a 1938 judgment of conviction for robbery
was reversed thirty-one years later, in 1969, because of the retroactive effect of *Bruton* v. *United States,*[11] a 1968 decision of the United States Supreme Court holding that the admission in evidence of a codefendant's extrajudicial statement violated a defendant's constitutional right to
confrontation. In reversing the 1938 judgment in 1969 Justice Lester Wm.
Roth of the California Court of Appeal wrote:

17

"Appellant's trial was not a miscarriage of justice. At his trial, appellant was afforded his full constitutional rights as such rights were interpreted by the courts prior to *Bruton* and *Hill*. However, these cases make retroactive the prohibition against receiving in evidence at a joint trial the unedited confessions of one codefendant, even though accompanied by proper limiting instructions." (1 Cal. App. 3d at p. 235)

These examples of retroactivity could be multiplied indefinitely, for a large part of the work of appellate courts today consists of retroactive and collateral review of cases whose judgments have long been final.

Often the application of retroactivity becomes nothing more than an exercise in form. For example, in 1969 the California Supreme Court in *People* v. *Daniels* narrowed its prior interpretation of the crime of kidnapping-for-robbery to exclude from the reach of the crime mere incidental movement of a victim during the course of a robbery.[12] The new interpretation was designed to limit convictions for kidnapping to instances of genuine abduction and to prevent routine escalation of the crime of robbery into the crime of kidnapping. This change in the interpretation of the law was soundly conceived, for as a result of experience it had become clear that the danger of a true kidnapper's escaping just punishment because of a narrow interpretation of the law was outweighed by the tendency of prosecutors to charge kidnapping in instances where only the charge of robbery was warranted. So far, all to the good.

However, in 1971 the California Supreme Court made its new interpretation of the crime of kidnapping-for-robbery retroactive to 1951. The dissenting justices on the court argued that dangerous criminals would be turned loose as a result of the decision. Not so, the majority justices replied: no dangerous criminals would be released, since all persons convicted of the crime of kidnapping-for-robbery would also have been convicted of the crime of robbery. If this surmise of the majority justices had proved correct, the retroactive application of the new rule to final judgments would have served no substantial purpose that could not have been better served by executive action of the Adult Authority or the Governor, for under California's Indeterminate Sentence Law the Adult Authority fixes the length of a felon's sentence and controls the term actually served, and the Governor, of course, has power to grant reprieves, pardons, and commutations of sentence.[13,14] Administratively, the sentences of those convicted under the earlier interpretation of the law could have been adjusted by the Adult Authority to achieve a harmonious result with the court's new interpretation of the kidnapping statute.

Unfortunately, the surmise of the majority justices that all persons con-victed of kidnapping-for-robbery would also have been convicted of rob-bery proved incorrect, for in 1971 the court found it necessary to declare that the granting of retroactive relief under *Daniels* could be conditioned on the imposition of punishment that might have been imposed for another offense but which had not been imposed because of the kidnapping sen-tence.[15] To accomplish this end, said the California Supreme Court, a court could order a suspended sentence into effect, vacate the reversal of a conviction set aside to avoid double punishment and impose sentence on the reinstated conviction, impose sentence for a lesser offense included in the accusatory pleading, and even recharge and retry offenses initially charged but subsequently dismissed. In effect, the past could be rewritten completely.

What happened here was that the court forgot there were other organs of government capable of dealing with problems that might arise from the court's changed interpretation of the kidnapping statute. In trying to con-trol everything itself the court promptly ran into difficulties. To extricate itself, it turned the courts into a species of administrative agency exercis-ing both prosecutorial and commutative powers.

In picking and choosing among the bewildering variety of possible rules for retroactivity the courts have entered foursquare into the field of legisla-tion. Justice Harlan of the United States Supreme Court, referring to what he called the Court's ambulatory retroactivity doctrine, said in 1971:

> "What emerges from today's decisions is that in the realm of constitu-tional adjudication in the criminal field the Court is free to act, in ef-fect, like a legislature, making its new constitutional rules wholly or partially retroactive or only prospective as it deems wise. I com-pletely disagree with this point of view. . . . Finality in the criminal law is an end which must always be kept in plain view. . . . [T]he Court in deciding these cases seems largely to have forgotten the limi-tations that accompany its functions as a court of law." [16]

The Transitoriness of Final Judgment

An important consequence of the development of retroactivity has been the blurring of the authority of a final judgment. The sharp focus of a judgment as a final determination in an action of the rights of the parties has faded into an ambiguous depiction rendered in the style of subjective impressionism. Even in theoretical form the concept of a final judgment has been discarded in certain cases, among them federal postconviction remedies, about which Justice Brennan of the United States Supreme Court has declared that "[c]onventional notions of finality of litigation have no place where life or liberty is at stake and infringement of constitutional rights is alleged." [17]

This view of the provisional nature of a final judgment has now been introduced into civil cases. For example, in *Gondeck* v. *Pan American World Airways, Inc.* the United States Supreme Court denied a petition for hearing in June 1962 and denied a petition for rehearing in October 1962, at which time the judgment in favor of Pan American became final.[18] Three years later, in 1965, the Supreme Court granted a subsequent petition for rehearing and reversed the judgment in favor of Pan American on the ground that finality of litigation must yield to the interests of justice and the decision be made to conform to later rulings. In this instance the court acted to reinstate an award in favor of Gondeck against Pan American. The latter, of course, is a rich corporation and able to pay. But it is inconceivable that the court would have acted as it did if the situation of the parties had been reversed, inconceivable to imagine that the court would have reversed a final judgment of three years' standing in favor of Gondeck to remedy an injustice against Pan American.

The weakness of retroactivity thus appears, for justice can only be rewritten after the fact at the expense of other important elements in law. Those sacrificed in *Gondeck* were uniformity of treatment by the law and equality of persons before the law, for it is quite evident that one party was treated differently from the way the other party would have been treated and that the even-handedness of justice was dispensed with in order to secure a particular result. In this instance equal justice under law was made dependent upon the identity of the parties.

One result of this erosion of the finality of judgment in the United States Supreme Court has been the phenomenon of the perpetual petition for hearing. In one instance a hearing in that court was sought and denied in the same case four times, and on the fourth time two justices voted in favor of a hearing.[19]

In criminal law the scope of relitigation of final judgments enlarges yearly. For example, in the case of *Nelson* v. *George*, decided by the United States Supreme Court in 1970, Nelson, while serving a sentence for robbery in California, insisted on his right to stand trial on another robbery charge pending against him in North Carolina.[20] Nelson was given his trial in North Carolina, he was convicted of robbery there, and his conviction was affirmed by the North Carolina Supreme Court. Nelson, having in the meantime been returned to California to complete the service of his California robbery sentence, then sought a hearing in the federal district court in California to challenge the validity of his North Carolina conviction for robbery and the validity of the detainer filed against him by North Carolina authorities. The United States Supreme Court declared that the federal district court in California had jurisdiction to consider Nelson's claims, in that the North Carolina detainer was a form of constructive custody, but that the federal district court in California should stay its action until the California state courts had acted on Nelson's claims. The decision thus visualizes three sets of reviews, for the validity of a final judgment of the North Carolina courts is to be reviewed by two other sets of tribunals, first by the state courts in California, and then by the federal courts in California.

Activity of this sort assumes the possibility of achieving ultimate certainty in litigation by eliminating the possibility of mistake. Yet certainty is an illusion, and mistake remains a possibility, no matter how frequent the reviews. Judge Learned Hand made the point with his observation that "due process of law does not mean infallible process of law." [21] If we insist that the object of review is to eliminate the possibility of mistake, we condemn ourselves to endless litigation that can never produce finality of judgment. The issue was well put by Justice Jackson of the United States Supreme Court in 1953:

> "Whenever decisions of one court are reviewed by another, a percentage of them are reversed. That reflects a difference in outlook normally found between personnel comprising different courts. However, reversal by a higher court is not proof that justice is thereby better done. There is no doubt that if there were a super-Supreme Court, a substantial proportion of our reversals of state courts would also be reversed. We are not final because we are infallible, but we are infallible only because we are final." [22]

21

3

PERFECTIBILITY AND PARALLEL

SYSTEMS OF COURTS

OPERATING ON THE

SAME SUBJECT MATTER

U_{NDER} the full flowering of perfectibility every criminal cause may now be completely reviewed at least twice. We take up the manner by which this dual review evolved.

In our federal scheme of government the American judicial system is comprised of two sets of courts, one maintained by the national government as a forum of limited jurisdiction for the enforcement of federal rights, the other by the state governments as a forum of general jurisdiction for the determination of all other rights. Within this system the United States Supreme Court performs two functions. It is the court of last resort for the federal courts and the ultimate authority on the division of power among the branches of the federal government; and it is the final arbiter of the federal constitutional system and the resolver of conflicts between federal and state authority. The theoretical operation of the federal courts within this judicial system has been described by Justice Black:

"While the lower federal courts were given certain powers in the 1789 Act, they were not given any power to review directly cases from state courts, and they have not been given such powers since that time. Only the Supreme Court was authorized to review on direct appeal the decisions of state courts. Thus from the beginning we have had in this country two essentially separate legal systems. Each system proceeds independently of the other with ultimate review in this Court of the federal questions raised in either system." [1]

Since Appomattox, in 1865, state sovereignty has been little more than a political slogan, but its continuing use in official and unofficial rhetoric reflects a deep-seated and widespread desire to retain regional governments possessing a high degree of autonomy and the capacity to exercise authority without reference to or dependence upon the national government.

In the field of criminal law a strict demarcation line between the two court systems was generally observed until about twenty years ago, when the United States Supreme Court began to expand the scope of federally protected rights, principally through the use of the due process and equal protection clauses of the Fourteenth Amendment. Those clauses, said the court, impose on state governments and on state courts most of the specific limitations imposed on the national government by the Constitution. Hand-in-hand with this expansion of federal rights there arose the notion that only judges of the federal court system were fully competent to adjudicate and protect federal rights. Since federally protected rights, or at least claimed federally protected rights, soon came to include all aspects of state criminal procedure, and since only federal courts could fully protect federal rights, in short order state criminal procedure in its entirety became reviewable in the federal courts. In theory, the scope of this review is restricted to federal constitutionality. In practice, the review has become unlimited and now embraces the entire body of state criminal law.

The year 1953 saw the beginning of this expansion with the decision of the Supreme Court in *Brown* v. *Allen*.[2] The court ruled that a defendant in a state criminal cause, whose conviction had been affirmed on direct appeal in the state courts and been rejected for hearing by the United States Supreme Court, could apply to a federal district court on habeas corpus for review of his claim that his federal constitutional rights had been withheld in the state proceedings. And if the federal district court should deny his petition for habeas corpus he could appeal that denial to the higher federal courts. In effect, under the authority of *Brown* v. *Allen* a state court defendant can obtain two sets of reviews of his conviction, for should he fail to overturn his conviction in the state courts on direct appeal, he may apply for relief in the federal courts under the banner of habeas corpus.

Nevertheless, the court in *Brown* v. *Allen* cautioned that the authority of a second review should be sparingly exercised. And in a concurring opinion Justice Frankfurter emphasized the need for restraint in the exercise of this new authority because " [a]buse of the writ may undermine the orderly administration of justice and therefore weaken the forces of authority that are essential for civilization." Yet Frankfurter remained convinced the new writ would be used with restraint, and he concluded it was ". . . a baseless fear, a bogeyman, to worry lest State convictions be upset by allowing district courts to entertain applications for habeas corpus on behalf of prisoners under State sentence."

Justice Jackson, disagreeing with the court's decision, foresaw grave dangers in using the writ of habeas corpus, whose historic function had been to relieve detention by executive authority, as a device to entertain collateral attacks on state criminal judgments. He observed:

> "The generalities of the Fourteenth Amendment are so indeterminate as to what state actions are forbidden that this Court has found it a ready instrument, in one field or another, to magnify federal, and incidentally its own, authority over the states. The expansion now has reached a point where *any state court conviction, disapproved by a majority of this Court, thereby becomes unconstitutional* and subject to nullification by habeas corpus.
>
> "This might not be so demoralizing if state judges could anticipate, and so comply with, this Court's due process requirements or ascertain any standards to which this Court will adhere in prescribing them. But they cannot. . . . [I]t is prudent to assume that the scope and reach of the Fourteenth Amendment will continue to be unknown and unknowable, that what seems established by one decision is apt to be unsettled by another, and that its interpretation will be more or less swayed by contemporary intellectual fashions and political currents." (Italics added.) (344 U.S. 443, at p. 534)

Jackson's warnings found no audience with his colleagues, and in 1963 the Supreme Court further broadened the scope of dual criminal review by its decisions in *Townsend* v. *Sain* and in *Fay* v. *Noia*.[3] All restrictions on habeas corpus as a further review of final state judgments of conviction were abandoned, and the Supreme Court decreed that a federal district court must grant an evidentiary hearing whenever a claim of violation of federal right has been stated on the face of a petition. In holding in *Townsend* v. *Sain* that federal courts should conduct evidentiary hearings to relitigate issues previously litigated in the state trial courts, affirmed on appeal in the state supreme courts, and denied a hearing in the United States Supreme Court, Chief Justice Warren declared that a federal court in habeas corpus must hold an evidentiary hearing whenever an applicant has not received "a *full* and *fair* evidentiary hearing in a state court." He then promulgated the following rule:

> "In other words a federal evidentiary hearing is required unless the state-court trier of fact has after a *full* hearing *reliably* found the *relevant* facts." (Italics added.) [4]

This rule, he added, superseded anything the court had said earlier in *Brown* v. *Allen.* This remarkable rule contains not one, but three, weasel words, i.e., words susceptible of qualitative interpretation. Whether a hearing is *full* [and *fair*] involves a qualitative judgment; whether a finding is *reliable* involves another; whether facts are *relevant* involves a third. Warren then delineated a series of detailed procedural rules for the guidance of district judges, and after repeating his basic rule he declared:

> "If he [the district judge] concludes that the habeas applicant was afforded a *full* and *fair* hearing by the state court resulting in *reliable* findings, he may, and ordinarily should, accept the facts as found in the hearing. *But he need not.* In every case he has the power, constrained only by his sound discretion, to receive evidence bearing upon the applicant's constitutional claim." (Italics added.) (372 U.S. 293, at p. 318)

Thus was given to every federal district court a roving commission to intervene in any state criminal case that caught its fancy, either as to law or as to fact. And in any case that failed to satisfy any one of the three weasel words of the rule in *Townsend* v. *Sain,* the district court was required to intervene and conduct an evidentiary hearing. The finality of every state judgment of conviction thereby received a wound not so deep as a well nor so wide as a church door but large enough to become undone.

In the companion case of *Fay* v. *Noia* the Supreme Court declared that habeas corpus is available to remedy any kind of restraint contrary to fundamental law. Conventional notions of finality in criminal litigation, said the court, cannot deny the fullest opportunity for plenary federal judicial review, and therefore petitioner need not have exhausted his remedies under state law and need not have appealed his conviction. State procedural rules, said the court, must yield to overriding federal policy.

In dissent, Justice Clark declared:

". . . the effective administration of criminal justice in state courts receives a staggering blow. . . . Essential to the administration of justice is the prompt enforcement of judicial decrees. After today state judgments will be relegated to a judicial limbo, subject to federal collateral attack—as here—a score of years later despite a defendant's willful failure to appeal." (372 U.S. 391, at p. 446)

Under the mandate of these rulings the scope of federal review of state criminal proceedings has entered a phase of unlimited expansionism. Something close to full federal control over a state's procedures for the administration of its criminal justice has been achieved, under the rubric that conventional notions of finality of litigation have no place where life or liberty is at stake and infringement of constitutional rights is alleged. A federal court may now review any confinement under a state judgment, may excuse a failure to exhaust state remedies, may try facts anew, and may disregard a prior denial of habeas corpus in order to serve the ends of perfect justice.

The consequence of these decisions has been to make all criminal cases in the state courts susceptible to two complete sets of reviews. To cite a few examples:

Oregon: An issue involving admissibility of evidence in a murder case was successively examined by the Oregon state court, the Oregon Supreme Court, the federal district court, the federal court of appeals, and the United States Supreme Court—a total of five reviews.[5]

Pennsylvania: An issue of search and seizure in a robbery case was successively examined by the Pennsylvania state court, by another Pennsylvania state court, by the Pennsylvania appellate courts, by the federal district court, by the federal court of appeals, and by the United States Supreme Court—a total of six reviews.[6]

Georgia: An issue of the admissibility of hearsay evidence in a murder case was examined by the Georgia state court and by the Georgia Supreme Court, and a hearing was denied by the United States Supreme Court; thereafter the same issue was again examined by the federal district court, the federal court of appeals, and the United States Supreme Court—a total of six reviews.[7]

Dual review in the garb of constitutional right has become such a commonplace it is now routine. But in recent years a further complication has been introduced into the system. If before trial the defendant in a state prosecution avers the state is about to invade his federal rights (either because its procedure is, or may be, defective under federal constitutional standards, or because its substantive law is, or may be, contrary to the federal constitution), he has positioned himself to argue that the normal system of review is inadequate, that he should not be required to stand trial under state law and then vindicate his federal rights under federal habeas corpus, and therefore the federal district court should enjoin his state prosecution in advance of any trial.[8] By use of this technique a defendant prosecuted under state law may ignore the state proceedings altogether and initiate federal proceedings to enjoin his prosecution. If he is unsuccessful in the federal district court, he may appeal to the court of appeals and then seek a hearing in the United States Supreme Court.

As a consequence of this dual review, state enforcement of criminal law has fallen into a condition that may charitably be described as chaotic. With parallel systems of courts operating on identical subject matter, a defendant can switch back and forth from one system to the other as his interests dictate, and, if fortune smiles, he may succeed in setting one system of courts in contention with the other. These maneuvers, of course, do not occur in every case, for only the celebrated case, the extensively publicized case, the case defended by a special-interest group, or the case of an accused with resources of his own or the support of a group with resources of its own, can stand the cost of such duplicitous litigation. Such a group may be a trade association (American Book Publishers Council), a labor union (Teamsters Union), a corporation (General Electric), a racial interest group (NAACP), a special-interest group (American Civil Liberties Union), a lobbyist group (Sierra Club), a political group (Communist Party), or attorneys who have adopted a particular cause as their hobby and made it their own. A defendant who secures such backing may postpone the day of final judgment to Armageddon.

The consequence of dual review has been an algebraic multiplication of collateral litigation. From 1940 to 1970 petitions from state prisoners seeking habeas corpus relief in the federal courts increased from 89 to over 12,000.[9] Judge J. Edward Lumbard of the federal court of appeals that sits in New York calls this judge-made business, and about it has said:

> "For all our work on thousands of state prisoner cases I have yet to hear of one where an innocent man had been convicted. The net result of our fruitless meddling in search of the non-existent needle in the ever-larger haystack has been a serious detriment to the administration of criminal justice by the states." [10]

Judge Lumbard's conclusion coincides with that of the author and of judges with whom the author has discussed the problem. Rather than resulting in the release of innocent men, such review merely brings about an endless rehash of events having some slight tangential relationship to the procedures used in the judgment under attack but none whatsoever to the merits of the cause. Consider the details of a representative case, the *Bates* and *Chavez* proceedings: [11]

Six persons died as a result of the throwing by Bates and Chavez of five gallons of gasoline and lighted matches into the Mecca Bar in Los Angeles on the night of 4 April 1957. Bates, Chavez, and others had been denied service at the bar and ejected for creating a disturbance. Swearing to get even, they purchased five gallons of gasoline in an open bucket, returned to the bar, threw the gasoline on the floor, and then threw a book of lighted matches on the gasoline. In the resulting flash fire five persons were killed by carbon monoxide, and a sixth was killed by asphyxia and burns. A jury convicted Bates and Chavez of six counts of murder and one count of arson, and death sentences were imposed. The judgments were affirmed in 1958 by the California Supreme Court, and hearings were denied in 1959 by the United States Supreme Court. Thus terminated the direct review of the case.

Collateral review immediately began in the federal courts with the filing by Bates and Chavez in 1959 of petitions for habeas corpus. Their petitions were denied by the district court, but in June 1960 the federal court of appeals ordered the district court to consider two issues—whether the written transcripts of orally recorded statements of the defendants were, as claimed, grossly inaccurate, and whether the photographs of the bodies of the victims were, as claimed, so excessively gruesome that their use amounted to prejudicial error.

Thereafter the district court found that the transcripts were substantially accurate and that the photographs were not excessively gruesome and denied the petitions for habeas corpus. This denial was affirmed by the federal court of appeals in 1962, and a hearing was denied by the United States Supreme Court.

In 1963, after an unsuccessful petition for a writ of habeas corpus in the California Supreme Court, Bates and Chavez filed new petitions for habeas corpus in the federal district court. Hearings on those petitions were held during 1964, and in June 1966 the petitions were denied.

Meanwhile the Governor of California commuted Bates' sentence to life imprisonment without possibility of parole and commuted Chavez's sentence to life imprisonment.

In 1967 the federal court of appeals affirmed the district court's denial of habeas corpus. But in 1968 the United States Supreme Court vacated the decision of the court of appeals and remanded the case for further consideration in the light of two recent Supreme Court decisions: *Burgett* v. *Texas,* a 1967 ruling that a defendant's earlier conviction while unrepresented by counsel cannot be used to support guilt or to enhance punishment, and *Bruton* v. *United States,* a 1968 holding that the admission of incriminating extrajudicial statements of a codefendant violates the defendant's right to cross-examination even though the jury has been instructed to disregard the statements with respect to the defendant himself.

In November 1971 the federal district court, in which the case had made its home for more than a decade, determined that neither the use of prior convictions to impeach the veracity of Bates' testimony nor the use of statements of codefendants in the cause amounted to prejudicial error, and the court again denied the petitions for habeas corpus. In 1973 an appeal from this denial was pending in the federal court of appeals. Should these issues be authoritatively resolved against defendants, doubtless new retroactive procedural issues will continue to be raised in the federal courts. It has never been controverted that Bates threw the gasoline on the floor of the Mecca Bar, that Chavez threw a book of lighted matches on the gasoline, and that six persons died in the ensuing holocaust. But sixteen years later interest in the innocence or guilt of Bates and Chavez of the murder of six persons in the Mecca Bar in 1957 has been wholly superseded by questions of correct procedure and of the retroactive application of correct procedure to a case where proof of guilt has always been overwhelming.

In its preoccupation with perfection in procedure the law has lost sight of its objectives. Perhaps Bates and Chavez have rehabilitated themselves. Perhaps their present potentiality for useful citizenship is good. Perhaps their exemplary conduct in prison has earned them the privilege of release. If these questions can be affirmatively answered, then it may well be that Bates or Chavez or both should be released from prison. The issues would be appropriate and useful subjects for inquiry. But to root around and worry old issues—such as the degree of gruesomeness of photographs in a trial conducted years earlier or the effect that Bates' prior convictions had on the credibility of his testimony before the jury sixteen years ago— couples release from prison to wholly fortuitous factors dependent on evolving views of correct procedure.

Meanwhile, like a perpetually reopened wound, the claim of unconstitutional conviction remains pending and unsettled. As a consequence of such uncertainty of adjudication many in our prison population can comfortably continue to believe themselves martyrs to the tyranny of an unjust legal system and thus avoid acceptance of any personal responsibility for the consequences of their acts—in the instance of Bates and Chavez the deaths of six innocent persons.

No detail of state procedure is too insignificant to acquire immunity from retroactive review. In *Whiteley* v. *Warden,* the United States Supreme Court in 1971 overturned petitioner's 1965 judgment of conviction for breaking and entering, a judgment which had become final on its affirmation by the Supreme Court of Wyoming in 1966.[12] Habeas corpus must be issued, said the court, because the warrant for petitioner's arrest in 1964 had not been supported by an affidavit setting forth sufficient facts to furnish probable cause for the issuance of the warrant, and consequently the stolen property found in petitioner's automobile at the time of his arrest should not have been received in evidence at petitioner's trial. Justice Black, dissenting, found probable cause for the arrest, and characterized the decision as "a gross and wholly indefensible miscarriage of justice," one calculated to make people believe the Supreme Court "enjoys frustrating justice by unnecessarily turning professional criminals loose to prey upon society with impugnity." After pointing out that ten judges had consistently and unanimously rejected petitioner's claim, he concluded that the reversal of the judgment amounted to "a travesty of justice."

The present situation has been summarized by George Cochran Doub, former Assistant Attorney General of the United States:

> "Conviction in the state courts now has become merely the starting point of interminable litigation. State appeals are followed by successive petitions for federal habeas corpus and successive federal appeals. What is involved is a repetitious, indefinite, costly process of judicial screening, rescreening, sifting, resifting, examining and reexamining of state criminal judgments for possible constitutional error. . . . No other nation in the world has so little confidence in its judicial systems as to tolerate these collateral attacks on criminal court judgments. . . . This comparatively new concept of federal habeas corpus has dangerously prejudiced the delicate balance of federal-state relations and has seriously degraded the authority of the states and their judicial tribunals." [13]

It should be added that this dual review has also paralyzed the ability of state criminal law to function effectively in important and celebrated cases. In turn this paralysis has further lowered in public esteem the authority of the states and their judicial tribunals—to the ultimate injury of the judicial process in its entirety.

30

Parallel Systems—the Glory of
Federal Habeas Corpus

Some commentators, recognizing the disruption brought about by federal review of state criminal judgments, would nevertheless retain federal review in certain instances. For example, Judge Henry J. Friendly, in his article "Is Innocence Irrelevant? Collateral Attack on Criminal Judgments," called for restrictions on the use of federal habeas corpus for collateral attacks on state judgments of conviction, but he would retain the use of the writ where colorable (i.e., plausible) claims of innocence are presented or where the attack concerns "the very basis of the criminal process." Federal habeas corpus should always be available, said Judge Friendly, to vacate a conviction in the state courts on evidence known by the prosecution to be perjured. In support of this proposition he referred to the case of *Miller* v. *Pate,* decided by the United States Supreme Court in 1967, as one of the glories of federal habeas corpus for state prisoners.[14] Since the *Miller* case was the principal example given to support this view, the case deserves a careful look.[15]

The *Miller* case arose from the rape-murder of an eight-year-old girl in Canton, Illinois, in 1955.[16] A concrete block and bloodstained clothing were found near the scene of the crime, and after the crime became known a witness named Betty Baldwin reported to the authorities that petitioner Miller had told her he was responsible for the little girl's death. Miller fled from Canton and was arrested two days later en route to Detroit. Thereafter he signed a full confession to the crime and admitted ownership of the clothing, including some shorts, found near the scene of the crime. Miller was convicted by a jury of murder and sentenced to death, and the judgment was affirmed by the Illinois Supreme Court in 1958. That court rejected an attack on the admissibility of Miller's confession, finding that the questioning which led to the confession had not been coercive. It also concluded that proof of guilt was "overwhelming." The United States Supreme Court denied hearing and rehearing in 1958.

A postconviction petition under Illinois law was dismissed in the trial court, the dismissal was affirmed by the Supreme Court of Illinois, and hearing and rehearing were denied by the United States Supreme Court. A second petition in the state trial court was also dismissed, this dismissal was affirmed by the Supreme Court of Illinois in 1961, and hearing was denied by the United States Supreme Court. Miller then applied for habeas corpus in the federal district court. His petition was dismissed, the dismissal was affirmed by the federal court of appeals, and hearing and rehearing were denied for the fourth time by the United States Supreme Court.

In 1963 a hearing was held in the state court on the issue of Miller's then mental condition, and a jury found him sane. That same year he applied for executive clemency and commutation of the death penalty, and his application was denied.

In 1963 Miller again applied for habeas corpus in the federal district court, asserting that in violation of his constitutional rights his confession had been improperly received in evidence, the prosecution had suppressed testimony favorable to him and knowingly used perjured testimony against him, and the prosecution witness Betty Baldwin had recanted her testimony. After a hearing the federal district court found that the confession was valid and had not been coerced, no new evidence had been produced that had not been reasonably available to Miller at the time of trial, the prosecutors had not knowingly presented perjured testimony against Miller nor had they suppressed testimony favorable to him nor had they deprived him of any of his federal constitutional rights, and the evidence presented by petitioner's expert that some of the reddish spots on the shorts were paint spots was not new testimony, "inasmuch as there had never been any dispute but what the shorts did contain paint spots."

> "The court finds that the evidence presented by petitioner's expert which tended to establish that some of the reddish-brown discolored spots on the shorts, State's Exhibit three (3) at the trial, were paint spots was not new testimony, inasmuch as there had never been any dispute but what the shorts did contain paint spots. The expert in question, on cross examination, stated that he was not qualified to say whether there were blood stains on the shorts at the time they were examined eight years ago and he admitted that blood disintegrates within a few days." (226 F. Supp. 541, 545)

The district court declared that if it had been the finder of fact, it would have found Miller guilty on the circumstantial evidence and on his confession without regard to the testimony of Betty Baldwin. However, said the district court, in view of Betty Baldwin's recantation of her testimony the court was unable to determine how the jury would have decided the case without her evidence. Accordingly, the court issued a writ of habeas corpus, concluding that "even though this court has found that the petitioner

32

had a fair trial in every respect and that his constitutional rights were in no way violated" the writ of habeas corpus should issue, and petitioner should be discharged or retried.

The federal court of appeals reversed this order, holding that in the absence of any violation of federal constitutional rights the district court had no power to issue the writ.

Certiorari was granted by the United States Supreme Court in 1966, and that court found itself in the following position: the federal district court had specifically found and ruled there were no violations of federal constitutional rights in the case; the reason given by the district court for overturning the judgment of conviction and issuing a writ of habeas corpus, viz., doubt about the persuasiveness of the evidence to a jury in the absence of the testimony of the recanting witness, was on its face an improper reason for the issuance of a federal writ, since the sufficiency of the evidence is a question for determination by the state courts. The cause, however, was a death penalty case.

The Supreme Court in effect turned itself into a trial court for the purpose of finding the facts. It sent for Exhibit 3, the shorts, and on examining them found them covered with paint. The court then adopted the testimony of petitioner's expert in the habeas corpus hearing in 1963 that at the time of the hearing he had not found blood on the shorts as a result of his examination of ten threads of the garment. The court then declared it had been highly prejudicial for the prosecution to refer in argument to Exhibit 3 as blood-stained shorts when in fact they contained paint. From this the court concluded the prosecution had misrepresented the evidence by referring to Exhibit 3 as blood-stained when in fact it was paint-stained and that " [t]he prosecution deliberately misrepresented the truth." Misrepresentation of the truth is equivalent to knowing use of false evidence, said the court, and the Fourteenth Amendment prohibits a state conviction obtained by knowing use of false evidence. In this manner the Supreme Court found a violation of the Fourteenth Amendment, viz., knowing use of evidence known to be false, and reversed the judgment. It did so in spite of the specific finding to the contrary of every trier of fact that had considered the case, including the federal district court that had issued the writ of habeas corpus. It did so by selective use of evidence, contrary to the fundamental rule that conflicts in evidence are to be resolved in support of a judgment.

Thus eleven years after the trial the prosecutors found themselves branded as having made knowing use of false evidence to obtain a conviction, an act that has been considered a heinous crime since the time of the Ten Commandments. In California the tender of evidence known to be

33

false is a felony, and the same rule prevails in Illinois.[17] The prosecutors were stigmatized as criminals without charges, without notice, without hearing, without opportunity to reply, *ex cathedra* by the highest court in the land.

Thereafter the Illinois State Bar Association on its own motion initiated an investigation of the prosecutors in order to determine whether disciplinary action against them was warranted. At the end of a nine-month investigation the grievance committee of the Illinois State Bar Association publicly exonerated the two prosecutors and declared it was the Supreme Court rather than the prosecutors which had misrepresented:

> "It became apparent to the Committee early in its investigation that the United States Supreme Court had misapprehended the facts of the case. At the trial, which took place in 1956, the State chemist testified that there *were* bloodstains on the shorts in question. Prior to the trial, the prosecutors had been given a laboratory report from the Illinois State Bureau of Criminal Identification and Investigation which disclosed that the shorts did, in fact, contain blood. The State chemist further testified at the trial that the blood on the shorts was type 'A' which was the same type as that of the victim.
>
> "The Committee found no reason to doubt that there was blood on the shorts at the time of the trial and no reason to doubt that the prosecutors in the case believed there was blood on the shorts. Accordingly, the Committee found that there was no basis for the view of the United States Supreme Court that the prosecution had been guilty of a misrepresentation when it asserted as a fact that the shorts contained blood.
>
> "The Committee investigation further disclosed that, in addition to the blood, there was paint on the shorts. It is clear that the prosecution knew, or at least assumed, there was paint on the shorts as well as blood, and the prosecutors contend that the difference was apparent. . . .
>
> "The Committee concluded that the decision of the U.S. Supreme Court was based entirely upon a portion of the testimony which had been given at the habeas corpus hearing in the United States District Court at Chicago. The Supreme Court rejected the testimony given at the original trial eleven years earlier, and ignored the testimony of the State chemist who again testified at the habeas corpus proceedings that there was blood on the shorts." [18]

The findings of the grievance committee on this subject thus coincided in every respect with the earlier findings of the federal district court.

Meanwhile Miller's case had been remanded to the federal district court, which ordered him discharged from custody and permanently restrained the State of Illinois from retrying him on the rape-murder charge. On appeal the court of appeals in 1970 reversed the order enjoining Illinois from retrying petitioner and in 1971 the United States Supreme Court denied a hearing.[19] By that time petitioner was said to be permanently residing in California.

The *Miller* case is the one that is described as the glory of federal habeas corpus. Under it the convicted rape-murderer of an eight-year-old child, the validity of whose confession has been upheld by every court which has considered the issue, whose proof of guilt was characterized by the Illinois Supreme Court as overwhelming, is now a free man, freed on a factual basis which had been rejected by every trial court which had considered the particular facts involved. The glory of federal habeas corpus turns out to be a morning-glory that wilts at first light of day.

Miller v. *Pate* is the prototype for what has become an all-purpose method of collateral attack on a prior state criminal judgment. The method is simplicity itself. First, counsel finds a conflict in the evidence at the trial, preferably, but not necessarily, on a matter directly in issue in the case. Second, he declares that the truth in the conflict lies entirely on one side, and therefore the opposite contention must be false. Third, he points out that the prosecutor argued the truth of the false contention. Fourth, he concludes that the prosecutor knew the contention was false (or should have known it was false) and therefore was guilty of the knowing use of false testimony, which is equivalent to the knowing use of perjured testimony, which is a crime as well as a violation of defendant's constitutional rights.

Some variations on this procedure are simpler. For example, counsel first finds a *contradiction* in the testimony of a prosecution witness. Second, counsel deduces that since there is a contradiction in the witness's testimony, the witness must have committed perjury. Third, since the prosecutor relied on this witness, counsel concludes that the prosecutor relied on a witness who the prosecutor knew (or should have known) perjured himself, and therefore the prosecutor knowingly used perjured testimony to obtain a conviction, in violation of the defendant's constitutional rights.

A third variation is even more elementary. First, counsel finds an *implausibility* in a witness's testimony. Second, he assumes without any evidence that the testimony must be false and hence amounts to perjury. Third and fourth, he proceeds as before.

The use of this technique is seen in the murder case of *California* v. *Im-*

35

bler, where a federal district judge in Los Angeles, eight years after the trial, without taking any evidence, without hearing any testimony, and without calling any witnesses, overrode the unanimous judgment of the California Supreme Court, and concluded that the prosecution had knowingly relied on false testimony and knowingly suppressed evidence favorable to defendant in order to secure a judgment of conviction.[20]

Essentially, what the federal district court did was simply to reweigh the credibility of witnesses on a reading of the transcript and re-evaluate the weight of the evidence in a case turning on identification. A federal court is not allowed to do this in reviewing a state case, but this legal prohibition is easily evaded by the device of casting the material in the mold of constitutional error and then determining that conclusions thought to be egregiously wrong are dishonest and therefore unconstitutional.

The *Imbler* case puts in sharp focus the extent to which the state criminal process has been subordinated to the federal district courts. Sufficiency of evidence, credibility of witnesses, sufficiency of proof, all matters formerly determinable by state courts of last resort, may now be reweighed and re-evaluated by a single federal district judge five years or more after the event. The unanimous conclusion of the highest state court in a state criminal case may be disregarded at will by a single federal judge who has done nothing more than read the reporter's transcript of the proceedings.

The vehicle for this assumption of authority by lower federal courts over state criminal cases is the Constitution. Yet in practical operation the mumbo jumbo of constitutional error is completely without meaning, for the concept of knowing use of perjured testimony has so rapidly lost all contact with reality that it now encompasses bits and snatches of inconsistency in fringe evidence at a trial. Since any examination at any length of any witness in any trial is bound to produce inconsistencies, every trial is now vulnerable to the claim of constitutional error. Or, more simply put, every state criminal trial has now been made subject to complete federal review by the adoption of the legal fiction that evidence not 100 percent accurate and true is perjured, and that such evidence must have been used with knowledge of its falsity. Judge Friendly's purported restrictions on the use of federal habeas corpus would merely produce some slight change in the language of the petitions filed, and two complete reviews of state criminal cases would continue to run their parallel courses.

4

PRECONVICTION SHUTTLES

BETWEEN PARALLEL

COURT SYSTEMS

PARALLEL review in state and federal courts provides opportunities to a defendant for offensive as well as defensive maneuvers and permits him to shift operations from one set of courts to the other. A defendant in state court criminal proceedings is not restricted to the use of postconviction remedies, nor is he required to await the outcome of his trial in the state courts before launching an attack in the federal courts on the state proceedings pending against him. At least four preconviction remedies are readily available within the federal court system for use by a resourceful litigant to delay, suspend, or halt the progress of a state criminal prosecution. These include injunctive relief, declaratory relief, federal civil rights actions, and petitions for removal to the federal court.

Injunction

An application for injunctive relief normally seeks an order of the federal court prohibiting the further prosecution of a state court accusation. Because the Eleventh Amendment to the Constitution prohibits suit against a state in a federal court, the application is usually directed at state officers and state prosecutors and seeks to enjoin them, not the state, from prosecuting a particular cause on the state's behalf.

37

The federal injunction against state prosecutions flowered at the turn of the century, and its principal beneficiaries were railroads, warehouses, shippers, and the like, which sought relief in the federal courts against enforcement of state regulatory laws asserted to be unconstitutional. This use of federal injunction received the formal blessing of the United States Supreme Court in 1908,[1] and as a consequence 150 such injunctive cases were pending in the federal courts in 1910.[2] Congress reacted to this situation by adopting legislation in 1911 that required the action of a three-judge court for the issuance of a federal injunction.[3] Following the passage of this legislation use of federal injunctive relief against state law enforcement remained relatively quiescent for two decades, the Supreme Court having adopted the view that " [a]n intolerable condition would arise if, whenever about to be charged with violating a state law, one were permitted freely to contest its validity by an original proceeding in some federal court." [4]

With the advent of the New Deal, federal courts once again began to issue injunctions in numbers against the enforcement of laws said to be unconstitutional, this time largely against laws of the federal government.[5] The prodigality with which such injunctions were issued by the federal courts was one of the specifics that precipitated Roosevelt's court-packing fight in 1937, and as a result of that fight a three-judge court was made mandatory for the issuance of injunctive relief against enforcement of acts of Congress.[6]

For the next quarter century the use of federal injunctive relief against state criminal prosecutions remained in disfavor. The prevailing view of the Supreme Court was articulated in a decision where the court refused to enjoin the use in a state criminal prosecution of evidence assertedly seized in violation of a defendant's federal constitutional rights.[7] In prophetic language Justice Frankfurter detailed the reasons against such an injunction:

> "If we were to sanction this intervention, we would expose every State criminal prosecution to insupportable disruption. *Every question of procedural due process of law*—with its far-flung and undefined range—*would invite a flanking movement against the system of State courts by resort to the federal forum,* with review if need be to this Court, to determine the issue. Asserted unconstitutionality in the impaneling and selection of the grand and petit juries, in the failure to appoint counsel, in the admission of a confession, in the creation of an unfair trial atmosphere, in the misconduct of the trial court—all

would provide ready opportunities, which conscientious counsel might be bound to employ, to subvert the orderly, effective prosecution of local crime in local courts." (Italics added.) (342 U.S. 117, at pp. 123–24)

Frankfurter, however, was destined to play the role of Cassandra, who foreseeing the future was doomed not to be believed. Within a generation Frankfurter's warnings had been forgotten, and injunctive relief against state law enforcement sprang to life once more, its target this time not regulatory laws affecting business enterprise but criminal laws relating to public order and security. The breakthrough came in 1965 when the Supreme Court declared in the case of *Dombrowski* v. *Pfister* that issuance of injunctive relief by a federal court against enforcement of state criminal law not only was proper but was compelled whenever the state law being enforced or about to be enforced was one which appeared unconstitutional on its face or one whose enforcement would have a chilling effect on the exercise of constitutional rights.[8] The phrase *chilling effect* appeared in the court's opinion three times, and promptly became a legal cliché interpreted to mean any type of discouragement to contemplated activity tied in some manner to the exercise of constitutional rights. With the filing of this opinion the doors of the federal courts opened wide to applications for injunctive relief against any type of state criminal prosecution that could plausibly be claimed to have a chilling effect on the exercise of some particular constitutional right.

As a consequence of *Dombrowski,* obscenity prosecutions, for example, have tended to follow a regular pattern. On the filing of a criminal action in the state court, the defendant immediately petitions the federal court to enjoin further prosecution of the state action on the ground the state law under which the prosecution has been brought is unconstitutional, and that a continuation of the prosecution under the state law will have a chilling effect on the defendant's exercise of his constitutional rights.[9]

If the defendant does not wish to litigate before a three-judge court he may seek an injunction against an unconstitutional *use* of state law (as contrasted with unconstitutionality of the law itself), for the requirement of a three-judge court to enjoin enforcement of an unconstitutional state law has been interpreted as not applying to an action to enjoin the unconstitutional *use* of the state law.[10] Under this interpretation a single federal judge can enjoin future prosecutions and suppress evidence in pending prosecutions if he finds either an unconstitutional *use* of state law, or some irregularity in the procedure *used* in the state prosecution.

In any event only one federal judge is required to convene a three-judge court. Relief can be sought in higher federal courts if a district judge refuses to convene a three-judge court.[11] If a three-judge court is convened and injunctive relief denied, the order of denial can be appealed to a higher federal court.[12] A case pending before one judge can be dismissed and refiled before another judge in order to secure a more sympathetic audience.[13] With the exercise of a modicum of diligence, a litigant can tie up a state obscenity prosecution for years, even though federal injunctive relief against the prosecution may ultimately be denied.

In 1971 the United States Supreme Court in *Younger* v. *Harris* disapproved the widespread use of federal injunctive relief against pending state criminal prosecutions and, in theory at least, sharply curbed the power of the lower federal courts to issue injunctions.[14] In vacating an injunction issued by a three-judge federal court against a state criminal prosecution, the court declared that national policy forbade federal courts from staying or enjoining pending state court proceedings except under "extraordinary circumstances" involving irreparable injury. In a companion case the Supreme Court also disapproved the suppression by federal district courts of evidence in pending state prosecutions. In vacating such an order Justice Black said it was "difficult to imagine a more disruptive interference with the operation of the state criminal process short of an injunction against all state proceedings." [15]

While the decision in *Younger* v. *Harris* may slow down the issuance of federal injunctions against state criminal prosecutions, each applicant for injunctive relief will doubtless insist that his particular application involves "extraordinary circumstances" of great and irreparable injury. In view of the benefits accruing to the average criminal defendant from delays in prosecution, it appears inevitable that applications for injunctions against state prosecutions will continue to be presented to federal district courts so long as the practice is permitted. The periods of delay are substantial. For example, in *Younger* v. *Harris* the state initiated its prosecution in 1966, and it was not until 1971 that the federal injunction against the prosecution was dissolved.

Declaratory Relief

A second preconviction remedy available in the federal courts to forestall state criminal prosecution is declaratory relief.[16] An applicant may seek a judgment of the federal court declaring that a state law is invalid in some respects or that some phase of a state prosecution is improper. An application for declaratory relief does not require a pending prosecution, perhaps not even a potential prosecution. All the applicant need do is convince the federal court that the existence of the state law has a chilling effect on his desire to exercise his constitutional rights in a certain manner, and the federal court, if favorably inclined, may issue a judgment declaring that the state law must be constitutionally interpreted in a certain manner.

In *Zwickler* v. *Koota* the applicant attacked a New York penal statute which required political handbills to contain the names of their sponsors.[17] A federal district court dismissed the complaint for declaratory and injunctive relief on the ground that the applicant could challenge the statute in the state courts. The United States Supreme Court reversed in 1967, stating that the federal district court should adjudicate the request for declaratory relief in view of the potentially chilling effect of the statute on the exercise of the constitutional right of free expression. The practical application of this doctrine may be seen in a case where the applicant, under prosecution in the Wisconsin courts for violating the state abortion law, secured a declaration from the federal district court that Wisconsin's abortion law was unconstitutional.[18] One judge has been held sufficient to issue a declaratory judgment, and a three-judge court may not be required.[19] If a federal district court refuses declaratory relief, or if it declares the law in a manner unsatisfactory to the litigant, the latter can appeal to the federal appellate court.[20]

In 1971 the Supreme Court in *Samuels* v. *Mackell* ruled that declaratory relief involving a pending state criminal prosecution is governed by the rules applicable to injunctive relief, and that such relief should ordinarily be withheld in the absence of "unusual circumstances." [21] However, the separate opinion of Justice Brennan implied that declaratory relief would be proper if sought prior to the commencement of a state criminal prosecution. If this latter view is correct, the availability of federal declaratory relief in state criminal prosecutions may often turn on the outcome of the race to the courthouse, and if a prospective defendant succeeds in filing his action for declaratory relief in federal court before the state prosecutor has filed an accusation against him in the state court, the remedy of declaratory relief may remain available to him to attack the subsequent state prosecution.

Civil Rights Action

A third preconviction remedy in federal district courts against state criminal prosecutions is that of a separate civil action against state police, state prosecutors, or state officials, charging them with having violated, or being about to violate, plaintiff's federal civil rights.[22] These claims can be framed around almost any aspect of the criminal process—investigation, surveillance, arrest, search, detention, identification, interrogation, prosecution—and the suspect, instead of awaiting the course of prosecution under state law, can seize the initiative and get the jump on his prosecutors by filing his own action in federal court, thereby reversing roles and casting the public authorities as defendants instead of himself. This practice received great impetus from the Supreme Court's decision in *Monroe* v. *Pape* in 1961, where the court upheld the filing of a federal civil suit against Chicago police officers for unreasonable search and seizure and for false arrest.[23] The same principle has now been extended to suits against federal officers.[24]

Considerable ingenuity is used in drafting civil rights complaints, and matters having only tenuous connection with traditional civil rights form the basis for many of the claims. For example, the right to possess obscene material is claimed as a civil right, and under color of this claim civil rights actions in the federal courts are routinely used to forestall state obscenity prosecutions.[25]

Removal

A fourth preconviction remedy available to a defendant in a state criminal prosecution is removal of the pending state case to the federal courts.[26] Under the federal Judicial Code, a defendant in the state courts can remove the case to the federal courts if it properly belongs there. Cases removable to the federal courts include those arising out of denials of federal civil rights.[27] Since here, again, the operation of practically every aspect of the criminal process can be depicted in terms of a denial of federal civil rights, a petition for removal of a case to the federal courts can almost always be filed with some degree of plausibility.

Whether or not the petition has merit, the mere existence of the right to apply for removal makes it possible to tie up a state criminal prosecution for substantial periods of time. One example is the case of *Maryland* v. *H. Rap Brown,* a criminal prosecution initiated in the state courts of Maryland in 1967 for arson, riot, and incitement to riot.[28] Removal of the case to the federal district court was sought by Brown under the claim that it involved his federal civil rights, and in 1969 Brown's petition for removal was denied by the district court. The denial was affirmed by the court of appeals, and in 1970 a hearing was denied by the United States Supreme Court. A second removal petition was then filed by Brown on a different ground. It, too, was denied by the federal district court, and this denial, too, was affirmed by the court of appeals. Yet the mere filing of these unmeritorious petitions for removal succeeded in delaying the progress of the state criminal prosecution for years.

Multiple Use of Preconviction Remedies

A litigant who does not wish to stand trial in the state court need not restrict himself to one of these preconviction remedies; he may pursue all of them simultaneously.[29] At the same time he may pursue comparable remedies in the state courts. And he may seek a particular preconviction remedy more than once, as did H. Rap Brown.[30] In this endeavor the litigant's objective is to juxtapose one system of courts against the other, or to set a higher court against a lower court within the same court system, thereby diverting attention from the pending accusation against him onto something else. With parallel systems of law operating on the same subject matter, a lawyer of only moderate ability has little difficulty in launching such procedures and keeping them afloat for months or years. In *LaRue* v. *State of California,* for example, bar owners and bar entertainers sought injunctive and declaratory relief and vindication of their federal civil rights against California's Department of Alcoholic Beverage Control when the latter attempted to enforce its rules prohibiting bars from featuring as entertainment bottomless dancers, simulated sex acts, and the exhibition of stag movies.[31] A three-judge federal district court granted the relief sought in 1971, a judgment, however, which was reversed in 1972 by the Supreme Court.

5

MULTIPLE TRIALS
OF THE SAME CAUSE

CENTRAL to the concept of perfectibility is the multiple trial. Ideally, a defendant is entitled to a perfectly presented defense, and to achieve this ideal the prosecution may be required to present its case against him over and over again until perfectibility in the defense, or some close approximation thereof, has been achieved. However, this vision of perfectibility looks in one direction only, and if in a criminal cause an unwarranted judgment is returned in favor of the defendant as a consequence of blunders on the part of the prosecution, or if the trial is aborted in some manner for which the defendant cannot be held responsible, that is the end of the prosecution because of the prohibition against double jeopardy found in the Fifth Amendment. This remains true even when the trial is cut short solely because of an error of the trial judge.

Under the concept that perfectibility may be achieved through multiple trials, the same case may be tried as many as five times. Consider the following:

TERRY killed a police officer in June 1960. His conviction for first-degree murder was affirmed on appeal, but the jury's imposition of the death penalty was reversed because improper argument had been made to the jury. In a *second* penalty trial the jury again imposed the death penalty, but this was reversed on appeal because of improper evidentiary rulings and because instructions and argument to the jury were deemed to have been erroneous in the light of retroactive application of a 1964 decision in another case. A *third* penalty trial ended in a hung jury. In the *fourth* penalty trial the jury once more imposed the death penalty, but the

44

sentence was reversed on appeal because potential jurors had been improperly excluded on account of their views on the death penalty, a result brought about by retroactive application of a 1968 decision in yet another case. A *fifth* penalty trial, pending in 1972, was mooted when the California Supreme Court held California's death penalty law unconstitutional.[1] In 1973 Terry had pending in the courts two petitions for habeas corpus, which, conceivably, could lead to a further trial.

SEITERLE [2] killed a man and his wife in a holdup in August 1960. He pleaded guilty to first-degree murder. On appeal the death penalty imposed by a jury was reversed because erroneous instructions had been given to the jury. A *second* jury again imposed the death penalty, and that judgment was affirmed on appeal. However, on collateral attack a third penalty trial was ordered because instructions given the second penalty jury were now deemed erroneous in the light of retroactive application of a 1964 decision in another case. A *third* jury again imposed the death penalty, and on appeal that judgment was affirmed. But on collateral attack a *fourth* penalty trial was ordered because potential jurors had been improperly excluded on account of their views on the death penalty, a result brought about by retroactive application of a 1968 decision in another case. When California's death penalty law was declared unconstitutional in 1972, Seiterle was sentenced to life imprisonment.

KETCHEL [3] and two others killed an off-duty policeman in June 1961. Three jury verdicts imposing the death penalty were each reversed on appeal. In 1972 Ketchel was sentenced to life imprisonment.

MODESTO [4] killed two little girls, ages nine and twelve, in October 1961. He was tried and convicted of these murders three times, and juries imposed the death penalty on him three times. A stay of execution remained in effect, and in 1972 Modesto was resentenced to life imprisonment.

ARGUELLO [5] killed an eighty-two-year-old widow in November 1961. He was tried and convicted of first-degree murder three times, but on collateral attack a *fourth* penalty trial was ordered. In 1972 Arguello was sentenced to life imprisonment.

HILLERY [6] killed a fifteen-year-old girl in March 1962. His appeal from a third penalty trial remained pending in 1973.

SEARS [7] killed his step-daughter and attempted to kill his wife and mother-in-law in May 1963. In a *fourth* trial for murder he was sentenced in 1972 to life imprisonment.

In none of these cases was there any doubt that the accused committed the act for which he was prosecuted. While these particular cases involved charges of murder and imposition of the death penalty, similar repetitive trials take place in other types of felony prosecutions—robbery, rape, burglary, aggravated assault, and the like. For example, in *United States* v. *Persico* a conviction for a 1959 robbery was affirmed in 1970 after five trials and two prior reversals.[8]

The underlying assumption of the multiple trial is that a case can be tried over and over again, and no harm will be done to the ideal of justice or to the participants. This assumption is incorrect. Witnesses die and evidence disappears, and frequently the case cannot be tried again. Yet the surface appeal of the notion that error will be banished from the case on a subsequent retrial appears irresistible to the judiciary, and as a result judges in the United States exhibit a certain degree of irresponsibility in their reversals of criminal judgments. Multiple prosecutions tend to produce irresponsibility on the part of everyone connected with the cause, because jurors, counsel, the trial judge, and the reviewing judges all know that any given judgment is only tentative and provisional. Judgments are reversed or vacated on slender, even frivolous, grounds, because the reversing court assumes that a clearly guilty defendant will be prosecuted and convicted again.

These multiple trials must appear strange to a nonlawyer when they are viewed in the light of the Fifth Amendment to the federal Constitution, which says:

> "Nor shall any person be subject for the same offense to be twice put in jeopardy of life or limb."

Similar provisions appear in most state constitutions. California's declares:

> "No person shall be twice put in jeopardy for the same offense" (art. I, § 13).

English law has always considered that the rule against double jeopardy means what it says, and it holds that a defendant whose cause has gone to a final judgment which has been reversed on appeal may not again be prosecuted.[9] Such was the view taken by Justice Story of the United States Supreme Court in 1834, who, sitting on circuit in *United States* v. *Gibert,* held that the double jeopardy clause of the Constitution prohibited the granting of a new trial after a jury had returned its verdict.[10] The common law prohibition against double jeopardy, he said, presents an insurmountable barrier to a second felony prosecution where there has been a verdict of acquittal or conviction regularly had upon a sufficient indictment. Were it otherwise, said Story in anticipation of present developments, the same party might be tried ten or twenty times for the same offense.

Although a second trial has long been considered proper when the jury is unable to reach a verdict,[11] the idea of a second trial after a final judgment of conviction is one of relatively recent origin. In 1896 the Supreme Court upheld the validity of a second trial when the defendant himself brought about the vacation of the original judgment.[12] The theory in justification of these multiple trials is that since the defendant himself has brought about a reversal of the judgment against him, he has waived double jeopardy and has nothing to complain about on retrial.

The flood of reversals of criminal judgments on technical grounds has inspired certain proposed solutions. California, in its attempt to stem this tide of reversals, amended its constitution in 1911 to provide:

> "No judgment shall be set aside, or new trial granted in any criminal case on the ground of misdirection of the jury or the improper admission or rejection of evidence, or for error as to any matter of pleading or procedure, unless, after an examination of the entire cause including the evidence, the court shall be of the opinion that the *error* complained of has *resulted in a miscarriage of justice.*" [13] (Italics added.)

For the phrase *miscarriage of justice* the California courts soon substituted the phrase *prejudicial error,*[14] and the constitutional provision rapidly sank into innocuous desuetude. The possibility of its resurrection in its original meaning, suggested by a California Supreme Court opinion in 1956,[15] was scotched by the holding of the United States Supreme Court in *Chapman* v. *California* in 1967 that where federal constitutional rights are involved a prohibition against reversal of judgments can only apply to cases where the error is *nonprejudicial beyond a reasonable doubt.*[16] The formulation of laws, rules, and remedies to protect federally guaranteed rights in state courts, declared the Supreme Court, could not be left to the states themselves.

Defendants who, like Persico, have been subjected to numerous trials and whose prosecutions have been pending a decade or more, now argue that they should be discharged because of the prohibition in the Eighth Amendment against cruel and unusual punishments. They argue that the pendency of unresolved charges for so many years is a form of torture that amounts to cruel and unusual punishment. The United States Supreme Court attempted to answer this argument in *Harrison* v. *United States* by stating:

> "Virtually all of the delays of which the petitioner complains occurred in the course of appellate proceedings and resulted either from

the actions of the petitioner or from *the need to assure careful review* of an unusually complex case." [17] (Italics added.)

Messrs. Persico and Harrison have a point, which although it may not amount to a valid legal argument certainly presents a powerful indictment of a system of criminal law that can tolerate and encourage these multiple trials. Suppose we reverted to the English system and adopted the rule that on a given charge a defendant could be tried to judgment only once. If he were acquitted, that would end the matter. If he were adjudged guilty and took an appeal, the reviewing court would have two choices. It could affirm the judgment of conviction, or it could reverse the judgment and discharge the defendant. There would be no retrial. If, despite errors in the trial of the cause, the reviewing court were reasonably certain that the correct result had been achieved and that the errors had no real bearing on the determination of the defendant's guilt, it would affirm the judgment. But if the reviewing court were not so satisfied and concluded that the errors did have a prejudicial bearing on the determination of defendant's guilt or innocence, it would reverse the judgment, and the defendant would go free.

These are exacting choices to make, but not impossible ones. Subsequently discovered mistakes, the hardships of a close case, and the occasional miscarriage of justice could be corrected by executive authority through use of its clemency and pardoning powers, as is done in England through the office of the Home Secretary. Rectifications in individual cases could be made on an individual basis without overturning valid judgments or creating bad law in order to achieve an equitable result in a particular case. Would not this be a better, fairer system than the present merry-go-round? Would it not sharpen the sense of responsibility of trial judges, of juries, of reviewing courts, and focus their attention on the ultimate issue of the guilt or innocence of the accused?

6

MULTIPLE REVIEWS
OF THE SAME ISSUE

MULTIPLE reviews of the same issue as a consequence of parallel operation of state and federal court systems have been discussed in earlier chapters. Yet even within a single court system a perpetual re-examination of the same issue can occur by reason of the proliferation of pretrial remedies, trial remedies, posttrial remedies, and extraordinary remedies, for in certain areas multiple review has been allowed to run its course uncurbed.

The opportunities to litigate the same issues over and over again may be visualized by an itemization of the successive attacks a criminal defendant in California may make on a particular state search and seizure under the claim that it violates the Fourth Amendment to the federal Constitution and the comparable provision in the California Constitution against unreasonable seizures and searches (Cal. Const., art. I, § 19).

Preliminarily, the validity of a particular search and seizure may be attacked even before criminal proceedings have begun. If a search and seizure has taken place pursuant to warrant, the validity of the warrant may be challenged and return of the seized property sought.[1] If search and seizure has taken place without a warrant, the courts will entertain an independent suit for return of the property and its suppression as evidence.[2] Additionally, a civil action for damages for wrongful seizure may be filed in the state courts,[3] and an action for invasion of civil rights may be filed in the federal courts under the Civil Rights Act.[4]

Once a prosecution is formally under way, the validity of a particular

49

search and seizure could be attacked by a criminal defendant on the following occasions: [5]

1. At the preliminary examination. If, disregarding improperly seized evidence, there is insufficient cause to hold the defendant, he must be discharged.

2. At a motion to set aside the accusation as having been brought without reasonable or probable cause. If on hearing the motion the court determines that evidence has been improperly seized and concludes that without this illegally seized evidence insufficient cause to charge the defendant is present, defendant must be discharged.

3. If the motion to set aside the accusation in step 2 is denied, defendant can apply for a writ of prohibition to the court of appeal.

4. If unsuccessful in step 3, defendant can apply to the California Supreme Court for the same writ.

5. Defendant can move for an evidentiary hearing to suppress the evidence he claims was unlawfully seized.

6. If his motion to suppress evidence is denied, he can apply for a writ of mandate or prohibition to the court of appeal. Ordinarily, prosecution of the cause will be stayed pending such review.

7. If unsuccessful in step 6, defendant can apply for the same writ in the California Supreme Court.

8. Defendant can seek to remove the cause to the federal district court on the claim that he has been denied his federal civil rights.

9. If removal is denied by the federal district court, he can appeal the order of denial to the federal court of appeals.

10. If the federal court of appeals rules against him, he can petition the United States Supreme Court for certiorari.

11. Defendant can initiate a new action in federal court charging violation of his civil rights and seeking injunctive relief, suppression of evidence, etc.

12. If preliminary relief is denied him in step 11, he can appeal the denial to the federal court of appeals.

13. Thereafter he can petition the United States Supreme Court for certiorari.

14. At his trial defendant can object to the admissibility of evidence on the ground it is the product of unlawful search and seizure. While California appellate courts have been firm in their rulings that a defendant who has previously been granted an evidentiary hearing is not entitled to a further evidentiary hearing at the trial nor entitled to renew an earlier motion, nevertheless he is entitled to object to admission of the material into evidence and is entitled to make a new motion based on new grounds, as

50

for example that the law has been changed by a later appellate ruling or that new evidence to support a motion to suppress has been discovered.

15. If defendant is convicted, he can renew his claims on a motion for a new trial. This motion is subject to the limitations mentioned in step 14. But again the possibility exists that some new mandatory retroactive interpretation of the law of search and seizure by some appellate court will require reconsideration of a former ruling.

16. Defendant can appeal his judgment of conviction to the court of appeal and obtain a further review of the lawfulness of the challenged search and seizure.

17. If the appeal in step 16 is lost, he can petition for a hearing in the California Supreme Court.

18. If the petition for hearing in the California Supreme Court is denied, or if that court affirms the judgment against him, he can petition for certiorari to the United States Supreme Court.

19. Thereafter, defendant can apply for postconviction relief in the California superior court on the ground that his conviction was obtained by means of unconstitutionally seized evidence.

20. If relief is denied, he is entitled to a free transcript of the hearing in the superior court to enable him to apply for the same relief to the court of appeal.

21. If relief is denied by the court of appeal, he can petition the California Supreme Court for the same relief.

22. Thereafter he can petition for certiorari to the United States Supreme Court.

23. Defendant can also pursue postconviction remedies in federal district court by seeking a writ of habeas corpus on the ground that his conviction was obtained through use of unconstitutionally seized evidence.

24. If the federal district court denies relief, he can appeal to the federal court of appeals.

25. Thereafter he can again petition for certiorari to the United States Supreme Court.

26. At any time he can petition the California appellate courts for an extraordinary writ to vacate the original judgment. These writs are variously entitled Petition to Recall Remittitur or Petition for Writ of Error Coram Nobis, and are principally used where there has been a retrospective change in applicable law.

In almost every one of the foregoing steps the losing defendant can petition for rehearing or reconsideration by the particular court that ruled against him.[6] Thus the theoretical number of instances of judicial review of the same point can rise to over fifty. Furthermore, at many of these steps a defendant may petition for rehearing more than once by filing a document with some such title as Motion to Reconsider Denial of Rehearing, and if that motion is denied, he may file a subsequent motion, perhaps entitled Motion to Vacate Denial of Motion to Reconsider Denial of Rehearing.[7] Writs of habeas corpus may be filed any number of times, for the principle of final adjudication does not apply to petitions for habeas corpus in either federal or state courts.[8] As the Supreme Court has said of postconviction reviews, "Conventional notions of finality of litigation have no place where life or liberty is at stake and infringement of constitutional rights is alleged."[9] Courts, of course, soon tire of reviewing matters which are precisely identical to those another court has acted upon; therefore in successive petitions slight variations will normally appear in the claims, or in the legal points, or in the factual issues raised.

From the defendant's point of view multiple review serves several purposes. First, it delays proceedings interminably, and a defendant who does not wish to stand trial on the merits expects to profit from delay. Witnesses and evidence may be lost, and memories may grow dim. Second, while the case is at a standstill, there is always the possibility the law will be changed in defendant's favor, either by new legislation or by new interpretation of existing law from the courts. Third, the more steps involved in the litigation, the more possibilities of ultimate error. If in one of these multiple reviews a valid claim of error can be developed, then the thrust of the litigation can be changed from an accusation against the defendant to an accusation against the court, the district attorney, or some public official based on the latter's failure to grant defendant his full legal and constitutional rights. For example, if during an evidentiary hearing on a motion to suppress evidence the court erroneously excludes certain testimony from the hearing, it is possible that at some later stage another court may consider this ruling so prejudicial that it will nullify all proceedings subsequent to the erroneous ruling.

Holdsworth, in his examination of the operation of English chancery courts in the early nineteenth century, found that under the equity rules, which aimed at the doing of complete justice regardless of any other consideration,

> " [t]he existing delays were aggravated by the system of rehearings and appeals which a determined litigant could demand upon the most trivial points. Any point arising in the course of a suit might be discussed—(1) Before the Master of the Rolls; (2) Before the same person by way of rehearing; (3) Before the Lord Chancellor; (4) Before the same person by way of rehearing; (5) Before the House of

Lords. Upon these appeals and rehearings, other than appeals to the House of Lords, new evidence could be adduced." [10]

With American efficiency we have expanded English chancery's five points of discussion into fifty.

To observe multiple review of the same issue in operation, consider the case of *Carafas,*[11] convicted of burglary and grand larceny by a New York state court in 1960. At his trial the defendant unsuccessfully argued that illegally obtained evidence had been introduced against him. His conviction was affirmed by the state appellate court, by the New York Court of Appeals in two opinions, and by denial of a hearing in the United States Supreme Court. Thereafter Carafas unsuccessfully applied for reconsideration in the state appellate court, and then litigated habeas corpus in the three tiers of the federal court system. On his second appearance in the federal district court that court, after a hearing, denied his petition on the merits. The federal court of appeals dismissed his appeal and denied rehearing. The United States Supreme Court then granted a petition for certiorari in 1967 and reinstated Carafas' appeal in the federal court of appeals for further consideration on its merits. Thus on thirteen different occasions the courts considered the same claim, more or less, involving the use of illegally obtained evidence.

With such possibilities for multiple review of the same issue a criminal defendant's opportunity to relitigate is limited only by the resourcefulness of his counsel and by the defendant's ability to stimulate counsel's interest in pursuing these remedies.

7

THE LAW'S DELAY—
SIDETRACKING AND
MAINLINING OF CAUSES

In addition to repetitive trials and repetitive reviews of the same issue as a result of attempts by parallel court systems to achieve perfectibility, the judicial process suffers from interminable delay. This comes about as a result of two kinds of activities—those which divert the inquiry into a collateral issue, and those which slow down the progress of the inquiry itself. These activities may be termed sidetracking and mainlining.

In the operation of a railway system to sidetrack a train is to switch it from the main line to a siding. In criminal law to sidetrack a cause is to divert the accusation from the pending issue to some other issue, any issue, and then keep the prosecution so occupied in litigating the side issue that the hearing of the accusation itself comes to a halt. In recent years opportunities for this type of diversionary activity have proliferated like crabgrass in the summer sun. Reference has been made in Chapter 4 to the possibility that a prospective defendant in a state prosecution may seize the initiative and seek federal injunctive or declaratory relief on constitutional grounds to establish a violation of his federal civil rights. Normally, however, a defendant will await the filing of an accusation against him before he undertakes to frame an issue to his liking.

Suppose a defendant has been indicted for the crime of murder. The issue raised by the indictment is, of course, the guilt or innocence of the defendant of the particular murder with which he is charged. If the defendant wishes to litigate the accusation against him, he has the constitutional right to a speedy and public trial,[1] and under California law he is entitled to come to trial within 60 days.[2] But if, as almost invariably happens, the defendant is not anxious promptly to litigate the issue of his guilt or innocence, he may undertake to develop a diversionary issue more to his liking and thereby sidetrack the hearing of the murder charge in favor of an issue of his own selection. The defendant has the choice of numerous switches he may throw in order to divert the cause from the main track onto a siding:

1. He may attack the court machinery that initiated the accusation against him and is scheduled to process his case. Such an attack may cover the legality of the process that brought him into court, the validity of any search or arrest warrants that were issued, the composition of the grand jury that returned the indictment, the validity of the indictment itself, the qualifications of the judge or judges assigned to the case, the competency of court-assigned defense counsel, and the composition of the prospective trial jury panel.

2. He may attack the law enforcement machinery and challenge the standing and conduct of investigators, of police, or of jailers. Such an attack may be directed against the manner of arrest, the validity of a search connected with the arrest, the validity of an admission or confession given the police, the conduct or composition of a lineup, the treatment of defendant in custody, and the sufficiency of his access to counsel.

3. He may attack the prosecutors and complain of the prosecutors' refusal to disclose the names and addresses of informers, the prosecutors' denial of access to tangible evidence, their intimidation of potential defense witnesses, their failure to locate witnesses sought by the defense, or their refusal to suppress evidence unfavorable to the defendant.

4. He may attack the constitutionality of the law against murder, as for example, its definition, its degrees, its mode of trial, its punishment, and he may tender an issue that the present law against murder denies him the equal protection of the laws, or violates due process, or discriminates against him on racial or ethnic grounds.

5. He may attack the news media for unfairly publicizing or sensationalizing the accusation against him, and he may claim that because of publicity it has become impossible for him to get a fair trial at that particular time and place.

6. If in pursuing these tactics the defendant meets an unfavorable ruling in the trial court, he can seek to overturn that ruling in the appellate courts. A defendant is not restricted in the number of attacks he may make, nor is he required to make them simultaneously. Rather he may

55

dole them out serially. The most fruitful methods for sidetracking a cause are those which require a hearing, and of these the very best for purposes of delay are those requiring an extended evidentiary hearing and the calling of witnesses.

The normal sequence of events, then, for a defendant who does not wish to answer the charge against him is to tender one or more side issues and then insist on his right to an evidentiary hearing. Let us consider some of these sidetracks.

Sidetracking

ATTACK ON THE GRAND JURY PANEL

Felony accusations in California are initiated by a grand jury indictment or by an information filed on a magistrate's preliminary commitment. A defendant who has been indicted by a grand jury may attack the composition of the grand jury that returned his indictment, and if his attack is unsuccessful in the trial court, he may seek to renew it in the appellate courts.[3] The charge currently favored for such an attack is racial discrimination contrary to the Fourteenth Amendment in the composition of the grand jury panel from which the grand jury was selected. If racial discrimination can be established, then the proceedings of the grand jury become a nullity, a result made mandatory by the United States Supreme Court in two leading cases. In *Cassell* v. *Texas* the court in 1950 set aside a Texas judgment of conviction of a Negro for murder because it found unconstitutional discrimination against defendant's race in the selection of the grand jury that indicted him.[4] In *Hernandez* v. *Texas* the court in 1954 set aside a Texas judgment of conviction of a person of Mexican descent for murder because it found that persons of Mexican descent had been systematically excluded from both the grand jury and the trial jury.[5]

Although discrimination based on race provides the principal ground for attacks on a grand jury, claims of unconstitutional discrimination need not be limited to matters of race, ancestry, or national origin. In *Hernandez* v. *Texas,* Chief Justice Warren declared that

> ". . . from time to time other differences from the community norm may define other groups which need the same protection. . . . When the existence of a distinct class is demonstrated, and it is further shown that the laws, as written or as applied, single out that class for different treatment not based on some reasonable classification, the

guarantees of the Constitution have been violated." (347 U.S. 475, at p. 478)

Thus any definable group to which a defendant belongs may be used as the basis for a claim of discrimination in the composition of the grand jury.

Under this expanded concept of group discrimination the composition of a grand jury can be attacked as discriminatory on almost any conceivable basis, not merely on racial and ethnic grounds but on the basis of age, sex, education, wealth, and residential location. In mounting such an attack the defendant's opening move is to demand an evidentiary hearing in order to prove discrimination against his particular group by the selectors of the grand jury panel. In Los Angeles County in 1973, for example, the proceeding unfolds in the following manner:

The grand jury in Los Angeles County consists of twenty-three persons whose names are drawn from a panel of persons nominated by the 161 judges of the superior court, each of whom has nominated two persons for the panel.[6] The defendant charges that members of his particular group have been systematically excluded from the panel of nominees from which the grand jury was drawn and demands a hearing to prove his charge. Since the judges have selected the nominees, the judges are the ones who have discriminated. If an evidentiary hearing is granted, the defendant has succeeded in putting the judges on trial rather than standing trial himself —and not merely one judge, but 161 judges. At such a hearing the 161 judges of the superior court may be subpenaed as witnesses, questioned about the factors they took into account in selecting their individual nominees for the grand jury panel and asked whether they systematically excluded from consideration persons of defendant's particular group. At such hearings defendants have sought to interrogate each judge on his own race, ethnic origin, and religion; to interrogate him on the race, ethnic origin, religion, wealth, and education of his nominees for the grand jury panel; and to inquire into efforts made by the judge to fulfill his affirmative duty to seek out potential nominees for the grand jury from all segments of the population.

By the initiation of such a hearing progress of the original murder accusation can be brought to a standstill. And if the attack on the composition of the grand jury panel should fail in the trial court, further review can be sought in the appellate courts. Pending appellate review the accusation against defendant rusts on its siding. Consider a few examples:

In *Montez* v. *Superior Court* petitioners were indicted by the Los Angeles grand jury in May 1969 for arson and related offenses.[7] Petitioners moved to quash the indictment on the ground that members of petitioners' group had been systematically excluded by the judges as nominees for the grand jury panel. Petitioners variously described the members of their group as Mexican-Americans, persons with Spanish surnames, persons with Latin-American ancestry, and Spanish-surnamed Mexican-American citizens. After a four-day hearing the superior court disallowed subpenas addressed to the judges and denied the motion, finding there had been no discrimination in the selection of nominees for the grand jury panel and finding that ten persons with Spanish surnames had been nominated for the 1969 Los Angeles grand jury. In August 1970 the California appellate court reversed, holding that petitioners should have been allowed to subpena all judges of the superior court as witnesses. The existence of Spanish-surnamed Mexican-Americans on the grand jury panel, said the court, did not eliminate the possibility of discrimination against the group; not even roughly proportional representation would disprove the possibility of discrimination. Thereupon, the case was returned to the superior court, and a two-month hearing was held at which 109 judges testified. In March 1971 petitioners' motion was again denied. Meanwhile, of course, the prosecution of petitioners for arson had been sidetracked for two years, and further sidetracking was still possible.

The same kind of challenge to the grand jury panel took place in *People* v. *Castro,* in which thirty-three judges testified during a hearing of fourteen trial days,[8] and in *People* v. *Sirhan,* in which a majority of the judges of the Los Angeles superior court testified as witnesses or by deposition on Sirhan's claim that members of his nationality and race, Palestinian Arab, had been discriminated against in the selection of nominees for the grand jury which had indicted him.[9]

Claims of group discrimination in the selection of nominees for the grand jury panel are limited only by the imagination and resourcefulness of defendants in devising classifications for themselves to fit into. Sirhan attacked the composition of the Los Angeles County grand jury panel on the ground that it discriminated against him in age (the panel was older than average), in education (the panel had above-average education), and in employment (the panel had above-average employment). He also complained that the panel overrepresented the western part of Los Angeles County and underrepresented the eastern part of the county.

In another case Huey P. Newton attacked the composition of an Alameda County grand jury panel on the ground that it unconstitutionally discriminated against young persons, low-income groups, and black persons.[10] Defendants in a San Luis Obispo case attacked the composition of the grand jury as not representative of, and discriminatory against, defendant's group in age and in "socio-economic-political" composition.[11]

Even when a grand jury or grand jury panel contains members of a particular group in proportion to the numbers of that group in the community, a claim of discrimination can still be made, for in *Cassell* v. *Texas* the Supreme Court stated that proportional representation of a group on the grand jury in order to reflect the numbers of that group in the general population is impermissible, since race cannot be taken into account as a basis for selection.[12]

It is difficult to imagine a situation where a claim of discrimination with respect to the composition of the grand jury panel cannot be plausibly made and a hearing demanded. This is so because the group claimed to have been discriminated against can be tailored with an eye to defendant's needs and its composition fitted to his purposes. Underrepresentation in the selected group can be attacked as discriminatory. If the group is represented in proportion to its numbers, unconstitutional proportional limitation can be claimed. If it turns out that the group is overrepresented, defendant can switch to another group, for the grand jury panel can never fully and proportionately represent all groups in the population. Finally, even if in a given case a court has held a full hearing and ruled that the panel from which the grand jury was drawn was not discriminatorily selected, such a ruling does not bind any defendant except the one in whose case the determination was made. Every other defendant can make the identical claim, demand a similar hearing and, if a hearing is granted, subpena as witnesses the 161 judges of the Los Angeles Superior Court.

Entirely apart from the advantages to a defendant of delay, an attack on a grand jury panel may bring rich dividends, as can be seen in *United States* v. *Zirpolo,* a case wherein multiple defendants, all male, were indicted in Newark, New Jersey, by a federal grand jury for violations of the federal antiracketeering statute.[13] The indictment became the target for more than forty pretrial defense motions, one of which was an attack on the grand jury panel on the ground that women had been underrepresented on the panel from which the indicting grand jury had been drawn. Defendants were tried and convicted of racketeering, but their convictions were later reversed by the federal appellate court on the theory that the indictments and the convictions had been rendered invalid by an underrepresentation of women on the grand jury panel.

ATTACK ON THE TRIAL JURY PANEL

A defendant may also initiate an attack on the composition of the trial jury panel and demand an evidentiary hearing to prove his claim.[14] For example, he may contend that use of voter registration lists as the source of trial jurors discriminates against persons from lower income groups, who do not register to vote in the same proportion as do persons from higher income groups. Or he may claim that because of literacy qualifications for jurors higher income groups are overrepresented on the trial jury panel. For example, Huey P. Newton attacked a trial jury panel on the ground that selection of jurors exclusively from voter registration lists resulted in discrimination against poor persons and black persons because such persons were less likely than others to register to vote.[15] If a jury panel has been drawn from the county as a whole, defendant may claim it should have been drawn from a particular segment of the county. If it has been drawn from a particular segment of the county, defendant may claim it should have been drawn from the county as a whole. An evidentiary hearing on these matters can tie up the case for weeks, or months, and if the ruling is unfavorable to the defendant, appellate review may be sought.

It is theoretically possible that attacks on jury panels could extend into perpetuity. In a murder case in Los Angeles two defendants attacked the composition of the Los Angeles grand jury panel and of the 1968 Los Angeles trial jury panel as well.[16] A hearing on these challenges extended over a period of six months, and in January 1969 all motions were denied. But meanwhile the new Los Angeles trial jury panel had been drawn for the year 1969. Defendants promptly filed new motions to attack the new Los Angeles trial jury panel, motions which were denied in February 1969.

ATTACK ON THE TRIAL JUDGE

In California a party is entitled to one peremptory challenge against the judge assigned to hear the case; a party is also entitled to challenge the judge for cause, i.e., bias or prejudice, and on such challenge the party is entitled to a hearing before another judge on the challenged judge's qualifications.[17] A party dissatisfied with the outcome of such a hearing may seek relief in the appellate courts.

ATTACK ON COURT-APPOINTED DEFENSE COUNSEL

An indigent defendant who has had counsel assigned by the court to represent him may launch an attack on the competency of his assigned counsel and demand appointment of a replacement. If properly timed, such an attack may result in substantial delay.

ATTACK ON LAW ENFORCEMENT MACHINERY

Each step in the process of law enforcement—such as arrest, search, identification, interrogation—can be attacked on grounds of unfairness, and an evidentiary hearing sought. Each contains the potential for effectively sidetracking the accusation and delaying the day of judgment. In each instance an unfavorable ruling of the trial court may be challenged in advance of trial in the appellate courts.[18]

ATTACK ON CONSTITUTIONALITY

Before any trial has occurred or any evidence has been presented, defendants now routinely attack the constitutionality of the laws under which they are prosecuted, and the courts have drifted into the habit of responding to such attacks in the broadest possible terms and determining in advance of trial all constitutional issues that might have some relevancy to the accusation. An attack on the constitutionality of a law need bear little relationship to the facts of the particular case before the court, for it is only necessary to discover in the law some "potential for unfairness" or some "possible fonts of injustice" in order to argue that regardless of the facts in the actual case before the court the law should be struck down.[19]

Through the device of a generalized attack on the law the facts of a particular prosecution may be diverted onto a siding while attention is focused on the operation of a statute under various hypothetical circumstances unrelated to the facts in the case. For an inquiry into the facts of the accusation there is substituted a speculative inquiry into potentially invalid applications of the statute under which the charge has been brought. Here, the capabilities for delay are limited only by the resourcefulness of counsel in conjuring up theoretical possibilities of unconstitutional applications of the law under attack. In *Younger* v. *Harris* and related cases the state criminal prosecutions under attack were delayed for periods up to five years on the basis of charges which in Justice Black's words amounted to "nothing more than speculation about the future." [20]

ATTACK ON HOLDING A TRIAL BECAUSE OF
UNFAVORABLE PUBLICITY

The defendant in a criminal prosecution may claim that because of unfavorable publicity or because of community prejudice he will be unable to get a fair hearing if he is brought to trial, and therefore his trial should not be held at its scheduled time or in its scheduled place. The impetus for this type of attack comes from *Sheppard* v. *Maxwell,* where the United States Supreme Court in 1966 set aside defendant's conviction for the murder of his wife in 1954 on the ground that extraordinary pretrial and trial publicity during the 1954 trial prevented defendant from receiving a fair trial consistent with the due process clause of the Fourteenth Amendment. The court noted the increasing prevalence of unfair news comment on pending trials and declared:

> ". . . where there is a reasonable likelihood that prejudicial news prior to trial will prevent a fair trial, the judge should continue the case until the threat abates, or transfer it to another county not so permeated with publicity. . . . If publicity during the proceedings threatens the fairness of the trial, a new trial should be ordered." [21]

In short, widespread publicity may preclude further prosecution of a case at its regularly scheduled time and place.

Under this expanded view of the effect of pretrial publicity, a defendant may routinely seek to postpone his trial or move it to another location. At a minimum he will secure an evidentiary hearing, whose validity he may then challenge in the appellate courts.[22] In authorizing such a procedure the California Supreme Court, somewhat optimistically, foresaw no significant delay in the trial of cases as a consequence of such review. What the court failed to foresee was the development of multiple and repetitive motions for change of venue, each with its own appendant appellate review.[23]

Of equal significance in the sidetracking of criminal trials is the new standard for determining qualifications of jurors to sit in a particular case. The new rule requires a change of venue or postponement of the trial whenever "potentially prejudicial material" relating to the defendant has circulated. The change is required because jurors cannot efface such material from their conscious and subconscious minds and hence a reasonable likelihood arises that a fair trial cannot be had. Today, the traditional view that a juror without *fixed* opinions is qualified for jury service has been superseded by the view that only a juror without *any* opinions, and who has not been exposed to potentially prejudicial material, is qualified to serve.[24] In celebrated cases this requirement is an impossibility, and under such a rule, if followed literally, England, France, and Norway could never have brought to trial William Joyce (Lord Haw-Haw), Pierre Laval, and Vidkun Quisling. In 1971 a Connecticut superior court dismissed murder charges against Black Panther Bobby Seale, partly on the ground the defendant was so notorious that an unbiased jury could not be found to give him a fair trial.[25]

Clearly, the opportunities for delay are practically unlimited whenever a hearing is launched to determine whether potentially prejudicial material has circulated among potential jurors and, if it has, to evaluate the effect of that material on the conscious and subconscious minds of potential jurors.

Applications to appellate courts to forestall pending prosecutions in advance of trial are a relatively recent development in the law. As late as 1940 the United States Supreme Court declared there could be only one appeal in each case and that applications to reviewing courts for provisional relief prior to judgment were improper. Finality of judgment, wrote Justice Frankfurter for a unanimous court, was a condition of appellate review.

> "To be effective, judicial administration must not be leaden-footed. Its momentum would be arrested by permitting separate reviews of the component elements in a unified cause. These considerations of policy are especially compelling in the administration of criminal justice. . . . The correctness of a trial court's rejection even of a constitutional claim made by the accused in the process of prosecution must await his conviction before its reconsideration by an appellate tribunal." [26]

In California this point of view, if not archaic, is, at least, antiquated.[27] Applications are routinely made to appellate courts to secure rulings in advance of trial on the narrowest evidentiary and procedural points, and such applications are limited neither in time nor in number. This algebraic multiplication of potential side issues available for a defendant's use has brought us close to the point where a defendant need not stand trial at all until he is willing to do so, for as long as he perseveres on collateral issues, courts are reluctant to require him to go to trial.

The present difficulties in bringing a defendant to trial are comparable in some respects to those of the late medieval English courts in conducting felony prosecutions. Under early medieval law a felony defendant had a choice of three methods of trial—trial by battle, trial by ordeal, or trial by jury (also known as trial by the country)—and the exercise of this choice was considered an absolute right.[28] In the course of development of English law, trial by ordeal was abolished, and trial by battle became obsolete. Yet the choice remained part of the law, and until the defendant exercised his choice by entering his plea, i.e., consented to trial by jury, the proceedings remained at a standstill, and the trial could not proceed. In instances of refusal to plead a defendant was returned to prison and subjected to stretching and pressing and fed only bread and water on alternate days until he either pleaded or died. Such obstinacy was fairly common, because successful refusal to plead avoided forfeiture of the defendant's estate to the Crown. Not for a number of centuries did English law arrive at the present practice of entering a not-guilty plea on behalf of a defendant who stands mute and allowing the proceedings to go to trial without his consent.

As long as we entertain the present view that until a defendant ceases to raise collateral issues it is unfair to force him to stand trial, we continue to permit the defendant to control the course of litigation and effectively sidetrack the prosecution.

Mainlining

Mainlining differs from sidetracking in that the progress of the accusation continues on the main track, but its speed is reduced to a crawl. The trial goes forward in slow motion with each phase of the proceeding becoming in itself a major undertaking.

In many jurisdictions selection of a trial jury may consume weeks or even months of the court's time. Prospective jurors are examined exhaustively on their background, education, employment, personal history, personal beliefs, familiarity with the law, and experience as jurors in other cases. On occasion they may be subjected to rigorous cross-examination by counsel who wish to excuse them for cause without using up peremptory challenges to remove them. In California the selection of a trial jury in a criminal cause often resembles a filibuster. In *People* v. *Finch* selection of a jury took four to five weeks on each of two occasions.[29] In *People* v. *Sirhan* selection of the jury in 1969 took six weeks.[30] In *People* v. *Manson* selection of the jury in 1970 took five weeks.[31] This prodigal expenditure of time in jury selection contrasts sharply with the practice in England, where there is no interrogation of jurors and where selection of a jury, even in the most celebrated cases, usually takes no more than a few minutes.[32] The theoretical justification for exhaustive interrogation of prospective jurors is that such questioning makes it possible to obtain a jury composed of persons who have no opinions on any issues relevant to the case. In practice, exhaustive jury examination is used to propagate a particular viewpoint and to suggest through repetitive and reiterative assertion by counsel the existence of facts which may never be proved at the trial.

When the stage for the production of evidence has been reached, each item of evidence and almost every question put to a witness can be made a subject for argument. Certain kinds of evidence, as for example a confession, may first require a full hearing by the trial judge outside the presence of the jury to determine whether the evidence is admissible, and then a second hearing before the jury at which the identical evidence is presented a second time.[33] Subsidiary issues arising during the course of the trial may be extensively explored. For example, if the validity of a prior criminal conviction becomes an issue, a hearing may be held outside the presence of the jury to determine whether the defendant had been properly advised of and properly waived his right to counsel in the former proceeding.[34]

Other subsidiary issues may include treatment of the defendant while in custody, facilities available to him in custody, news media publicity and coverage of the cause, sequestration of the jury, sequestration of witnesses, statements by counsel inside and outside the courtroom, continuances for further preparation, continuances to interview witnesses, and the like. In California, criminal trials lasting for months are routine and in one instance a jury trial continued for nine months.[35] This dilatoriness sharply contrasts with the practice in England, where the longest criminal trial on record, the great mail train robbery, lasted only forty-eight days.[36]

Advantages to a defendant from these long, drawn-out trials are several. First, something may turn up to improve his situation; for example, a witness may recant, a witness may die, or the law may change. Next, the tolerance of the jury for the crime involved may grow with the passage of time on the principle made familiar by Pope. If a jury is forced to listen month after month to a brutal multiple murder or a child rape, it may become somewhat accustomed to the particular facts of the crime and perhaps deal more leniently with the defendant than it might have done on first acquaintance. Additionally, if the trial of a relatively simple case can be spun into months, some jurors may begin to believe there is more to the case than meets the eye. If the issues are simple and straightforward, reasons a certain type of juror, the court would not have allowed the case to consume the time it has taken. Therefore, some mysterious factor must be at work, a factor which the juror doesn't understand but which is important. Once a juror has acquired this frame of mind, he lays himself open to irrational suggestion of all sorts and becomes prime material with which to hang a jury. For the prosecution the dangers of overtrying a case, i.e., confusing the jury with a torrent of evidence, are well known. For a defense with nothing meritorious to bring forward, overtrial may be the most effective tactic possible.

Finally, a mainlining defendant is tying up court facilities for a great length of time, and other causes begin to pile up awaiting their day in court. Traffic may back up all the way to the station, and the entire line become choked. A prosecutor who knows that the trial of a particular case will occupy months of trial-time may be tempted to compromise his case by accepting a plea of guilty to a lesser charge. Thus, a murder accusation may end up with acceptance of a guilty plea to involuntary manslaughter. Dilatory tactics by defense counsel are not seriously frowned upon by the legal profession; rather, in the present climate of opinion they are routinely admired on the theory that counsel who employ them are putting up the best possible defense for their clients.

Mainlining thus serves a defendant's purpose and will continue to serve it so long as it is tolerated by the courts.

8

THE LAW'S DELAY—
PROCRASTINATION AT HOME
IN THE COURTS

THE extent of procrastination in criminal cases must be experienced to be believed. The bare statement that it takes so many months or so many years to bring a cause to judgment does not carry the impact on the reader that it should, for today's reader is so overwhelmed with statistical data that he tends to build up massive resistance to statistical shock. Yet the dilatory course of criminal proceedings is scandalous. The scandal lies not merely in the handling of the celebrated case, but extends to disposition of the routine, run-of-the-mill case involving neither extraordinary issues of law or fact. The most effective way to visualize the extent of this delay is to follow the chronology of a routine California case, *People v. Esparza,* in which defendant was caught in the act of burglary on 7 December 1968.[1] The reader is invited to imagine himself a participant in the case, either as witness, counsel, or presiding judge, and in that capacity to follow each step in the chronology as though he were personally involved. Following Esparza's arrest on 7 December 1968 these proceedings occurred:

1968
30 December. Information filed charging sundry robberies, burglaries, rapes, kidnappings, and sexual offenses.

1969

6 January. Defendant arraigned and pleaded not guilty.

3 February. Information amended to charge prior offenses. Trial continued to 4 March.

4 February. Arraignment and plea continued to 10 February.

10 February. Arraignment and plea continued to 13 February.

13 February. Defendant arraigned and pleaded not guilty. Trial date remained 4 March.

28 February. On defendant's motion trial continued to 2 April.

2 April. On defendant's motion trial continued to 24 April.

24 April. On defendant's motion that his counsel was elsewhere engaged, trial continued to 1 May.

1 May. On defendant's motion trial continued to 9 May.

9 May. On defendant's motion that his counsel was elsewhere engaged, trial continued to 14 May.

14 May. On defendant's motion that counsel was elsewhere engaged, trial continued to 15 May.

15 May. On defendant's motion trial continued to 20 May.

20 May. Defendant pleaded guilty to three counts of the information. Probation and sentence set for 13 June.

13 June. Mentally disordered sex offender proceedings initiated, and proceedings continued to 10 July.

10 July. Defendant's motion to withdraw guilty plea granted, and not-guilty plea reinstated. Cause continued to 18 July for trial setting.

18 July. On motion of defendant, cause continued to 1 August for trial setting.

1 August. On motion of defendant, cause continued to 8 August for trial setting.

8 August. On motion of defendant, cause continued to 29 August.

29 August. Prosecution moves to vacate order reinstating defendant's not-guilty plea. On motion of defendant cause continued to 5 September.

5 September. By stipulation cause continued to 1 October.

1 October. Prosecution's motion to vacate order reinstating not-guilty plea denied. Cause continued to 8 October for trial setting.

8 October. Trial set for 2 December.

13 November. Hearing on defendant's discovery motion; motion granted in part.

26 November. Defendant's motion to dismiss two kidnapping

counts granted as to one. Trial date of 2 December vacated, and cause continued to 3 December for trial setting.

3 December. Cause set for trial on 21 January 1970.

1970

21 January. Defendant's motion to relieve deputy public defender is denied. Defendant's motion to suppress evidence continued to 22 January.

22 January. Cause continued to 23 January.

23 January. Hearing on motion to suppress evidence continued to 26 January.

26 January. Motion to suppress evidence granted in part. Hearing held on motion to dismiss lineup evidence. Later, motion is denied. Trial continued to 27 January.

27 January. Trial begins.

9 February. Jury returned verdicts of guilty.

4 March. Judgment and sentence.

In Esparza's prosecution fourteen months elapsed from filing of the accusation to entry of judgment. But California law contemplates that criminal causes will be brought to trial within two months. Penal Code section 1382 states that if the defendant is not brought to trial within sixty days, the action shall be dismissed unless the delay has been caused or consented to by defendant. And Penal Code section 1050 requires that

> "all proceedings in criminal cases shall be set for trial and heard and determined at the earliest possible time, and it shall be the duty of all courts and judicial officers and of all prosecuting attorneys to expedite such proceedings to the greatest degree that is consistent with the ends of justice."

Yet despite these provisions delays beyond the statutory period are routine.

Defendants almost invariably procrastinate. Prosecutors likewise procrastinate, for a case that has been dismissed for lack of timely prosecution may be reinstated by filing a new accusation.

It should be noted that in Esparza's prosecution no fewer than twelve continuances of the proceedings were granted at defendant's request. The wasted time of witnesses, counsel, and trial judge as a result of these continuances is incalculable. Yet California has a strong statutory policy against continuances in criminal cases. Penal Code section 1050 states:

"No continuance of a criminal trial shall be granted except upon affirmative proof in open court, upon reasonable notice, that the ends of justice require a continuance. . . . No continuance shall be granted for any longer time than it is affirmatively proved the ends of justice require."

In the light of this statutory policy against continuances the reader may wonder why continuances are granted so readily by trial judges. The answer is found in the readiness with which appellate courts reverse judgments of conviction for refusals to grant continuances. It is axiomatic that a trial judge can never go wrong granting a further continuance, but if he denies a continuance it is possible that he may subsequently be reversed. Consider a few examples: In *People* v. *Maddox* the judgment of conviction was reversed because, when on the day of trial defendant discharged the public defender and undertook to represent himself, he was denied a sixty-day continuance.[2] In *Jennings* v. *Superior Court,* even though evidence at the preliminary hearing constituted sufficient cause to hold defendant to answer charges in the complaint, the information was ruled invalid because defendant had not been allowed a continuance at the preliminary hearing to attempt to locate a witness.[3] In *People* v. *Crovedi* the judgment of conviction was reversed because the trial court, after having continued the trial for two weeks, refused an additional continuance of at least seven more weeks so that defendant could be represented by counsel who was recovering from a heart attack.[4] In *People* v. *Murphy,* a prosecution for pimping and statutory rape, the information was amended on the morning of the trial to change the names of the two customers alleged to have been involved in defendants' criminal activities from Jim Prince and Jim McDonald to John Doe William and John Doe Bob.[5] The trial court's denial of defendants' request for a continuance formed the basis for the subsequent reversal of the judgments of conviction.

Criminal cases proceed at an equally leisurely pace on appeal. In 1969 the median delays for the various divisions of the California Court of Appeal, Second District, between notice of a criminal appeal and the filing of an opinion were twelve to twenty-five months.[6] In 1970 similar median delays were fourteen to seventeen months.[7]

Why such delays?

Defendants procrastinate. Professor Delmar Karlen has summarized the reasons for procrastination by defendants:

"Why should the accused in a criminal prosecution plead guilty? More than likely he is free on bail or on his own recognizance, for this is becoming more and more the practice in the United States; he is probably well advised by counsel, supplied at public expense; and he knows that the case will not be reached for trial for six months or a year, possibly longer. The prosecution witnesses may forget or disappear, and the victim of the crime may become so disgusted with delays and adjournments that he will drop the charges if he can or fail to appear at the trial when it is finally reached. . . . Because delay yields such rich dividends, it pays to demand a trial, quite apart from the chance of winning the case either at the trial or the appellate level." [8]

Trial judges, court clerks, and court reporters procrastinate. Consider a routine example, *People* v. *Grant.*[9] Grant was sentenced to prison for robbery on 4 May 1969. On the day of his sentence he filed a notice of appeal. Although Rule 35 of California Rules of Court requires that the record of the trial be filed in the appellate court within thirty days, the record was not filed until 22 September 1969, a delay four times as long as that contemplated by the rule. The reporter's transcript was of average length (260 pages), and no reason for the delay was apparent other than procrastination.

Lawyers procrastinate. Procrastination is the occupational disease of the legal profession. Consider the further progress of *People* v. *Grant* after the record was filed with the court of appeal. The briefing of this appeal, instead of the eighty days contemplated by the California Rules of Court,[10] took fourteen months. Meanwhile Grant continued to languish in state prison.

Such lawyer procrastination is ordinary, not extraordinary.

Judges procrastinate. As erstwhile lawyers, judges bring habits of procrastination with them when they assume the bench. The California Constitution requires a cause to be decided within ninety days of its submission, and a judge who does not comply with this provision is not entitled to collect his salary.[11] But the effect of the requirement may be avoided by resubmission of a cause or by delayed submission of a cause.

In particular cases judicial procrastination can be profligate. In *Castro* v. *Superior Court* petitioners were charged in March 1968 with offenses arising out of demonstrations at public high schools.[12] In January 1969 petitioners applied to the court of appeal for an extraordinary writ to prevent the superior court from proceeding to trial on their indictment. Eighteen months later in July 1970 the court of appeal decided the petition for the writ, holding invalid and insufficient on constitutional grounds some but not all the charges brought against petitioners. The court itself conceded:

71

"As a result of our decision in this writ proceeding and the passage of time, several of the petitioners who, according to the evidence presented to the grand jury, clearly committed or aided and abetted in the commission of several misdemeanors, may never be tried for those crimes. We share the view of anyone who thinks that this is a most undesirable result." (9 Cal. App. 3d 675, at p. 677)

Judicial procrastination is not limited to California. In *Harrison* v. *United States* defendant's appeal from his second conviction was argued in the federal appellate court in the District of Columbia in December 1963. The cause was reargued in June 1965, and remained under submission in the court of appeals until December 1965, a period of two years between initial argument and decision.[13]

Excuses for failure to meet legal deadlines tend to be sympathetically received by the courts. Although under the California Rules of Court a notice of a criminal appeal must be filed within sixty days of the judgment,[14] acceptance of delay of a year or more is common.[15] On one occasion the sixty-day period to file an appeal was extended to almost ten years. This occurred in *People* v. *Flores,* where defendant was convicted in 1961 of participation in an armed robbery.[16] In 1970 the California Supreme Court granted his petition for delayed appeal on the ground that he had not learned the English language until after he had spent some years in prison and therefore had not known of his right to appeal. On his delayed appeal his conviction was affirmed in March 1971.

When all these delays are put together in one case the legal process, like Joshua's sun, appears to stand still. In *People* v. *Dobson,* a routine assault and battery, two-and-one-half years elapsed between arrest of the defendant and affirmance of his conviction on appeal.[17] At no stage did the proceedings conform to time schedules established by statute and by rules of court. It must be emphasized that this was a routine representative case, in no way extraordinary.

9

ERROR—INCOMPETENCY OF
COUNSEL AND
SELF-REPRESENTATION

Incompetent Counsel

UNDER the Sixth Amendment an accused is entitled to assistance of counsel for his defense. In California free counsel have been provided for indigent felony defendants since 1872, long before the 1963 decision of the United States Supreme Court in *Gideon* made free counsel for indigent felony defendants a constitutional requirement under the Fourteenth Amendment.[1] Initially, assistance of counsel was interpreted to mean the assistance of an attorney licensed to practice law and in good professional standing within the jurisdiction in which the accusation was pending. But the ideal of perfectibility envisages counsel in each case who function at maximum effectiveness with the smoothness, precision, energy, and skill of, say, a John W. Davis. Under the thrust of this conception California has adopted the view that an accused is entitled to the assistance of, not just any counsel, but competent and diligent counsel, whose absence from a particular trial reduces it to a farce and a sham and compels reversal of a judgment of conviction.[2] The practical implementation of this view requires qualitative evaluation of the performance of defense counsel in each case, in order to determine with the aid of hindsight whether the performance came up to a theoretical standard of excellence attributable to counsel of first chop at the bar. With the full flowering of this doctrine, incompetency of counsel has come to embrace any arguable deficiency in strategy or tactics in the conduct of a case that might have had some effect on its outcome.

In California incompetency of trial counsel has become a routine ground for appeal, a ground supplemented in later appeals and in postconviction remedies by the further claim of incompetency of counsel on appeal. In evaluation of these claims innocence or guilt of the defendant becomes largely immaterial. Thus a defendant goes to trial and loses. On appeal he argues incompetency of trial counsel. He loses his appeal. On further appeal he argues incompetency of appellate counsel on his earlier appeal. He loses again. On collateral attack he argues denial of due process of law because of absence of competent counsel on his further appeal. And so on into infinity.

These gymnastics received a large boost from the United States Supreme Court in 1967 when, having previously decided that all indigents are entitled to free counsel on appeal,[3] it undertook in *Anders* v. *California* to analyze the duty of appointed appellate counsel.[4] Because of the requirement of equal protection of the laws contained in the Fourteenth Amendment, said Justice Clark, appointed counsel may no longer advise the court the appeal has no merit:

> "The constitutional requirement of substantial equality and fair process can only be attained where counsel acts in the role of an active advocate in behalf of his client. . . . Of course, if counsel finds his case to be *wholly frivolous,* after a conscientious examination of it, he should so advise the court and request permission to withdraw. That request must, however, be accompanied by a *brief* referring to anything in the record that might *arguably* support the appeal. . . . This procedure will assure penniless defendants the same rights and opportunities on appeal—as nearly as is practicable—as are enjoyed by those persons who are in a similar situation but who are able to afford the retention of private counsel." (Italics added.) (386 U.S. 738, at pp. 744–45)

The California Supreme Court has enlarged the *Anders* requirement of effective assistance of counsel on appeal, and *In re Smith* it vacated the affirmance of a judgment of conviction on the ground of incompetence of appellate counsel.[5] In opting for imaginative appellate advocacy the court catalogued what it termed plausible assignments of error which might have been argued and then declared:

> "We have catalogued the arguments which petitioner's counsel failed
> to offer on behalf of his client, *not because we conclude that peti-*
> *tioner was likely to obtain a reversal on appeal,* but only to demon-
> strate that his appellate counsel did not render the thoughtful assis-
> tance to which he was entitled. *Petitioner need not establish that he*
> *was entitled to reversal in order to show prejudice in the denial of*
> *[competent] counsel."* (Italics added.) (3 Cal. 3d 192, at p. 202)

Obviously, the court was not concerned with the merits of the appeal, but
only with the vigor with which plausible arguments should have been presented. It follows that in many cases a defendant is better served at his
trial by a bad lawyer than a good one, for with the bad lawyer he can center subsequent inquiries on the lawyer's inadequacies and postpone or
sidestep an examination of the charges on which he was convicted.

The author knows no instance where counsel who had been judicially
declared incompetent in a particular California proceeding has been required to defend his right to continue to practice law or been prevented in
any way from further imposing his incompetence on other clients in other
causes. Indeed, an attempt by a trial judge to remove appointed counsel
from a pending murder trial on the ground counsel was not competent to
try a murder case and had previously been found incompetent by another
judge to try a marijuana possession case was disapproved by the California
Supreme Court. In reinstating appointed counsel, that court concluded that
the trial judge had exceeded his powers, had infringed upon defendant's
right to counsel of his choice, and had compromised the independence of
the bar.[6]

As a result of the *Anders* and *Smith* decisions, defense counsel who
wish to avoid subsequent charges of incompetency tend to argue every
conceivable point, whether or not it possesses the slightest merit. Consider,
for example, the following argument on an appeal in behalf of one Miyamoto from a judgment of conviction for rape, to the effect that defendant
had been represented by incompetent counsel at his trial because trial
counsel had not raised the issue of defendant's insanity:

> "No sane person would criminally assault a woman and then tell her
> that he wants to be friends with her husband. It is further submitted
> that no sane person would tell a woman that he wants to help her
> when he means he wants to rape her. . . . It is therefore submitted
> that defense counsel deprived Miyamoto of a crucial defense, namely,
> the defense of insanity. . . . While it may be contended that it does

not conclusively appear from the record that Miyamoto is legally insane, it is submitted that it is at least an arguable issue." [7]

The weakness of the *Anders* opinion is that after pointing out that rich men can take frivolous appeals while poor men cannot, it wrongly concludes that constitutional equality under the Fourteenth Amendment requires that everyone be allowed, even encouraged, to take frivolous appeals.[8] The sensible way to achieve the desired goal of equality would have been to cut down on frivolous appeals by the rich, not extend them to the poor. Justice Clark, the author of the *Anders* opinion, on his retirement from the Supreme Court commendably undertook service on the trial bench for the first time. In a subsequent newspaper interview about his experiences, Clark identified one of the causes of legal delay as the "appeals courts being nearly swamped with frivolous cases and matters that should be disposed of with a simple order, rather than a time-consuming hearing." [9] About this conclusion from the author of the opinion that launched a thousand frivolous appeals, the comment of Justice Frankfurter seems apt: "Wisdom too often never comes, and so one ought not to reject it merely because it comes late." [10]

Self-Representation

The accused in a criminal prosecution, in addition to his right to assistance of counsel, has a right to appear and defend in person. This means he may act as his own counsel, a right actually older and of longer standing than his right to assistance of counsel.[11] But imposed on both these rights is the new constitutional requirement that an accused be represented by effective, competent counsel, a requirement now guaranteed him by the Sixth and Fourteenth Amendments.

Because of the existence of this requirement of competent counsel, California courts have ruled that the right of self-representation may be exercised only by a defendant who is competent to represent himself. Before a defendant will be permitted to waive his right to counsel, the trial court must first determine his competency to represent himself. This the court does by conducting an inquiry into the defendant's understanding of the nature of the charges, the elements of the offense, the available pleas and defenses, and the punishments that could be imposed. The inquiry normally covers defendant's education and experience, his prior acquaintance with the law, his familiarity with courtroom procedure, and his understanding of substantive law. The California Supreme Court has said it "will not accept a mere superficial inquiry," [12] and in order to properly carry out this mandate the trial court must conduct a minitrial on the question of the accused's competency to represent himself.

If the trial court fails to conduct a sufficiently searching inquiry, or if it conducts a sufficient inquiry but reaches an incorrect conclusion, then a subsequent conviction of the defendant will be reversed, and the charges against him may be dismissed. Thus has come into being a game available to defendants entitled Waive the Lawyer, which, if skillfully played, may vitiate the consequences of an unfavorable verdict. Sophisticated defendants have undertaken to play the Game for reasons summarized by Justice Otto M. Kaus of the California Court of Appeal:

"We can take judicial notice [citation] that in case after case the obvious purpose of the defendant's request to be permitted to represent himself is not a sincere desire that the motion be granted, but rather the hope that it will be granted or denied after an inadequate inquiry concerning the defendant's competency to waive counsel or that, if the inquiry is sufficiently exhaustive, the court will make a ruling which a higher court will, later on, find to have been erroneous." [13]

The Game becomes particularly elaborate when codefendants are involved who periodically raise questions of self-representation, appointment of counsel, and appointment of separate counsel for each defendant at successive stages of the proceedings.[14] A further refinement of the Game developed by imaginative players involves the gambit of a *conditional* demand for self-representation. In *People* v. *Carter,* during the four months immediately prior to trial defendant was granted numerous continuances and changes of counsel.[15] On the day of the trial defendant demanded the right to represent himself, which was granted, but he also demanded further time for preparation and for the use of a law library, which were denied. The California Supreme Court concluded that the waiver of counsel was *conditional,* that the failure of the trial court to accept the condition or advise defendant it intended to reject the condition was error which deprived defendant of his constitutional right to counsel and required reversal of the judgment of conviction.

In appellate review of cases involving the dichotomy of right to counsel and right to self-representation, the guilt or innocence of the defendant becomes wholly immaterial. To paraphrase Cardozo, if the trial judge blunders, the accused goes free.[16] Under the operation of this doctrine a defendant's conviction for grand theft with five prior felony convictions was reversed on appeal and the prosecution dismissed—because defendant had been improperly denied the right to represent himself.[17]

The game of Waive the Lawyer may continue into subsequent proceedings. For example, in *People* v. *Newton,* the defendant, on trial in 1968 for murder, and charged with a prior conviction in 1964 of assault, filed a motion at his 1968 trial to strike his prior assault conviction on the ground that his waiver of counsel in 1964 had been constitutionally ineffective.[18] In 1964 Newton had insisted on representing himself, and his conviction in that case had been affirmed by an appellate court, which found he had validly waived counsel. In view of this affirmance, the trial court in the 1968 proceeding denied defendant's motion to strike his 1964 conviction. But in 1970 the appellate court (which reversed Newton's conviction for manslaughter on other grounds) found this denial erroneous because the trial court in 1968 had not held an evidentiary hearing to determine whether the trial court in 1964 had sufficiently inquired into defendant's capacity to represent himself in order to make his then waiver of counsel constitutionally effective. Black Panther Huey P. Newton did not, of course, claim he had been incompetent to represent himself in 1964. He merely claimed that the trial court in 1964 had not made sufficient inquiry into his capabilities to represent himself, and consequently his 1964 conviction had been rendered constitutionally invalid. The governing principle here is that failure to conduct the *inquiry* renders the conviction constitutionally invalid, regardless of the defendant's actual capabilities.

One more point in this Alice in Wonderland of *People* v. *Newton:* The requirement for an evidentiary hearing was first laid down by the California Supreme Court in 1967. Thus the trial court in *Newton* was supposed to hold an evidentiary hearing in 1968 to determine whether another trial court in 1964 had conducted a sufficient hearing on defendant's ability to represent himself (and thereby waive his right to counsel) and to judge the sufficiency of the 1964 hearing by standards first promulgated by the California Supreme Court in 1967.

The basic vice of the restrictions on self-representation is that they force counsel on an unwilling defendant. By-products of such unwanted representation include physical assaults, interminable quarrels between defendant and counsel over the latter's competency, and endless motions by defendant to dismiss his appointed counsel for incompetency.

A sensible resolution of the problem created by the Game should not prove difficult. Since a defendant is entitled to represent himself, all defendants should be allowed to do so except those who are certifiably insane or who are suffering from patent mental or physical disability. If a defendant wishes to exercise his right of self-representation and thereby acquire a fool for a lawyer, he should be allowed to do so as long as he conducts himself in an orderly manner. To force an unwanted lawyer on him is an exercise in paternalism reminiscent of revolutionary zeal:

> SPEAKER: Comes the revolution, comrades, we'll all have strawberries and cream.
> LISTENER: But I don't like strawberries and cream.
> SPEAKER: Comes the revolution, comrade, you'll *have* strawberries and cream—and *like* it.

An offshoot of the right of self-representation involves prisoners and persons in custody awaiting trial who undertake to represent themselves. Since a defendant is entitled to be represented by effective, competent counsel, it is argued that a defendant in confinement who undertakes to represent himself is entitled to facilities necessary for that purpose. Principally these involve access to a law library and time to use its law books. In California, law library facilities are maintained at central metropolitan jails and in state penal institutions, and prisoners are permitted to purchase law books of their own and keep limited quantities of them in their cells.[19] The sufficiency of the law library facilities in the state's custodial institutions was attacked in the federal court,[20] and the latter characterized the issue as a substantial question of constitutional law arising out of the due process and equal protection clauses of the Fourteenth Amendment. With respect to prisoners in California the federal district court reasoned that

> ". . . the affluent are guaranteed the right to communicate with private counsel [Calif. Pen. Code, § 2600(2)], and to buy personal law books without restriction save as to space limitations. The indigent, however, are relegated to seeking out fellow inmates with legal knowledge, and to the resources of the prison law library, the contents of which are severely limited under the regulation now under attack. . . . This neglect of one class, when contrasted with the attention paid to the rights of others, raises serious equal protection questions." (319 F. Supp. 105, at p. 111)

Because the federal district court found law-book facilities for indigent California state prisoners inadequate, it enjoined the California Director of Corrections from enforcing prison regulations dealing with law libraries and ordered him to file new regulations with the federal district court, presumably regulations which would provide a greater number of law books and would allocate additional public funds for their purchase.

The logical steps that make adequacy of prison law libraries a constitutional issue under the Fourteenth Amendment derive from two legal fictions: that a nonlawyer with access to an adequate law library becomes the equal of a competent lawyer, and that an inmate confined in prison or in jail can enjoy access to legal facilities equivalent to that enjoyed by a free man on the outside. Since neither fiction possesses substance in fact, facilities for self-representation in confinement will never prove adequate, and controversy over their adequacy will continue so long as courts examine the problem from the viewpoint of a fictitious equality.

10

ERROR—OPEN SWITCHES
THAT DERAIL THE CAUSE

T HE attempt to achieve technical perfection in the trial of causes has fostered a technique that may be termed open-switching. An open switch is one which may derail a trial no matter what action is taken by the presiding judge. In criminal trials the art of open-switching consists in creating a dilemma of such a nature that whichever way the judge rules it can be argued later that his ruling was erroneous. The more dilemmas introduced into a trial, the more the likelihood of reversible error.

One such dilemma involves disruption of the trial by the defendant, by defense counsel, or by both.[1] The trial judge confronted with disruption has, basically, two choices. He can be punitive, or he can be permissive. If he takes the punitive approach and imposes sanctions for misbehavior, the sanctions will almost inevitably interfere to some extent with the presentation of defendant's case and the conduct of the trial. On appeal defendant can vigorously argue that the sanctions were excessive, arbitrary, and vindictively conceived, that their imposition invaded his constitutional rights and prevented him from obtaining a fair trial. When the trial judge follows a punitive course it frequently happens that he will be later faulted by the reviewing court for not using different sanctions or for not applying them in a different fashion. On the other hand, if the trial judge takes a permissive approach, the disruption tends promptly to escalate, and the judge may lose all control over the proceedings and its participants. When this happens the trial is discredited, the system of justice is blackened, and on appeal the reviewing court is apt to criticize the trial judge for excessive

81

indulgence and for a failure of moral mastery that produced chaos rather than a fair trial.[2]

A tactic comparable to disruption, often of equal effectiveness and involving less personal risk, is the refusal of defendant, or his counsel, to participate in the proceedings, usually on the ground of unfairness after some specific demand has been refused by the court. The resulting dilemma of the trial judge is both genuine and immediate. If the judge goes ahead with the trial without defendant's or counsel's participation, the proceedings soon acquire a certain noxious appearance. If the judge succumbs to the demands, he has opened himself to further blackmail and to the charge of wishy-washiness. Once again we take an example from the game of Waive the Lawyer (see Chapter 9). In *People* v. *Jones,* defendant, charged with indecent exposure and two prior convictions for the same offense, sought to act as his own counsel, but the trial judge denied his request on the ground he was not qualified.[3] Defendant thereupon announced he would refuse to cooperate with the public defender and would not present a defense. After some further discussion the trial judge relented and allowed defendant to dismiss the public defender and conduct his own defense. Defendant's conviction was reversed on appeal, because, said the appellate court, the trial judge should not have allowed defendant's threat of noncooperation with counsel to sway him into allowing defendant to dismiss the public defender and represent himself.

On the other hand, if the judge stands firm and conducts the trial without defendant's participation, more probably than not a judgment of conviction will be reversed on appeal.[4] In such cases appellate courts search the record minutely in order to find reversible error in the proceedings— for a trial in which the defendant does not participate bears so little resemblance to the ideally perfect trial that the reviewing court is likely to consider it no trial at all. Once again we find a modern application of the principle of medieval English jurisprudence that a defendant who does not consent to trial may not be brought to trial. The theoretical hope of the court that reverses a conviction involving nonparticipation is that the defendant will ultimately be persuaded to collaborate with the trial court in producing some semblance of the perfect trial.

Open-switching is a particularly effective tactic in cases where multiple defendants are involved, for the court can be presented with dilemmas at every stage of the trial. For example, in *People* v. *Chacon* four defendants were represented by the same attorney at their arraignment.[5] At their next appearance one defendant asked the court to appoint separate counsel to represent him, which was done, and two other defendants moved to represent themselves, which was allowed. Thus prior to the time of trial two of four defendants were represented by separate, appointed counsel, and the other two defendants had obtained the right to represent themselves. On the day of trial the latter two defendants informed the court that they now wished to be represented by the particular counsel who represented one of the other defendants. The court granted their request, and at the trial these three defendants were convicted. On appeal, their convictions were reversed because the three had not been specifically told on the day of trial that appointment of separate counsel for each of them might have been sought. The California Supreme Court declared that conflicts of interest necessarily exist when penalties must be fixed for more than one defendant, and it concluded that defendants with conflicting interests who have been represented by the same counsel have been denied the effective assistance of counsel. Yet had the trial court refused to permit the requested representation and insisted on appointment of separate counsel for each defendant, it is easy to visualize a reversal of the same cause for violation of defendants' right to be represented by counsel of their own choice.[6]

Multiple defendants represented by the same trial counsel are in an unusually favorable position to maneuver the court into an open switch. For example, two defendants represented by the same counsel may go through an entire trial and submit their cases to the jury without making any complaint about joint representation. If they are acquitted, that ends the matter. If they are convicted, then on motion for a new trial they can argue for the first time that they had a right to separate counsel, because the difference in their degree of culpability created a conflict of interest between them.[7]

When there are multiple defendants, one of them may demand one course of action; his codefendant may insist on the exact opposite. For example, one defendant may request sequestration of the jury; his codefendant may oppose sequestration on the ground that it produces an unrepresentative trier of fact. One defendant may press for an early trial; another may seek a continuance.[8] Whatever ruling the judge makes may later be found to be reversible error. Where multiple defendants are involved the trial court can be maneuvered into a triple open switch. For example, defendant A may move to postpone the trial in order to mitigate the effect of unfavorable publicity. Defendant B may move for a change of venue on the ground of prejudice in the local community, and defendant C may insist on immediate trial in the place where the accusation is pending. Here the nominal odds are two to one that the trial court's ruling may later be held erroneous. It is, of course, possible that the trial of the cause could be severed into three parts. This brings us back to considerations relating to length of trial discussed in Chapter 7 under the heading "Mainlining."

Another technique of open-switching is to set up a conflict in the duties of the court. An instance of this appears when a defendant produces a witness who himself may be subject to criminal liability for the offense with which the defendant is charged. If the court fails to call the witness's attention to the dangers of self-incrimination, the court may be criticized as derelict in the performance of its duty.[9] But if the court vigorously instructs the witness on the possible dangers of self-incrimination, the court may discourage the witness from testifying and thus prejudice the defendant who sought to call the witness. Thus the open switch: discouraging the witness is prejudicial to the defendant; not discouraging the witness is prejudicial to the witness.

Jury instructions on the law provide prolific sources for open-switching. The traditional view has been that the court's instructions to the jury on the law are derived from proposed instructions submitted by the parties to the court. But in recent years appellate courts in California have ruled with increasing frequency that the trial court must instruct the jury on certain subjects whether or not the defendant requests or desires such instructions. For example, in *People* v. *Newton* a conviction for manslaughter in a shoot-out with a policeman was reversed because the court had not instructed the jury on unconsciousness as a defense.[10] At the trial defendant had withdrawn his request for this instruction. Nevertheless the appellate court ruled that the trial court should have given the instruction on its own initiative. Thus, the open switch. If the trial court volunteers an instruction on a subject the defendant does not solicit, defendant can later argue his conviction should be reversed because of an unsolicited instruction. Contrariwise, if the instruction is not given, as in *Newton,* defendant can argue for reversal for failure properly to instruct the jury.

In *People* v. *Hood* a police officer in uniform responded to a call for help and was jumped by defendant and shot twice with the police officer's own gun.[11] The California Supreme Court held it reversible error for the trial court in a prosecution for assault with a deadly weapon *on a peace officer* (maximum punishment, fifteen years) not to have instructed the jury on its own initiative on the lesser included offense of assault with a deadly weapon (maximum punishment, ten years). Although defendant had not requested such an instruction, the reviewing court concluded that defendant might have thought the officer was preparing to use excessive force against him and therefore would not have been acting within the scope of his duties as a police officer, as a consequence of which defendant's bullets would have been directed against the officer as an individual and not as a police officer.

Even entry of a guilty plea by a defendant represented by counsel may be made a subject for open-switching.[12] The trial judge is now required to interrogate at length a defendant who wishes to enter a guilty plea, even though defendant is represented by counsel present in court. The interrogation must show that the plea is intelligent and voluntary, that defendant has waived his privilege against self-incrimination, that defendant has waived his right to a jury trial, that defendant has waived his right to confront his accusers, and that defendant possesses a full understanding of the connotations and consequences of his plea. The United States Supreme Court has made these requirements a matter of constitutional law, and each right must be separately enumerated and each response personally elicited from the defendant. In California a trial judge is also required to explain to the defendant the full import of a guilty plea.

These requirements add up to a considerable volume of improvised and extemporaneous legal advice that the trial judge is required to give the defendant in rough-hewn form. In a busy trial court conducting a variety of legal business, errors and omissions in such advice are always possible. For example, in one instance a defendant pleaded guilty to two of five narcotic charges after an hour's conference with the prosecutor, defense counsel, and the judge to whom the case had been assigned. The judgment of conviction was reversed because at the conference the judge had given mistaken advice on the legal implications of the defense of entrapment and on the judge's discretionary power over sentence.[13] When a judge gives legal advice to the defendant about the factors to be weighed in entering a plea, his advice must be both accurate and complete. In another case a defendant was found guilty of burglary after the case had been submitted to the court on the transcript of the preliminary hearing. The judgment of conviction was reversed on appeal because at the time of submission the judge had not advised defendant of the punishment for burglary, and the appellate court declared it could not assume that defendant's counsel had done so.[14] Unquestionably, a broad highway lies here for future attacks on guilty pleas and submissions.

In recent years the trend of appellate decisions has been to combat asserted incompetence of defense counsel by making the trial judge an associate defense counsel and requiring him to tender legal advice to defendant to protect the latter's interests, even against defendant's or defense counsel's own views of those interests. If, as is bound to happen on occasion, the trial judge's extemporaneous views on the defendant's situation are inaccurate or incomplete or ill-advised, then a firm basis has been laid for future reversal, this time not for incompetency of counsel but for incompetency of judge. And with reason, for the judge is ill-equipped and ill-placed to carry out the functions of defense counsel.

III

Perfect Justice
in Operation

11

DUE PROCESS, SHOCKED
CONSCIENCE, AND EMANATIONS
INTO THE PENUMBRA

ⅠN previous chapters we have seen how the ideal of perfectibility has manifested itself within the judicial process in the form of retroactive review, parallel review, multiple trial, multiple review, inordinate delay, and technical reversal. The consequence of this mechanical proliferation and duplication of the elements of the judicial process has been a corrosion of the sanctions within our legal system and a weakening of the law's power of compulsion. But the ideal of perfectibility has embarked upon a journey of further expansion—this time into the substance of the law itself. The demarcation line between form and substance has always been blurred at the boundary, and expansionist-minded legal theorists, operating under the banner of procedural right, have succeeded in moving the frontier deep into the territory of substantive law. From there a further march has taken them to the citadel of statute law. The chapters that follow discuss the legal doctrines through whose use this expansion has been achieved, explore the consequences that have resulted in certain areas of law, and suggest the desirability of fundamental change.

The basic authority employed by the courts to exercise control over substantive law is the Constitution of the United States, and the legal doctrines used to justify the exercise of federal control over state law are found in the Fourteenth Amendment to the Constitution. The use of the

Fourteenth Amendment to expand federal court control over state activity has centered upon two phrases in that Amendment, *due process of law* and *equal protection of the laws*. The historical development and current use of these phrases are briefly discussed in this and the succeeding chapter.

The phrase *due process of law* made its first appearance in the federal Constitution in 1791 with the adoption of the Fifth Amendment, which prohibits the federal government from depriving any person of life, liberty, or property without due process of law. The original meaning of due process comprehended law in its regular course of administration through courts of justice, and the due process clause originally operated merely to place certain procedures beyond the reach of the legislative process. In the words of Story, "This clause in effect affirms the right of trial according to the process and proceedings of the common law." [1]

Up to the time of the Civil War the phrase *due process of law* was used only once by the United States Supreme Court to limit the substantive content of federal legislation. That one use occurred in the Dred Scott case, where Chief Justice Taney, in holding limitations on slavery in the Missouri Compromise unconstitutional, reasoned that a statute which deprived "a citizen of the United States of his liberty and property, merely because he came himself or brought his property into a particular Territory of the United States, and who had committed no offence against the laws, could hardly be dignified with the name of due process of law." [2] Neither the Dred Scott decision nor Taney's argument were well received by the country, and this initial use of the phrase *due process of law* to regulate the substance of legislation was a resounding failure.

The Fourteenth Amendment to the Constitution, adopted in 1868, provides that no state shall deprive any person of life, liberty, or property without due process of law, nor deny any person within its jurisdiction the equal protection of the laws. When this amendment was first considered by the Supreme Court in the *Slaughter-House Cases* in 1873, the court gave due process of law its traditional procedural meaning in holding that state laws prohibiting all groups of butchers except one from exercising their trade in New Orleans did not deprive the excluded butchers of property without due process of law. [3]

But in later years of the nineteenth century the phrase *due process of law* began to be used by the Supreme Court as authority to weigh the substantive content of state laws, and with respect to laws that interfered with liberty of contract or with property rights, the phrase became authority to justify an evaluation of the basic fairness and equity of the interference rather than the regularity of the legal form employed. In the unfolding of

90

this doctrine, unjustifiable interference by state law with liberty of contract became a deprivation of property without due process of law and therefore unconstitutional, as the court held in the leading case of *Allgeyer* v. *Louisiana*.[4] The use of the due process doctrine to invalidate the substance of state law reached full flower in *Lochner* v. *New York,* in which a New York law restricting employment in bakeries to ten hours a day or sixty hours a week was held unconstitutional in 1905 as an interference with liberty of contract,[5] and in *Coppage* v. *Kansas,* where a Kansas statute outlawing yellow-dog contracts (i.e., agreements not to join a union) was found invalid in 1915 as an unconstitutional interference with freedom of contract.[6] Restrictions of due process of law were also applied against substantive legislation of the federal government, and in *Adkins* v. *Children's Hospital* a District of Columbia minimum-wage statute for women and children was held unconstitutional in 1923 as a violation of the due process clause of the Fifth Amendment.[7]

The theory behind the doctrine of substantive due process is that arbitrary power which injures persons or property is not law in any true sense, no matter how enacted, and against the exercise of arbitrary power the courts have a duty under the Constitution to protect persons and property, even when that power is exercised in the name of the government and through the government's own agencies. But who is to decide what power is arbitrary? Under the doctrine as it has developed, quite obviously it is the courts who decide. And how are the courts to determine when a law reflects arbitrary power and when it does not? Justice Holmes, dissenting in *Lochner,* would, in general, leave that decision to popular majority opinion which has embodied its views into statute law:

> "It is settled by various decisions of this court that state constitutions and state laws may regulate life in many ways which we as legislators might think as injudicious or if you like as tyrannical as this, and which equally with this interfere with the liberty of contract. . . . The Fourteenth Amendment does not enact Mr. Herbert Spencer's Social Statics."

Yet even Holmes paid tribute to the notion of substantive due process of law, for in the same opinion he said:

> "I think that the word liberty in the Fourteenth Amendment is perverted when it is held to prevent the natural outcome of a *dominant* opinion, *unless it can be said that a rational and fair man necessarily*

91

would admit that the statute proposed would infringe fundamental principles as they have been understood by the traditions of our people and our law." [8] (Italics added.)

In opting for the natural outcome of dominant opinion, Holmes spoke only for a minority of the court, and in the years immediately preceding the constitutional crisis of 1937 the Supreme Court more and more assumed for itself the role of ultimate adjudicator of the merits and wisdom of state and federal legislation.[9] Through its use of the doctrine of substantive due process the court played an accelerated role in thwarting effective government regulation of the economic affairs of the country, either by the states, or by the national government.

In 1937 President Roosevelt presented to Congress his proposal to reorganize the Supreme Court through the appointment of extra judges and thereby precipitated a six-month constitutional battle. At the height of the turmoil the Supreme Court took judicial notice of the strength of dominant opinion, and in rapid order it overruled its earlier decisions on the unconstitutionality of minimum-wage laws for women; it upheld the constitutionality of the National Labor Relations Act; and it overruled its earlier decision that injunctive relief must remain available to prohibit peaceful picketing.[10]

As a result of the Supreme Court's timely shift in direction, the court reorganization bill was defeated, and with changes in personnel of the court the constitutional crisis of the New Deal era subsided into history. One casualty of the battle, however, was the use of substantive due process of law as a measuring rod for the fairness of legislation. The new orthodoxy was reflected in Justice Frankfurter's declaration that it is not the function of courts to exercise their own judgment whether a legislative policy is within or without the vague contours of the due process clause.[11]

But the doctrine of due process of law remained moribund only a few years. Its revival was initiated in *Adamson* v. *California* in 1947 by a dissenting opinion of Justice Black, who argued that the restrictions on the power of the federal government contained in the first ten amendments to the Constitution (the Bill of Rights) had been incorporated by the due process clause of the Fourteenth Amendment as restrictions on the power of the states.[12] By adhering to this position over a period of years Black eventually persuaded a majority of the court to make a selective incorporation of the restrictions in the Bill of Rights into the Fourteenth Amendment, and thereby make these restrictions binding upon the states.

Counterpoised to the theory of due process of law defined by the Bill of Rights and incorporated as restrictions on the states by the Fourteenth

Amendment, arose another theory: the due process clause of the Fourteenth Amendment, although not incorporating restrictions on the federal government as restrictions on the states, does restrict the states from using laws which violate standards of fundamental decency and fairness or which violate generally accepted precepts of natural law. Proponents of this theory, among them Justice Frankfurter, argued the superiority of their view of due process over the incorporated due process theory, in that their view recognized the federal nature of our legal system and gave the states the flexibility needed to bring about change and reform. This natural law theory of due process was wholly unacceptable to proponents of the incorporated theory of due process, and Justice Black viewed the natural law theory as itself unconstitutional. In his *Adamson* dissent he declared:

> "And I further contend that the 'natural law' formula which the Court uses to reach its conclusion in this case should be abandoned as an incongruous excrescence on our Constitution. I believe that formula to be itself a violation of our Constitution, in that it subtly conveys to courts, at the expense of legislatures, ultimate power over public policies in fields where no specific provision of the Constitution limits legislative power." (332 U.S. 46, at p. 75)

This doctrinal warfare continued for fifteen years until the war was finally settled with adoption by the Supreme Court of both doctrines.

Substantially all protections of the first eight amendments were selectively incorporated through the due process clause of the Fourteenth Amendment as restrictions on the power of the states. Among these were exclusion of illegally seized evidence (*Mapp* v. *Ohio*); requirement of free counsel (*Gideon* v. *Wainwright*); requirement of free counsel on appeal (*Douglas* v. *California*); privilege against self-incrimination (*Malloy* v. *Hogan*); comment on defendant's failure to testify (*Griffin* v. *California*); restrictions on custodial interrogation (*Miranda* v. *Arizona*); right of confrontation (*Pointer* v. *Texas*); probable cause for issuance of search or arrest warrant (*Ker* v. *California*); prohibition against double jeopardy (*Benton* v. *Maryland*); jury trial in criminal cases (*Duncan* v. *Louisiana*).[13]

But at the same time that selective incorporation was being put into effect, the Supreme Court expanded its practice of declaring unconstitutional any law or procedure that offended its notions of acceptable justice or that infringed what it considered to be fundamental principles of natural law. Formulation of the natural law doctrine first achieved prominence in *Rochin* v. *California,* a case in which narcotic agents used a stomach pump to retrieve morphine capsules petitioner had swallowed at the time of his arrest.[14] In reversing petitioner's conviction, the court held that the use of evidence obtained by conduct which "shocks the conscience" violates the due process clause of the Fourteenth Amendment. Convictions brought about by methods which offend a sense of justice, fair play, and decency, said the court, violate due process of law. Thus shock-to-conscience, also described as violation of the fundamentals of ordered liberty and as violation of the canons of decency and fairness, became embodied within the term due process of law. Gradually at first, more frequently in later years, this general concept of fairness came to be widely applied, and it was used to overturn the New York procedure for submitting the issue of voluntariness of a confession to the jury (*Jackson* v. *Denno*),[15] to declare unconstitutional the use of television over the objection of a defendant in a heavily publicized case (*Estes* v. *Texas*),[16] and to declare unconstitutional courtroom identification of a defendant by a witness if pretrial identification has occurred at a lineup without the presence of counsel (*United States* v. *Wade*).[17]

In the current revival of substantive due process as a restriction on the power of state and federal governments, emphasis has been placed on personal rights and freedom from personal restraint. The new due process with its emphasis on personal rights is always differentiated from the old substantive due process represented by the discredited *Allgeyer-Lochner-Coppage-Adkins* doctrine, which protected property rights and safeguarded liberty of contract. Of this more later.

Although the majority of instances of use of due process, both that of selective incorporation and of fundamental fairness, related to due process in connection with court procedures, use of the doctrine began to spread to other areas. In *Schware* v. *Board of Bar Examiners,* licensing of attorneys by the states became a field for federal supervision under the due process clause of the Fourteenth Amendment.[18] Refusal by a state to license an applicant to practice law "on a wholly arbitrary standard . . . that offends the dictates of reason offends the Due Process Clause." The Supreme Court thus assumed what Justice Harlan later termed a general oversight of state investigatory procedures relating to bar admissions.[19] The due process clause was also used to invalidate a state law prohibiting secrecy of membership in an association (*NAACP* v. *Alabama*),[20] thus overruling an earlier application of a similar law to the Ku Klux Klan; [21] to supervise state employment of school teachers (*Shelton* v. *Tucker*); [22] to invalidate an Illinois law regulating currency exchanges (*Morey* v. *Doud*); [23] to invalidate a state's regulation of its attorneys with respect to solicitation of clients and business (*NAACP* v. *Button*).[24]

94

Periodically, however, the Supreme Court has said it would never revive the discredited doctrine of substantive due process of law reflected in *Lochner* and *Adkins,* that it could never return to the day when it would invalidate state laws because they were unwise, improvident, or out of harmony with a particular school of thought.[25] Yet with respect to the professions of attorney and school teacher the court has done exactly that, and it has reinstated the nineteenth century interpretation of the due process clause of the Fourteenth Amendment as its authority to review state issuance of occupational licenses and state regulation of occupations, the very question at issue in the *Slaughter-House Cases* (see p. 90). Where the Supreme Court leads subordinate state and federal courts follow, and the latter have once again begun to refer and cite with approval the *Coppage* decision invalidating a statute against yellow-dog contracts, and the *Allegeyer* decision upholding liberty of contract.[26]

But the expanded concept of due process of law has not stopped with incorporated due process and with fundamental-fairness due process In *Griswold* v. *Connecticut* the Supreme Court in 1965 in effect cut loose entirely from the restraints imposed by a written constitution and created a new constitutional right of privacy made binding upon the states by the due process clause of the Fourteenth Amendment.[27] As the precursor of new doctrine the case merits close attention. In *Griswold,* defendants challenged as contrary to the due process clause of the Fourteenth Amendment Connecticut laws which forbade the use of contraceptives and forbade the giving of contraceptive advice. Defendants ran a clinic which gave information to married persons about means of preventing conception. In invalidating these laws the Supreme Court, speaking through Justice Douglas, declared that the Constitution included not only specifically named rights but also peripheral rights, and that particular amendments had penumbras which surrounded their particular guarantees:

> "The foregoing cases suggest that specific guarantees in the Bill of Rights have penumbras, formed by emanations from those guarantees that help give them life and substance." (381 U.S. 479, at p. 484)

The court then found that the Connecticut statutes on contraception violated the zone of privacy surrounding the marriage relationship protected by several fundamental constitutional guarantees, among them those of the First, Third, Fourth, Fifth, Ninth, and Fourteenth Amendments.

Concurring justices agreed with the invalidation of the Connecticut laws for a variety of reasons: Justice Goldberg, because the concept of liberty protects fundamental personal rights and is not confined to the specific terms of the Bill of Rights; Justice Harlan, because the laws violated basic values implicit in the concept of ordered liberty protected by the due process clause of the Fourteenth Amendment; and Justice White, because the Connecticut statues deprived married couples of liberty without due process of law in violation of the Fourteenth Amendment.[28]

In dissent, Justice Black pointed out that the court had done what it said it would never do and had returned full circle to the discredited doctrine of *Lochner* and *Adkins,* i.e., that the court may declare unconstitutional those federal and state laws it finds arbitrary, capricious, unreasonable, or offensive to its notions of natural justice and civilized standards of conduct. He thought the Supreme Court was now claiming for itself and the federal judiciary "power to invalidate any legislative act which the judges find irrational, unreasonable or offensive," and he foresaw that the adoption of such a loose, flexible, and uncontrolled standard for holding laws unconstitutional would amount to a great shift of power to the courts, which, he was constrained to say, would be bad for the courts and worse for the country. He then quoted a dissenting opinion of Justice Holmes to the effect that the Fourteenth Amendment was not intended to give the majority of the court carte blanche to embody its own economic or moral beliefs in its prohibitions. Justice Stewart, also dissenting in *Griswold,* denied there was any general right of privacy in the Constitution, and said that although he thought the Connecticut law uncommonly silly, it was the province of the legislature and not of the courts to repeal it.[29]

This expanded concept of due process of law appeared again in *Shapiro* v. *Thompson,* a case which found a constitutional right in welfare recipients to obtain welfare benefits from the jurisdiction of their choice without satisfying a residency requirement of one year.[30] First, the court ruled that because of the constitutional right to travel from one state to another a waiting period of one year established by the *states* for eligibility for relief amounted to an invidious discrimination against indigents which denied them the equal protection of the laws under the Fourteenth Amendment. Then the court disposed of the similar one-year residency requirement adopted by Congress for the District of Columbia by holding that this *federal* restriction violated the due process clause of the Fifth Amendment and was therefore unconstitutional. Unjustifiable discrimination, said the court, violates due process of law.

Thus a constitutional right to travel joins a constitutional right to privacy as an engine under the due process clause to invalidate legislation thought improvident or undesirable by the Supreme Court. Due process of law now possesses three faces: (1) incorporated due process, (2) shocked-conscience and fundamental-fairness due process, and (3) interference-with-a-newly-emanated-constitutional-right due process.

Subordinate tribunals have been quick to respond to this expansion of power suggested by the Supreme Court. For example, in *Baird* v. *Eisenstadt* a federal court of appeals declared unconstitutional a Massachusetts statute that prohibited the sale or delivery of a contraceptive device except to a married person on prescription of a registered physician.[31] Among other grounds the court found the Massachusetts prohibition against contraception arbitrary, discriminatory, and in conflict with fundamental human rights. What clearly appears from the decision is the court of appeals' dislike for the state law, its refusal to await legislative action, and its willingness to invalidate statute law by the creation of yet another constitutional right—right of privacy (extramarital phase). As in Aesop's fable of the wolf and the lamb, if a court dislikes a law and wants to devour it, any excuse will serve. Thus substantive due process has reappeared, stronger than ever.

In the field of state criminal law and procedure the imposition of federal standards of incorporated due process, shocked-conscience due process, and emanations-from-the-penumbra-of-constitutional-rights due process has resulted in enactment by the United States Supreme Court of a detailed code of state criminal procedure, any deviation from which may suffice to overturn a criminal judgment years after the judgment has become final. Of this process the most famous example is *Miranda* v. *Arizona,* which deals with the subject of custodial interrogation.[32]

Once the Supreme Court has adopted a particular provision of its code of criminal procedure, the new procedure becomes embalmed in the Constitution, and there it remains until the Supreme Court itself decides to change it. For example, in *Katz* v. *United States* the court in 1967 made eavesdropping by federal agents on a person's use of a telephone booth unconstitutional under the Fourth Amendment, and in doing so it overruled its earlier decisions to the contrary handed down in 1928 and 1942.[33] Under current doctrine this ruling automatically extends to state criminal procedure.

The consequence of this expansion of federal power over state criminal procedure through the creation of flat prohibitions and rigidly ritualistic rules has been to elevate formalism to constitutional right, to complicate every significant phase of criminal procedure to the point where in some instances the system of criminal law has difficulty functioning and in others it turns loose persons who are patently guilty.

Yet rehabilitation of the doctrine of substantive due process proceeds apace. The opinions of the long-discredited Justice McReynolds have ac-

97

quired current respectability, and are now cited with approval by the Supreme Court.[34] And learned legal commentators in academic circles call for judges to impose their views on legislatures in such fields as abortion, pornography, gambling, homosexuality, and marijuana, through the engine of substantive due process.[35]

12

EQUAL PROTECTION OF
THE LAWS AND EQUALITY

Tₕₑ second doctrine on which heavy reliance is placed to achieve perfectibility in the legal order is that of *equal protection of the laws*. This phrase, like due process of law, finds its immediate source in the Fourteenth Amendment, which in a clause that fortifies the prohibition of the Thirteenth Amendment against slavery declares that no state shall deny "to any person within its jurisdiction the equal protection of the laws." The equal protection clause is designed to prohibit discriminatory legislation in favor of particular persons as against others in like condition, and to prohibit discriminatory law enforcement among persons similarly circumstanced, i.e., unequal treatment of equals. Such was the original interpretation of the clause by the Supreme Court in 1886 in *Yick Wo* v. *Hopkins,* where a San Francisco municipal ordinance made unlawful the operation of a laundry in a wooden building without the consent of the board of supervisors, and the board of supervisors customarily denied consent to Chinese nationals while granting it to others.[1] To discriminate in this manner solely on the basis of nationality, the court ruled, is to deny equal protection of the laws. But in 1896 the Supreme Court in *Plessy* v. *Ferguson* held that a state statute which required separate but equal accommodations on railroads for white and colored persons did not deny equal protection of the laws.[2] Thus the doctrine of separate-but-equal came into being and remained the law of the land for fifty-eight years. Use of the equal protection clause to review the substance of legislation was largely relegated to tax matters.

The revival of the equal protection clause began in 1942 with invalida-

99

tion by the Supreme Court of an Oklahoma law providing for sterilization of habitual criminals on the ground the law denied equal protection in that it applied to thieves but not embezzlers and thus discriminated without reason against the former in favor of the latter.[3] In later cases the court used the equal protection clause to hold that restrictive racial covenants on residential property could not be enforced by a state,[4] and to invalidate a California statute that withheld commercial fishing licenses from persons ineligible for citizenship (resident alien Japanese).[5]

These cases were followed in 1954 by the landmark decision of *Brown* v. *Board of Education,* in which the Supreme Court overruled *Plessy* v. *Ferguson* and held that racial segregation in public schools pursuant to state law denied Negro children the equal protection of the laws guaranteed them by the Fourteenth Amendment.[6] In repudiating the separate-but-equal doctrine the court declared that equality of facilities was not equivalent to equal protection of the laws under the Constitution, since segregation fostered the perpetuation of an inferior position and status for Negro children. The segregation of Negro children from others of similar age and qualifications solely because of race, declared the court, generated a feeling of inferiority about their status in the community, for a policy of separating the races by law is usually interpreted as denoting the inferiority of the Negro group. Where a state has undertaken to provide an opportunity for education, the opportunity must be made available to all on equal terms.

The cornerstone of the court's holding that racially segregated education denies the equal protection of the laws to Negro children is found in the hypothesis that racial segregation by law connotes inferiority of status. This implies, and the court in a series of cases has so ruled,[7] that racial segregation by law of other public facilities likewise amounts to denial of the equal protection of the laws. Thus legalized segregation on the basis of race or nationality has been found unconstitutional as a denial of equal protection of the laws. However, an expansive interpretation of the statement in *Brown* v. *Board of Education* that education "is a right which must be made available to all on equal terms" [8] has tended to confuse the idea of equal protection of the laws with the idea of equality. Some general discussion of the various meanings of equality may help clarify recent legal developments in this field.

The classic statement of Aristotle in reference to equality is that equals should be treated equally and unequals treated unequally. Aristotle categorizes the two types of equality as numerical equality and proportional equality.[9] Under numerical equality each person receives the same benefit, pays the same fee, pays the same tax, and casts the same vote. Under proportional equality a benefit or tax is allocated in proportion to need or ability to pay. But it is obvious that in addition to these two categories of equality a third category exists, one that may be termed subjective equality. Under subjective equality the extent of the benefit or burden is determined by the circumstances of the person to whom it is attached. A classic example of subjective equality is found in the Biblical parable of the widow's mite, whose farthing contribution was a greater gift than the much money cast into the treasury by the rich. Examples of numerical equality, of proportional equality, and of subjective equality may readily be found in the tax laws. Numerical equality is seen in an airport departure tax, which imposes the same fee on each passenger, rich or poor. Proportional equality is seen in the income tax as originally adopted, which taxed a flat percentage of personal income, and in a purchase or use tax, which taxes a flat percentage of the price of goods purchased or used. Subjective equality is seen in the graduated income tax, adopted in World War I and subsequently extended in World War II to impose a 91 percent tax on income above $200,000. Subjective equality is also seen in excise taxes on such luxuries as liquor, furs, and jewelry, which are normally taxed at considerably higher rates than other goods.

A moment's reflection makes it evident that with respect to each type of equality—numerical, proportional, and subjective—equality in one sense produces inequality in the others. A tax that satisfies numerical equality will not fall proportionally on taxpayers of different means, a tax that is proportionally equal will not require subjective equality of sacrifice from taxpayers of different means, and a tax that is subjectively equal in its application to different taxpayers will not qualify as numerically equal. Thus equality in one sense amounts to inequality in the others. To interpret the constitutional provision for equal protection of the laws in terms of equality we must first determine what type of equality is involved.

A second aspect of the constitutional application of equal protection of the laws takes into account the existence of inequalities among persons, situations, and things, and recognizes the justice of Aristotle's directive that unequals should be treated unequally. A mother on welfare with four dependent children should receive greater benefits than a similar mother with two. An ocean liner should pay a canal toll many times greater than that paid by a two-man fishing boat. In these instances unequals are recognized as such and are given unequal treatment. The law validates this unequal treatment because the inequalities arise from some valid factor that justifies different treatment. Within the same class, however, persons, situations, and things must be treated equally, that is to say, the ocean liner must pay the same toll as other ocean liners of the same size, and the fishing boat the same toll as other comparable fishing boats. In this manner we

101

arrive at classification, and with it the legal rule that a class must consist of persons, situations, and things which are similarly situated. If a class is too wide, or, conversely, if a class is too narrow, it may not qualify as a valid classification and hence may run afoul of the equal protection clause. These deficiencies in classification have been described in legal terminology as overinclusion and underinclusion.

To visualize the theory of overinclusion and underinclusion, consider the law against wife-beating (Cal. Pen. Code, § 273d). A defendant charged with an offense under the statute might attack the statute as inclusive of too large a class, and hence invalid by reason of overinclusion, in that a husband who pounds his wife on the back when she has a fishbone in her throat or slaps her in the face when she has hysterics falls within the terms of the statute. Alternatively, the same defendant might attack the statute as inclusive of too small a class, and hence invalid by reason of underinclusion, in that the prohibition of the statute is limited to infliction of bodily injury and does not cover injury brought about by mental torture or verbal assault, both of which may produce greater suffering than mere physical beating. A defendant charged with wife-beating is not precluded from launching an attack on the statute because his own conduct falls squarely within the prohibition of the statute, a point illustrated by the case of *Street* v. *New York*, where a conviction for flag-burning was reversed by the Supreme Court because the New York statute against flag-burning might have been wrongly interpreted to punish contemptuous words about the flag.[10] If the wife-beating defendant can convince the court that the statute is too broad or too narrow, then its classification is invalid and the statute may unconstitutionally deny him the equal protection of the laws. Why? Because this particular defendant has been discriminated against when his offense is considered in relation to, say, the husband who tortures his wife mentally but not physically.

Nor is this all; in addition to overinclusion and underinclusion, an even broader objection might be made to the statute against wife-beating: it could be argued that the statute is grounded on a suspect classification in that the statute has no application to husband-beating, and it is always possible that a large, muscular wife could inflict serious bodily injury on her small, frail husband. Today, sexual discrimination is closely akin to racial discrimination as a suspect category, and a male defendant charged with violation of the wife-beating statute could argue with some plausibility that the statute invidiously discriminated against him on account of his sex.[11] If a court should agree with him, it might very well hold the entire statute invalid as a denial of equal protection of the laws.

It is obvious that the concepts of numerical equality, proportional equality, subjective equality, overinclusion, underinclusion, and suspect classification are of practical value in solving specific legal problems only when kept under rigorous control and only when used with utmost restraint, for the concepts themselves furnish an unlimited opportunity and a never-ending temptation for those who use them to indulge in manipulation and frame a particular issue to achieve a preconceived end. Consider, for example, the problem in 1909 of Horace D. Taft, headmaster of a school in Connecticut attended by Robert A. Taft, son of William Howard Taft, at that time President-elect of the United States. Young Robert wanted desperately to attend the inauguration of his father as President, but unfortunately the school had strict rules against excusing students from classes during term-time. The problem was solved by adoption of a new rule: all boys whose fathers have been elected President of the United States may be excused from classes to attend the inauguration.[12]

It is evident that a great portion, perhaps the major portion, of the work of any legislative body consists in classification, definition, and delineation. A pays a tax, B does not; C's conduct subjects him to civil liability, D's does not; E's acts are criminal, F's are not; G is entitled to a benefit, while H is not. Additionally, this process of inclusion and exclusion forms the backbone of every organized body of science and of every rational scheme designed to bring order out of chaos. Since its use is so pervasive and so central to the creation of law, it is understandable why courts formerly left classification in the hands of the legislature and strongly resisted attempts to use the judicial process to revise classifications hammered out through legislative action. The undesirability of judicial revision of the legislative process by use of the equal protection clause was once so well accepted that Justice Holmes declared it was "the usual last resort of constitutional arguments to point out shortcomings of this sort." [13] In the Holmes view the equal protection clause was an instrument whose function was to strike down discrimination based on race or national origin.

The critical break with past practice came in 1964 with the full-blown entry of the United States Supreme Court into the field of political representation in *Reynolds* v. *Sims*.[14] The court adopted a one-man, one-vote requirement for state legislative representation and found unconstitutional any departure from equal population apportionment in the creation of state electoral districts. All such departures, the court held in a companion case, were invalid, even though a majority of the voters in a state might have approved by plebiscite unequal representation in one house of the state legislature.[15] These decisions rested squarely on a constitutional requirement of numerical equality of representation. In taking this position they rejected any concession to proportional equality or subjective equal-

103

ity, ideas of equality which in the past have met felt needs, both in representative government and in private associations that function on a representative basis. Obviously, numerical equality can be achieved only at the expense of other kinds of equality. For example, numerical equality ignores the factor of geographic dispersion when it requires all legislative representation to be established on a single basis. Prior to *Reynolds* v. *Sims,* isolated rural districts in California, such as the Owens Valley, had a substantial voice in the state senate, where they were overrepresented in proportion to their population. The same was true of the Neighbor Islands in Hawaii, similarly overrepresented in the Hawaiian senate. Under a one-man, one-vote allocation for both houses of the state legislature it seems highly doubtful that in Hawaii, for example, 150,000 persons scattered throughout the Neighbor Islands can effectively make their voices heard in legislative matters as against 600,000 persons concentrated in metropolitan Honolulu.

Subsequent to the *Reynolds* decision in 1964 the requirement of equal numerical representation has been expanded to all organizations that function in any governmental capacity, and it now covers such local entities as school boards, water districts, assessment districts, and the like. The decisions of the Supreme Court have not, of course, altered the inequalities of representation in the United States Senate. Thus, under the equal protection clause of the Fourteenth Amendment, state representative government, once called by Justice Brandeis a laboratory for experiment,[16] is now required to be more Catholic than the Pope.

Reynolds v. *Sims* relied on numerical equality. Another group of cases decided by the Supreme Court emphasizes proportional equality. In *Harper* v. *Virginia Board of Elections,* the court in 1966 declared unconstitutional a Virginia poll tax which treated all persons in numerically similar fashion with respect to the amount of a poll tax.[17] The basis for this ruling was the precise opposite of that in *Reynolds.* The court held that payment of an annual fee of $1.50 denied poor voters the equal protection of the laws under the Constitution because it drew lines between voters based on wealth and property and the lines it drew amounted to invidious discrimination. In this instance the court rejected the standard of numerical equality and held that nothing less than proportional equality would satisfy the requirement of equal protection of the laws. Significantly, the court found that a classification based on ability to pay an annual poll tax of $1.50 invidiously discriminated between rich and poor. In dissent, Justice Black deplored the use of the general language of the equal protection clause as a handy instrument to strike down state laws which the Supreme Court felt were based on bad governmental policy. The court was employing the equal protection clause, he said, to write into the Constitution its notions of good governmental policy.

In a third group of cases dealing with criminal procedure the Supreme Court held it a denial of equal protection of the laws for a state to require an indigent defendant who appealed his conviction to purchase a stenographic transcript of the proceedings,[18] and a denial of equal protection for a state to refuse to provide free counsel for indigents who wanted to appeal.[19] In these cases the court followed the standard of subjective equality, under which a state is constitutionally required to pay the cost of a stenographic transcript and the cost of counsel on appeal for a person who is indigent, but is not required to do so for a person who can afford to pay these costs.

Fed by the rhetoric of invidious discrimination the equal protection clause has flourished like the green bay tree. All a litigant need do is find someone better off or someone worse off than he is as the result of the operation of a particular law, and then argue he has been denied equal protection of the laws. Furthermore, it is not really necessary to find an actual someone, because imagining someone may be enough. The type of classification that can be made the basis for a claim of invidious discrimination, once limited to race and nationality, has now expanded to the point where it is coterminous with legislative classification itself and may even extend to classifications not yet reached by the legislature, for the creation of a given class is limited only by the imagination of the person conjuring up the class.

Differentiation based on sex has come under attack as a constitutional violation of the equal protection of the laws, and courts in California have ruled that the Constitution does not allow women to be excluded from tending bar,[20] or from working on the railroad.[21] This development has brought about a paradoxical reversal in the trend of the law. At the turn of the century a major objective of the Progressive Movement was the passage of legislation that would protect women by prohibiting their employment at heavy labor, for excessive hours, or for sweat-shop wages. With the help of Brandeis and others, laws for the protection of women workers were pushed through the state legislatures, and with such exceptions as the District of Columbia minimum-wage law held unconstitutional in *Adkins* v. *Children's Hospital*,[22] these laws were generally upheld by the courts. In *Muller* v. *Oregon* in 1908 the Brandeis sociological brief made its most famous appearance.[23] The current tide now flows strongly in the opposite direction, and laws previously adopted by state legislatures for the protection of women have come under heavy attack in the courts as discriminatory against women and hence unconstitutional. In many instances the ad-

105

vocates of change, instead of seeking amendments in the legislatures, resort directly to the courts, where they frequently find a sympathetic audience. Indeed, some of the courts now say very harsh things about the earlier decisions upholding protective laws for women, and in the lady bartender case the California Supreme Court referred to the United States Supreme Court's opinion in *Muller* v. *Oregon* as one resorting to "openly biased and wholly chauvinistic statements." (5 Cal 3d 1, at p. 17)

The net result of this expansive interpretation of the equal protection clause during the past decade has been to propel the courts pell-mell into the field of classification and differentiation, and to condition the courts to the idea that they should declare outworn or debatable legislative classifications unconstitutional, rather than refer the litigants back to the normal legislative process of revision and amendment. In effect, courts have become ready, willing, and eager to act as super-legislatures whenever litigants in particular causes can persuade them that legislative revision is presently desirable. Equal protection of the laws has become the chosen instrument to rewrite practically any law to the court's desire, for every classification may be found to contain arbitrary and invidious discrimination against some particular group and hence amount to a denial of equal protection of the laws. A few examples will give the flavor of current use of the equal protection clause as a device to vacate or annul laws that are not to the court's taste.

In *Dept. of Mental Hygiene* v. *Kirchner,* the California Supreme Court in 1964 held it a denial of equal protection of the laws to require an adult child to contribute to the care of a mentally ill parent.[24] Such a requirement, said the court, arbitrarily charges the cost of care of one group of society (mentally ill patients with adult children) to a particular class (the children), while the cost of care for mentally ill patients without adult children is borne by the state as a whole. Part of the reasoning which led to the court's conclusion that the charge was arbitrary and unconstitutional was grounded on the proposition that at common law a child has no legal obligation to support a parent. Since other mentally ill patients are supported by the citizenry at large through taxes, the court found it violated equal protection of the laws to require adult children of mentally ill parents to contribute to a species of taxation not imposed upon others.

In *County of San Mateo* v. *Boss* the California Supreme Court held in 1971 that an adult son had no duty to contribute twenty dollars a month as partial reimbursement of old age payments made by the county to his mother.[25] Such legislative classification, said the court, imposed an arbitrary charge on one class of society in violation of equal protection of the laws, since adult children are under no duty to support their parents. Although California has had a statute since 1872 imposing a duty on children of poor persons to maintain such persons to the extent of their abilities (Cal. Civ. Code, § 206), the court found the statute inapplicable in this case because the mother was not a poor person in that she owned a house. The court then reasoned in the following manner:

> "Therefore, defendant owes his mother neither a statutory nor a common law duty of support. Accordingly, there exists no rational basis to sustain the inclusion of defendant within a class which bears a disproportionately large burden of defraying the costs of the old age security aid program. As applied to defendant, the imposition of liability pursuant to sections 12100 and 12101 constitutes a denial of equal protection of the laws." (3 Cal. 3d 962, at p. 971)

The specific ruling in the case held it unconstitutional to require an adult son earning $800 a month to contribute $20 a month to the support of his mother.

In *Parr* v. *Municipal Court* the city council of Carmel had passed an ordinance which prohibited persons from sitting on the grass on public property.[26] The California Supreme Court in 1971 found that the ordinance denied the equal protection of the laws and hence was unconstitutional because the city council's motive in adopting the ordinance had been to halt the infiltration of undesirable transients into the city, particularly those undesirable and unsanitary persons known as hippies, a motive whose existence the court deduced from the city council's urgency clause making the ordinance effective immediately. The discriminatory purpose of the ordinance invalidated the measure, said the court, because it singled out a social group and stigmatized its members as undesirable and unsanitary. As an added fillip to support its holding, the court foresaw as inevitable a discriminatory enforcement of the keep-off-the-grass ordinance, and it envisioned state encouragement of private discrimination against hippies as a probable impact of the ordinance. Equal protection of the laws, said the court, is a constitutional verity which protects not only racial groups but also groups in current disfavor because of their attitudes, and the Carmel ordinance had been designed to "encourage private discrimination against the members of a cultural minority whose life style is disturbing to the majority." (3 Cal. 3d 861, at p. 870)

The current storm center in the use of the doctrine of equal protection of the laws is found in the field of public education, and the eye of the controversy swirls around the statement in *Brown* v. *Board of Education*

107

that opportunity for public education is a right which must be made available to all on equal terms.[27] This statement has been used to support a constitutional theory that public education must produce equal results for all its recipients, and from this has evolved the hypothesis that compensatory education is constitutionally required for pupils whose achievements fall below the norm. This theory assumes that public education should turn out pupils of uniform educational attainment and that, constitutionally, moneys and effort must be spent in a manner to achieve this result.

Thus a constitutional requirement of equality of opportunity has been transformed into one of equality of result. Such a subjective equality could be achieved, if at all, only by reversing the normal educational process and concentrating the best teachers and best facilities on those pupils least able to profit from education. In the popularization of this concept of equality public schools of superior standing and demonstrated merit, such as Lowell High School in San Francisco and Baltimore Polytechnic Institute in Baltimore, schools which have long accepted the brightest pupils from an entire school system solely on the basis of academic ability, have come under heavy attack and been charged with antidemocratic and racist orientation. Ignored is the fact that the existence of these schools has made it possible for a poor boy or girl to get a first-class free education in San Francisco and Baltimore. If a society undertook to train musicians and gymnasts by assigning the best instruments and the best teachers to the least promising pupils, it seems doubtful it would turn out many superior musicians and gymnasts. At least that was the view of Aristotle and Plato.[28] Past experience and common sense suggest that society will continue to find it most profitable to concentrate its best facilities on students who display the greatest aptitudes for the particular discipline involved. But it continues to be currently fashionable to argue that such rational selection violates a constitutional principle of equality. The type of equality meant is never specified.

A further development of the theory that equal protection of the laws requires equality of results is found in the notion that a particular race or group is entitled by reason of race or group alone to a proportionate share, or quota, of jobs in a given industry, of posts in public offices, of places in institutions of limited enrollment, such as law schools and medical schools, and of senior positions in public and private employment. In past years the Supreme Court has set its face against racial quotas and proportional representation, holding, for example, in 1950 with respect to trial juries:

"Proportional racial limitation is therefore forbidden. An accused is entitled to have charges against him considered by a jury *in the selec-*

tion of which there has been neither inclusion nor exclusion because of race." (Italics added.) [29]

The sponsors and supporters of racial quotas purport to find considerable support for their position in efforts of the United States Supreme Court to eradicate the effects of past legal segregation in public education. In the course of such eradication the Supreme Court has upheld busing of pupils by race, assignment of teachers by race, and establishment of racial quotas for pupils and teachers in particular schools. Yet in each instance the court has been careful to relate such moves to the prior existence of legalized segregation and to identify these moves as remedial devices available for use to eliminate the present effects of past legalized segregation. [30] Beyond this the court has not gone, and in view of the long constitutional history against discrimination based on race, it is difficult to imagine how the court could sanction racial quotas in employment or in selective admissions.

Other organizations, however, have failed to show similar restraint. The Board of Education in San Francisco undertook to promote and demote its administrative personnel on the basis of race in order to achieve an increased proportion of Negro administrators. [31] It does not require a profound legal scholar to conclude that a white administrator, whose services have been terminated solely because of the color of his skin in order to retain a black administrator junior to him and thereby increase the percentage of black administrators in the system as a whole, has a valid claim of unlawful discrimination on the basis of race, for the Civil Rights Act of 1964 makes it unlawful for an employer to discharge any individual because of that individual's race. In college faculty employment unmerited preference given to women and minority applicants has acquired the name *reverse discrimination,* that is, discrimination against white males, and the subject has become one of official government concern. [32] When racial discrimination ran the other way, the United States Supreme Court had no difficulty finding such discrimination unconstitutional, as in *Guinn* v. *United States* in 1915, where an exemption from the literacy requirement for voting given to those whose ancestors could vote before 1866 (grandfather clause) was held an invalid discrimination in favor of white illiterates and against Negro illiterates. [33]

The surface allure of racial quotas as a solution to racial problems has produced a type of double-think which from time to time passes itself off as current orthodoxy. For example, the American Bar Association's publication, *American Bar News,* in the same issue on the same page (October 1971, p. 3) reports ABA activity to uphold the use of racial quotas for admission of applicants to law schools, and also reports other ABA activity to prevent racial discrimination in the hiring of law school graduates. Under ABA theory, schools may discriminate on the basis of race but employers may not.

At least one member of the United States Supreme Court apparently would require racial quotas in public life. In *Carter* v. *Jury Commission* the court refused to require the Alabama governor to appoint county jury commissioners on the basis of race.[34] Dissenting from this holding, Justice Douglas declared he would strike down the jury commission because it did not provide proportional representation between whites and Negroes. Douglas referred with approval to legislation in India, which has authorized quotas for races and castes in legislatures, public offices, and public educational institutions. In the light of the tragic course of events in India following independence and the division of that country into three warring parts, it is difficult to understand how anyone could look upon India as a model for the correction of racial discrimination.

Proponents of racial quotas for employment and for selective admissions apparently assume that majority groups will never demand similar quotas for themselves. They theorize that each minority will achieve its proportionate share of jobs and admissions on quota and simultaneously remain free to exceed its proportionate share on merit—a theory which can work only if the majority foregoes its own claims. But quotas, once instituted, cannot rationally or logically be limited to minorities, and demands for quotas from majority groups are bound to ensue. A quota system necessarily imposes restrictions on overrepresented groups, including overrepresented minority groups whose members have achieved disproportionate success in a particular field. Such was the lot of Jewish applicants for admission to medical schools in New York during the 1930s, whose admissions were limited in numbers in order to preserve a quota of gentile students in medical schools in proportion to the latter's numbers in the general population.

A contemporaneous example of the phenomenon of quotas for majority groups is found in the activities of the Los Angeles Economic and Youth Opportunity Agency, an arm of the federal Office of Economic Opportunity engaged in the antipoverty program.[35] In 1971 the composition of the area staff of EYOA was:

	PERCENT
Black	45
Mexican-American	25
Anglo	23
Oriental and other	7

At that time the poverty population of the area was:

	PERCENT
Black	25
Mexican-American	30
Anglo	40
Oriental and other	5

Staff, board membership, and spending of funds were ordered "realigned" by the agency in order to reflect the ethnic proportions of the poverty population served, a realignment, however, which was to be achieved through "goals" rather than quotas. Yet regardless of the terminology used the consequences would come out the same—Blacks would be fired and Anglos would be hired, and a majority group quota established.

The distinction should be kept in mind between the use of racial quotas for competitive employment and selective admissions and the use of racial quotas to allocate persons within a system who are already members of that system. A school board or governing authority may adopt a policy of mixing different races as a long-term investment in racial harmony, and it may carry out its policy by redrawing school boundaries and allocating pupils on the basis of race. Such activity is proper and constitutional. In *Swann* v. *Charlotte-Mecklenburg Board of Education,* the Supreme Court said:

> "School authorities are traditionally charged with broad power to formulate and implement educational policy and might well conclude, for example, that in order to prepare students to live in a pluralistic society each school should have a prescribed ratio of Negro to white students reflecting the proportion for the district as a whole. To do this as an educational policy is within the broad discretionary powers of school authorities; absent a finding of a constitutional violation, however, that would not be within the authority of a federal court." (402 U.S. 1, at p. 16)

Equally proper are direct efforts to eliminate racial discrimination in labor unions, in public housing, in government employment, and in private employment. Use of racial quotas, on the other hand, attacks one discrimination by the creation of another discrimination against a different person or group. The latter can then justifiably claim a denial of equal protection of the laws.

In resisting invitations to enter the sphere of classification, the Supreme Court has declared again and again it does not sit as a super-legislature.[36]

But, like Lord Byron's Julia, who "whispering 'I will ne'er consent'—consented," it has assumed a posture from which it is difficult to fend off suitors. In *Shapiro* v. *Thompson* the court found a Connecticut law denying welfare benefits to residents of less than a year unconstitutional as an invidious discrimination between eligible and ineligible welfare beneficiaries.[37] The court thus put itself squarely in the legislative business of classification. One year is too long? What about three months? One month? Ten days? In dissent, Justice Harlan commented:

> "Today's decision, it seems to me, reflects to an unusual degree the current notion that this Court possesses a peculiar wisdom all its own whose capacity to lead this Nation out of its present troubles is contained only by the limits of judicial ingenuity in contriving new constitutional principles to meet each problem as it arises. . . . This resurgence of the expansive view of 'equal protection' carries the seeds of more judicial interference with the state and federal legislative process, much more indeed than does the judicial application of 'due process' according to traditional concepts . . ." (394 U.S. 618, at p. 677)

Because equality under one standard is inequality under others, any classification of any sort is subject to attack as a denial of equal protection, for necessarily the classification denies either numerical equality, or proportional equality, or subjective equality. And subjective equality, closely examined, turns out to be nothing more than another name for special privilege and special burden. This accordionlike notion of the equal protection of the laws is capable of furnishing suitable music for any occasion. *In re King* was the case of a father convicted of failure to support his children under a penal statute which classified such failure as a misdemeanor under ordinary circumstances but as a felony if the father remained out of the state for thirty days during the period of violation.[38] In 1970 the California Supreme Court found the statute arbitrary and contrary to the equal protection clause in that it invidiously discriminated between nonsupporting fathers who traveled and nonsupporting fathers who stayed at home. The classification, said the court citing *Shapiro* v. *Thompson,* lacked constitutional sanction because it violated "the individual's [nonsupporting father's] constitutional right to choose his own domicile and to travel freely throughout the country." (3 Cal. 3d 226, at p. 234)

What has happened is that under the rubric of equal protection courts have substituted their own views of enlightened social philosophy for those of the legislatures. Justice Harlan with his usual felicity of phrase referred to the equal protection rationale as a wolf in sheep's clothing, "no more than a masquerade of a supposedly objective standard for *subjective* judicial judgment as to what state legislation offends notions of 'fundamental fairness.' " [39]

From this brief review of the modern development of the doctrine of equal protection of the laws two critical constitutional developments take shape—first, the tendency of courts to cut loose entirely from a written constitution and follow what they believe to be the spirit of the laws, and second, the willingness of courts to supersede legislatures in the field of classification in order to promote the courts' own views of egalitarianism. These twin developments are discussed in the following chapter.

13

THE RETREAT FROM WRITTEN
LAW AND THE DECLINE
OF LEGISLATIVE AUTHORITY

THROUGHOUT history two fundamental demands have consistently shaped the development of the law. One is the demand for law in written form, a demand that law be made known, be established, and be publicly recorded. Moses, the great lawgiver, put fundamental law on two tablets of stone and later codified in written form the entire body of law governing the children of Israel. In Greek and Roman times the demand for written recorded law to replace unwritten law interpreted by the rulers periodically surfaced as a political issue, a demand that led in Rome to the adoption of the Twelve Tables. The leaders of the American revolution were responding to that same demand when they formulated a written constitution and embraced the doctrine of a government of law and not of men. The second fundamental guiding the evolution of law has been an insistence that new law be created by popular assembly, not by the monarch and not by a privy council. The history of the English parliament furnishes the best-known example of the transfer of the power to make new law from the hands of the monarch into those of a popular assembly.

During the past decade the supremacy of written, recorded law has been sharply challenged by the growth in popularity of the legal theories discussed in earlier chapters. Written law is now routinely qualified, rewritten, or repealed by the courts acting under the authority of natural law, fundamental law, or divine revelation. New rights have been created by the courts, rights which wholly supersede the provisions of written, recorded law. The scope and coverage of these newly created rights can only be declared by the courts, since the rights themselves are unwritten and derive entirely from the spirit of a Constitution whose interpretation lies within the exclusive province of the courts.

This supersession of written, recorded law by unwritten law has been most starkly revealed in *Griswold* v. *Connecticut,* the case which invalidated the Connecticut law against the use of contraceptives on the basis of a constitutional right to privacy, specifically marital privacy, a right created by the court out of emanations from the penumbra of specific constitutional guarantees (see Chapter 11). According to Justice Black's dissent, the technique for "diluting or expanding a constitutionally guaranteed right is to substitute for the crucial word or words of a constitutional guarantee another word or words, *more* or *less* flexible and *more* or *less* restricted in meaning" (italics added).[1] Through the use of this device broad, abstract, ambiguous concepts are substituted for specific provisions of the written constitution, and the latter's terms may thereby be expanded or contracted at the pleasure of the judges to achieve a predetermined result. Similar reliance on unwritten law emanating from the spirit of the Constitution appears in *Shapiro* v. *Thompson,* where the court nullified welfare residential requirements created by statute on the ground that they infringed an inherent constitutional right to travel,[2] and in *Harper* v. *Virginia* where the court found that classifications based on wealth or property were disfavored under the Constitution and overturned poll taxes which had been part of our written law since the earliest years of the Republic.[3] In the latter case Justice Black again called attention to the court's disregard for the written constitution and characterized the ruling as "an attack . . . on the concept of a written constitution." When a political theory embodied in the Constitution becomes outdated, he said, a majority of the nine members of the court not only are without constitutional power to choose a new constitutional political theory but are far less qualified to act than the people proceeding in the manner provided by the Constitution.

The viewpoint that the Supreme Court should be guided by the spirit of the laws was articulated in 1970 in *Oregon* v. *Mitchell* by four justices, who declared that they considered the Fourteenth Amendment a broadly worded injunction to be interpreted by future generations in accordance with the visions and needs of those generations.[4] Justice Douglas went further and declared that on the problem then before the court the history of the Fourteenth Amendment was irrelevant, a statement that completely astounded Justice Harlan and that contradicted an earlier assertion by Justice Holmes that a constitutional amendment should be read in a sense most obvious to common understanding at the time of its adoption.

The dangers of vague rulings based on unwritten law found in emanations from the penumbra quickly became apparent in *Baird* v. *Eisenstadt*.[5] There, petitioner's conviction in the state court for violation of a Massachusetts law prohibiting the sale or delivery of contraceptives except to married persons on prescription was invalidated by the federal court of appeals (1) on substantive due process grounds, because insofar as the statute reflected the legislature's belief in the immorality of contraceptives "such a view of morality . . . conflicts with fundamental human rights"; and (2) on equal protection grounds, because the statute discriminated without reason between married and unmarried persons in allowing the former but not the latter to obtain contraceptives on prescription. Thus we learn from the court in *Baird* that the right of marital privacy upheld in *Griswold* had nothing to do with marriage; but that if it did have something to do with marriage, it amounted to a denial of equal protection of the laws by discriminating without reason between married and unmarried persons. The *Baird* decision was later affirmed on equal protection grounds by the vote of four justices of the Supreme Court.

Such reliance on the instincts of judges as a source of public law is wholly at odds with Hamilton's view of the Constitution in *The Federalist,* where in reference to the courts he said:

> "To avoid an arbitrary discretion in the courts, it is indispensable that they should be bound down by strict rules and precedents, which serve to define and point out their duty in every particular case that comes before them. . . ." [6]

Law as the product of a popular assembly has also entered a period of decline. During the past decade, the habit has grown apace of replacing legislative acts of a popular assembly with decrees of a privy council, more specifically decrees of the courts. In this devaluation of written law and of legislative authority of popular assemblies, courts have boldly undertaken to rewrite laws of every description, from criminal procedure,[7] to rights of inheritance,[8] to regulation of personal conduct,[9] to state and federal election laws,[10] to parole revocation,[11] to abortion.[12] In entering upon such legislative tasks the courts find themselves creating, determining, selecting, and applying policy; choosing among various kinds of equality; weighing the benefits and burdens for particular groups; and then working out uniform schemes to carry out the policies they have deemed worthy of adoption. In superseding the legislative process the courts have demonstrated a willingness to employ constitutional doctrine to promote a policy of

116

subjective equality, a development noted in Justice Harlan's dissent in *Harper* v. *Virginia Board of Elections:*

> "Property and poll-tax qualifications, very simply, are not in accord with current egalitarian notions of how a modern democracy should be organized. It is of course entirely fitting that legislatures should modify the law to reflect such changes in popular attitudes. However, it is *all wrong,* in my view, for the Court to adopt the political doctrines popularly accepted at a particular moment of our history and to declare all others to be irrational and invidious, barring them from the range of choice by reasonably minded people acting through the political process. It was not too long ago that Mr. Justice Holmes felt impelled to remind the Court that the Due Process Clause of the Fourteenth Amendment does not enact the *laissez-faire* theory of society, *Lochner* v. *New York,* [citation]. The times have changed, and perhaps it is appropriate to observe that neither does the Equal Protection Clause of that Amendment rigidly impose upon America an ideology of unrestrained egalitarianism." [13] (Italics added)

This same tendency of the courts to supersede statute law with unwritten law appears again in *Boddie* v. *Connecticut,* where the court in 1971 held it unconstitutional for Connecticut to require payment of a court filing fee by an indigent who wished to file an action for divorce.[14] A majority of the justices thought the statutory requirement of a filing fee violated the due process clause, and a concurring minority thought it also violated equal protection of the laws because for them wealth, like race, had become a suspect classification for the determination of rights.[15] In one of his last dissents Justice Black declared that the case had been decided merely on the personal views of fairness held by the majority, "on a philosophy that any law violates due process if it is unreasonable, arbitrary, indecent, deviates from the fundamental, is shocking to the conscience, or fails to meet other tests composed of similar words or phrases equally lacking in any possible constitutional precision." Black then continued:

> "Such unbounded authority in any group of politically appointed or elected judges would unquestionably be sufficient to classify our Nation as a government of men, not the government of laws of which we boast. With a 'shock the conscience' test of constitutionality, citizens must guess what is the law, guess what a majority of nine judges will believe fair and reasonable. *Such a test wilfully throws away the certainty and security that lies in a written constitution,* one that does

not alter with a judge's health, belief, or his politics. . . . The people and their elected representatives, not judges, are constitutionally vested with the power to amend the Constitution. Judges should not usurp that power in order to put over their own views." [16] (Italics added.)

With this decline of legislative authority a certain reversal of function between legislature and courts has taken place. Instead of the legislature instructing the courts on the general rules of law that the courts should follow in deciding particular cases, the courts have been instructing the legislature on what laws the legislature can adopt and how those laws should be written. As a consequence of such judicial expansionism, in many fields of law the legislature merely echoes legislative acts that have been initially enacted into law by the courts. Consider two examples:

In *Townsend* v. *Sain* the United States Supreme Court in 1963 laid down a series of detailed procedural rules for exercise by federal courts of habeas corpus jurisdiction in the review of state criminal judgments.[17] Thereafter, Congress in 1966 amended the United States Code to paraphrase and restate the rules set out in *Townsend* v. *Sain,* thereby enacting the dictates of the Supreme Court into federal statute law.[18] Here the traditional division of authority between the legislative and judicial branches of the government was reversed, and instead of Congress through legislation determining the jurisdiction of the courts and establishing the manner of its exercise, the courts settled their own jurisdiction and decreed what legislation Congress should enact.

In *Roth* v. *United States* the United States Supreme Court undertook in 1957 to define and delineate obscenity.[19] Thereafter in 1961 the California legislature rewrote its obscenity statutes to define obscenity in the language used by the United States Supreme Court in *Roth*.[20] Once again the courts created new law, and the popular assembly had little choice but to ratify the new law created by the courts. In the obscenity field the California legislature has been hard put to keep pace with the obscenity views of the United States Supreme Court and of the California Supreme Court, and its obscenity statutes have required almost annual amendment in order to reflect current attitudes of the courts.

In recent years legislative declension and court ascension have accelerated their movements. An example is found in the death penalty cases in the California Supreme Court. In 1968 that court rejected an attack on the death penalty as cruel or unusual punishment, declaring that " 'the fixing of penalties for crime is a legislative function. What constitutes an adequate penalty is a matter of legislative judgment and discretion . . .' " [21]

A concurring justice wrote of his personal opposition to the death penalty and his temptation to yield to his predilections. But to do so, he said, "would be to act wilfully 'in the sense of enforcing individual views instead of speaking humbly as the voice of law . . .'" Slightly more than three years later the California Supreme Court again reviewed the same case, and this time the court found the death penalty invalid under the California Constitution as cruel or unusual punishment.[22] While the legislature may specify the punishment for crime, said the court, "the final judgment as to whether the punishment it decrees exceeds constitutional limits is a judicial function." Three of the justices who made up the court majority in the earlier case concurred in the new holding that evaluation of the propriety of the death penalty is a judicial function. Quite obviously, these justices succumbed to the temptation to yield to personal predilection and displace the legislature as the source of new law.

Why is this metamorphosis of courts into active legislatures, in the words of Justice Harlan, "all wrong"?[23] The basic reason is clear enough —courts are awkwardly positioned to carry out legislative functions, and they lack appropriate personnel and proper tools to do effective legislative work.

The medium of judicial legislation is the Constitution, and a court's effective exercise of power lies in a declaration that a particular act is unconstitutional. Such a declaration is an exercise in negation, a Thou-Shalt-Not. Although in exceptional instances a court may declare it unconstitutional for someone not to perform a particular act, and thereby order the execution of a positive act by a double-negative commandment, the usual rule of constitutional law relies on Thou-Shalt-Not. Hence a judicial solution to a general problem tends to be indirect, awkward, obscure, and incomplete. Often the solution appears to be one devised by Professor Henry Higgins' Frenchman, who doesn't care what you do so long as you pronounce it properly.

A major reason for the poor quality of most judicial solutions to legislative problems is that courts are extraordinarily inept instruments for political brokerage. Ordinarily, a court's members possess a similar background, a similar education, and a similar professional training. They are accustomed to working with ideas, phrases, and words rather than with people, organizations, and things; and they possess the occupational weaknesses of those who deal with problems secondhand. Because they are out of touch with many aspects of contemporary life, they are periodically astounded at the furor raised by some of their decisions.

Courts have limited access to information that is essential to effective solution of general problems. Usually the court's information about a gen-

119

eral problem comes from two partisans, each with an ax to grind, who appear before the court and make outrageous claims on behalf of their particular causes. Normally, neither partisan has any great interest in devising a workable solution for the general problem or in considering any aspect of the problem except the one needed to secure a favorable disposition of his case. If a convicted murderer can escape the consequences of his act through adoption of a new rule of law, it is of no moment to him that a hundred other murderers will go unpunished.

Frequently, a court is shown a tiny segment of a general problem and solemnly assured by the partisans before it that the tiny segment comprises the entire problem. These partisans shape the cause by such evidence and dramatization as suits their purpose and then invite the court to issue a sweeping decree on a subject about which the court is basically uninformed. Courts have a limited staff to assist them, almost no money, and little access to accurate information. As a consequence they tend to fall back on what they know best and on what they are most familiar with— the printed word, the published article, the learned report, the scholastic text. Partisans are quick to furnish whatever literature will promote their cause, and a cottage industry has grown up in the preparation of the sociological brief, a collection of references to published materials which lend generalized support to the contentions of the brief's author. This material is of uneven quality, unverified, untested by cross-examination; and its use as evidence would not satisfy the most elementary test of due process. Its true function is to imply popular support and scientific approval for a decision the partisan hopes the court will arrive at through personal predilection.

This narrow, limited presentation normally focuses the decision of a court on a single aspect of a general problem. But the problem itself remains, and as with the hydra, as soon as one head is cut off, nine others appear. The court is then forced to attack the nine other heads, and in so doing it tends to pile complication on complication until what should be simple, clear, and direct becomes complicated, obscure, and tortuous. Consider, as an example, the draft laws. With the best of intentions courts placed an enormous premium on calculated equivocation, multiplied the inequities of the law between rich and poor, and made even-handed enforcement of the draft all but impossible.

In sum, judicial legislation is all wrong because it is ineffectual. Experience has shown, and if the past is an accurate guide it will continue to show, that legislatures are better equipped, better informed, possess greater sensitivity, and exercise a broader vision in making new law than do the courts.

14

THE IRRELEVANCE
OF GUILT

THE phrase *the irrelevance of guilt* is one used by Lord Diplock of the British House of Lords in referring to the American rules of criminal law that require suppression of all evidence obtained by unlawful, improper, or irregular means. Suppression of evidence lies at the heart of the concept of perfectibility. As much as any single rule it has led to the shift of emphasis in a criminal proceeding from the determination of the guilt or innocence of the accused to the determination of the correctness of the procedure used in his prosecution. In this latter determination guilt becomes irrelevant.

The policy sought to be served by the suppression of relevant evidence is discouragement of the police from violating the law while they are engaged in seeking proof of law violations by others. The federal courts in 1914 adopted a policy prohibiting use in federal prosecutions of evidence that had been illegally obtained by federal officers.[1] The California Supreme Court in 1955 adopted a policy prohibiting the use in California courts of illegally obtained evidence.[2] The assumption behind these policies was that the incentive of officers to break the law would largely disappear if the illegally obtained evidence could not be used in court. These earlier rulings were primarily based on court policy, and as such they could be modified if they did not work out. But in 1961 the United States Supreme Court ruled in *Mapp* v. *Ohio* that as a matter of constitutional law under the Fourth and Fourteenth Amendments illegally obtained evidence could not be admitted in any state criminal prosecution.[3] Because the ruling was made on a constitutional basis, flexibility in the admission or exclusion of evidence disappeared.

A critical offshoot of the rule against use of illegally obtained evidence was that involving incriminating statements and confessions of a suspect obtained as a result of police interrogation. In the famous case of *Miranda* v. *Arizona* the United States Supreme Court laid down as a constitutional requirement for the states the rule that any statement given by a suspect during custodial police interrogation is inadmissible as evidence by virtue of the Fifth and Fourteenth Amendments unless prior to the time of the statement the police have advised the suspect of four matters: he has a right to remain silent, anything he says can be used against him in court, he is entitled to the presence of counsel, and if he cannot afford counsel, free counsel will be provided him.[4] The constitutional requirement that the suspect be given this exact advice has been made absolute, and any failure to meet this requirement renders a subsequent incriminating statement or confession inadmissible as evidence.

The primary theory behind such a rigid requirement is that a court policy which makes it unprofitable for the police to overreach will discourage improper police activity and tend to purify criminal investigative procedure. This theory assumes that police questioning, more often than not, is unduly coercive and that it is impractical for a court to differentiate between coercive and noncoercive police questioning. From these assumptions the theory concludes that in order to enforce a policy against coercive questioning, all custodial police questioning of suspects must be fitted into a uniform constitutional framework. A secondary theory in justification of the *Miranda* requirement is that compulsory warnings tend to equalize the position of rich suspects and poor suspects. This theory assumes that rich suspects know their legal rights and have ready access to counsel, whereas poor ones are ignorant of their rights and cannot afford counsel; therefore to put rich and poor on the same footing *Miranda* warnings must be given in all instances of police questioning of suspects under restraint.

Under *Mapp* and *Miranda* and related cases evidence must be suppressed:

> If it consists of admissions or confessions of a suspect questioned without warning under restraint;
>
> If it has been obtained as a result of a detention or arrest without sufficient cause;
>
> If obtained by entry on premises without proper permission;

If obtained by means of a search or arrest warrant issued without probable cause;

If obtained as a result of a defective search or arrest warrant;

If obtained as a result of an untimely search or too extensive a search;

If obtained as a result of improper wiretapping or improper eavesdropping;

If obtained under authority of an invalid statute;

If obtained at a lineup considered unfair or at which the suspect did not have counsel.

The suppression of all such evidence is compulsory as a matter of constitutional law, and no discretion or leeway is given the trial judge to suppress or not.

In many instances the rules for suppression of evidence are so complicated and their nuances so subtle that judges of the highest courts, years after the event, divide among themselves, five to four, or four to three, on the legality of a particular search or interrogation. For example, in *Coolidge* v. *New Hampshire* petitioner's conviction for a 1964 murder was reversed in 1971 by a five-to-four vote of the United States Supreme Court because a search warrant for petitioner's automobile issued by the chief investigator, the Attorney General of New Hampshire acting under New Hampshire law as a justice of the peace, was invalid under the Fourth Amendment in that the warrant had not been issued by a neutral magistrate, and because the seizure and search of petitioner's automobile could not otherwise be justified, and therefore the evidence obtained from the automobile had been illegally seized evidence which should have been suppressed.[5]

Thus far we have been discussing evidence which itself has been illegally obtained. The rules for suppression of evidence, however, cover not only the original illegally obtained evidence but all derivative evidence obtained as a result of leads secured or inferences drawn from the original illegally secured evidence. This derivative evidence has acquired the name Fruit of the Poisonous Tree, and it, too, like the original illegally obtained evidence, must be suppressed. If, for example, the location of a murder weapon or of the body of a victim has been discovered as a result of improper interrogation of a suspect, neither the murder weapon nor the circumstance of the discovery of the body may be used as evidence, since the discovery is tainted by the illegality of the original evidence.[6]

To the rule requiring the exclusion of tainted evidence, an exception exists known as attenuation. If a court concludes that the discovery of the subsequent evidence has been attenuated, i.e., it would have been discovered anyway or was discovered because of other factors, the connection between the subsequent evidence and the illegally obtained evidence may be disregarded, and the subsequent evidence admitted. Such complicated and elaborate rules produce highly theoretical, abstract exercises which revolve around such questions as these: Would the murder weapon have been found in a later search? Apart from illegal interrogation did the police have other valid clues which would have enabled them to discover the body of the victim? If fact A (the illegal seizure or interrogation) led to the discovery of fact B, which in turn led to the discovery of fact C, which then led to fact D, is there sufficient attenuation from A to D to make D constitutionally admissible evidence?

These inquiries have been formalized by the courts into standard routines that undertake to evaluate the sufficiency of probable cause for the detention or arrest, the legality of the entry into the house, the sufficiency of the affidavit to support the search warrant issued by the magistrate, the reliability of the informant whose information furnished probable cause for the arrest, the care and accuracy with which the *Miranda* warnings were given the suspect, and the validity of the lineup. Often a lower court has admitted evidence which a higher court subsequently determines to have been illegally obtained and hence constitutionally inadmissible. The critical question on appeal then becomes whether, after the subtraction of the illegally seized evidence, sufficient evidence remains to make it probable beyond a reasonable doubt that the jury would have returned a verdict of guilt on the lesser quantity of evidence.

Often the evidence has to be weighed by a process of double-think. In *People* v. *Blakeslee* the murder weapon had been classified as illegally secured evidence because the suspect had not been given the *Miranda* warnings prior to the time she told the police of its location.[7] Both the trial court and the appellate court were required to resolve the issue as to whether the remaining evidence was sufficient to sustain a conviction, and in doing this they were required mentally to blot out the discovery of the murder weapon. Mental gymnastics of this kind prompted Lord Diplock's observation about the irrelevance of guilt. Perhaps fifty percent of the work of the trial courts and eighty percent of the work of appellate courts in criminal cases is now taken up, not with evaluation or analysis of the guilt or innocence of the defendant, but with a determination of the legality of the methods used to secure the evidence.

Fruit of the Poisonous Tree received its greatest impetus from *Wong Sun* v. *United States,* a 1963 Supreme Court case in which the arrest of defendant Toy led to the arrest of defendant Yee, which in turn led to the arrest of Wong Sun.[8] After analyzing each of these phases in the proceedings the court concluded that Wong Sun was entitled to a new trial because it was not clear whether, after the subtraction of improperly obtained evidence and the subtraction of evidence secured as a result of leads from improperly obtained evidence, Wong Sun's confession had been sufficiently corroborated by other evidence. Such Chinese puzzles are now standard fare for appellate courts.

For example, in *People* v. *Johnson* the California Supreme Court reversed a conviction for burglary in 1969 by a four to three vote on the ground that a confession had been induced by illegally obtained evidence. Justice Stanley Mosk, for the dissenting justices, summarized the ever-widening ramifications of the doctrine:

> "In the style of *Jacula Prudentum* the majority in this case extend almost ad infinitum the 'fruit of the poisonous tree' doctrine: the law enforcement officers unlawfully broke into the premises occupied by one Ciabattari; because they broke in unlawfully the arrest of Ciabattari was unlawful; because the arrest of Ciabattari was unlawful, the seizure of the stolen television set was unlawful; because the seizure of the set was unlawful, the arrest of Howard was unlawful; because the arrest of Howard was unlawful, the confession of Howard was unlawful; because Howard's confession was unlawful, the arrest of Johnson was unlawful; because the arrest of Johnson was unlawful, the confession of Johnson was unlawful. The majority reap a prolific harvest of fruit from a tainted tree." [9]

Attenuation produces issues that would have delighted the medieval scholasticists who once debated how many angels could stand on the point of a needle. Consider the situation where the victim of a crime has identified the defendant at a pretrial lineup at which the suspect did not have counsel, and then later identifies him again in open court. Under such circumstances the trial court is required to decide whether the victim would have been able to identify the defendant in court if the earlier, invalid lineup had not taken place. In *United States* v. *Wade* the artificiality of such an exercise was vigorously attacked by Justice Black, who termed such a determination a practical impossibility and asked how a witness could be expected to probe the recesses of his mind to draw a sharp line between a courtroom identification due exclusively to an earlier lineup and a courtroom identification due to memory not based on the lineup.[10] What kind of clear and convincing evidence could the prosecution offer to prove upon what particular events memories rest? How long would trials be delayed while judges turn psychologists to probe the subconscious minds of witnesses? All these questions, said Black, were posed but not answered by the court's opinion.

A technical and mechanical interpretation of the requirements for the suppression of illegally obtained evidence purports to reduce to computer formula the legality of investigative efforts used by law enforcement officers to solve crime. As a consequence we have such bizarre results as *Whiteley* v. *Warden,* where a final judgment of conviction for burglary was vacated on collateral attack seven years after petitioner's arrest because of defects in the affidavit used to obtain the warrant for petitioner's arrest; *Foster* v. *California,* where petitioner's robbery conviction, established by the testimony of a confederate in the robbery and by courtroom identification by the victim, was reversed because of suggestiveness in the conduct of a pretrial lineup; and *Orozco* v. *Texas,* where petitioner's murder conviction was reversed because when investigating officers went to petitioner's home to ask him about a shooting which had occurred earlier that night, they had not first given him the *Miranda* warnings, for, said the court, petitioner was as much under restraint at home as he would have been at the police station.[11]

Admission of illegally seized evidence may be collaterally attacked years after the judgment of conviction has become final.[12] And once a final judgment has been overturned and a case set at large, then there may come into play other new rules and procedures, as has been discussed earlier in Chapter 2.

The American rule on the subject of illegally obtained evidence has flip-flopped from one that suppresses no evidence to one that suppresses all illegally obtained evidence, and throughout its use in this country the rule has been generally applied in an all-or-nothing fashion. Prior to 1914 American jurisprudence took the view that evidence relevant to the issue before the tribunal was admissible evidence regardless of its source and regardless of the means by which it had been brought before the tribunal. This point of view was comparable to that taken by the Israeli court in the Eichmann trial, where the fact that Eichmann had been kidnapped from another country was considered irrelevant to the requirement that he answer charges in the tribunal in which he was then found. But since 1961 exclusion of illegally obtained evidence has been compelled in all cases as a matter of constitutional law, and the requirement for the suppression of such evidence, including incriminating statements and confessions, has been inflated into formidable dimensions by the added constitutional requirement that the fruits of illegally obtained evidence be suppressed as well.

It may be instructive to examine how the problem of suppression of incriminating statements and confessions has been handled in England. The English likewise require that a warning be given a suspect prior to police interrogation, a requirement that has been formalized in instructions to the police known as Judges' Rules.[13] These rules direct that as soon as a police officer acquires evidence which would afford reasonable grounds to suspect that a person has committed an offense, the officer must caution that person before questioning him further in relation to the offense. While the caution required under Judges' Rules is roughly comparable in content to that required under *Miranda,* a vital distinction exists between the operation of English Judges' Rules and the American procedure compelled by *Miranda.* If the English police have failed to comply with Judges' Rules, nevertheless the proof they have secured may still be received in evidence, for under English practice it is discretionary with the trial court to exclude, or not exclude, evidence secured in violation of Judges' Rules.[14] The criterion used by the English courts in determining whether or not to suppress evidence against the accused is that of fairness, and if in a particular case a court believes the police have acted unfairly or oppressively toward the accused, it will suppress the evidence.

English courts evaluate the problem of suppression of evidence as one of striking a balance between the individual's interest in freedom from intrusion and society's interest in maintaining order and suppressing crime, and purely technical violations of Judges' Rules do not foreclose the use of evidence obtained in violation of the Rules. There thus exists in the English system a flexibility wholly lacking in the American system. At the same time there is reason to suppose that the existence of Judges' Rules accomplishes as much to deter the police from unlawful conduct as does the absolute exclusionary rule of American constitutional law.[15]

The English practice, which makes the admission or exclusion of evidence optional with the trial court, undoubtedly furnished the model for that provision in the federal Omnibus Crime Control and Safe Streets Act of 1968 which states that a confession voluntarily given may be received in evidence in a federal prosecution if the trial judge on consideration of all the circumstances determines that the confession is truly voluntary.[16] Factors such as advice given the defendant before questioning and assistance of counsel during questioning are relevant but not conclusive on the issue of the voluntariness of the confession. The statute amounts to a direct revision of *Miranda* for federal prosecutions and an implied revision of

127

Miranda for state prosecutions. The presently unsettled question is whether the Supreme Court will recognize the weaknesses of the existing exclusionary rules, revise its position, and accede to this action of Congress.

Section 5 of the Fourteenth Amendment provides suitable authority for the revision of *Mapp* and *Miranda* if the Supreme Court is so inclined, for the section states that "Congress shall have the power to enforce, by appropriate legislation, the provisions of this [amendment]." The Supreme Court could declare that *Mapp* and *Miranda* only applied in the absence of federally adopted congressional standards indicating the scope of the Fourteenth Amendment on a particular subject, and that once Congress had enacted appropriate standards of its own on a particular subject, such as admissibility in evidence of confessions, then compliance with congressional standards would satisfy the requirements of the Fourteenth Amendment.

Since in past decades the Supreme Court has successfully buried *Adkins* v. *Children's Hospital* (unconstitutionality of minimum wages for women and children in the District of Columbia), and *Plessy* v. *Ferguson* (constitutionality of separate-but-equal facilities for different races), no insurmountable reason exists why it could not similarly dispose of *Mapp* and *Miranda*.[17] Of the nine justices who comprised the court at the time of its decision in *Coolidge* v. *New Hampshire* in June 1971, three dissented from the original *Miranda* decision (Harlan, Stewart, White); [18] one has questioned the value of the entire exclusionary rule (Burger); [19] and two have questioned the use of an exclusionary rule under the Fourth Amendment (but not the Fifth) to regulate police procedure (Black and Blackmun).[20] In view of this fragmentation of opinion, of subsequent changes in the personnel of the court, and of the bizarre results brought about by the exclusionary rules themselves, it is not difficult to predict that the exclusionary rules—both *Mapp* and *Miranda*—will be radically revised in the future. Justice Harlan wrote in *Coolidge* of the "intolerable . . . state of uncertainty" and the "serious distortions" in the law of search and seizure and suggested the law was due for an "overhauling," one that he said should begin with the overruling of *Mapp*.[21] This overhauling will undoubtedly extend to all exclusionary rules of evidence. It would be a pity if the Supreme Court were to ignore the sensible rule of evidence set out in the 1968 Act merely because Congress formulated it first.

15

TRIVIALIZATION OF
THE CONSTITUTION

$\mathbf{A}$LL rights tend to declare themselves absolute to their logical extreme," said Justice Holmes.[1] Similarly, all doctrine tends to arrogate to itself a universal coverage and a transcendental application. In constitutional law this tendency produces the phenomenon known as trivialization, a description used by Justices Frankfurter and Jackson.[2] Trivialization sets in when the language of fundamental constitutional right begins to be routinely used by the courts to justify judicial regulation of administrative decisions of the smallest moment—with the consequence that a sort of Gresham's Law operates under which bad judicial decisions drive good ones from public notice. The result, as with the boy who cried wolf too often, is to give the entire body of constitutional law a somewhat inconsequential and frivolous cast.

The Rosetta stone of current trivialization in the use of the Fourteenth Amendment is found in *Tinker* v. *Des Moines School District,* a case decided by the United States Supreme Court in 1969.[3] School children, one eight years old, one eleven, one thirteen, and two fifteen, undertook an organized effort to demonstrate to their fellow pupils their opposition to the war in Vietnam by wearing black armbands to school and in the classroom. When school officials forbade the demonstration, the children sought injunctive relief against the school officials in the federal district court on the ground their constitutional rights under the Fourteenth Amendment had been violated. The Supreme Court upheld their suit, finding that peaceful demonstration without disruption is a form of symbolic speech protected by the First and Fourteenth Amendments to the Constitution. Neither students nor teachers, said the court, lost their constitutional rights of freedom of speech or expression at the schoolhouse gate. Warming to its subject, the court declared that "state-operated schools may not be enclaves of totalitarianism," that pupils—while in school, as well as while away from school—are persons possessed of fundamental rights which the state must respect, that the classroom is peculiarly the marketplace of ideas, and that the nation's future depends on a vast exchange of ideas which discovers truth out of a multitude of tongues rather than through any kind of authoritative selection.

Justice Black, dissenting in *Tinker,* declared that the court had ushered in an entirely new era in which the ultimate power to control the conduct of pupils had been transferred to the Supreme Court. In his view the court was returning to a discredited due process concept under which the court held laws unconstitutional whenever it believed the legislature had acted unwisely. Black also raised the question as to what extent teachers and students may use the schools at their whim as a platform for the exercise of free speech. In the case before the court, said Black, disruption of classwork occurred in exactly the way school officials had foreseen it would— the armbands took the pupils' minds off their classwork and diverted their thoughts to the highly emotional subject of the Vietnam War. One need not be a prophet or the son of a prophet, Black concluded, to foresee that continuous difficulties in school operations would result from the court's decision.

A generation ago Justice Jackson declared that the Supreme Court does not "accept the role of a super board of education for every school district in the nation." [4] Yet following the decision in *Tinker,* federal courts have become preoccupied with school regulations to an unbelievable extent. Long-standing state regulations against student membership groups (fraternities, sororities, and social clubs), regulations upheld as a proper exercise of state power by the Supreme Court in 1915,[5] have come under attack as an interference with freedom of association, at least where the purposes of the clubs are political. Demonstrations in schools cannot be banned by school authorities until there has been a clear finding that the demonstrations will be disruptive. In *Butts* v. *Dallas Independent School District* a federal court enjoined the Dallas school district from interfering with petitioners' wearing of black armbands to school to protest the Vietnam War.[6] In defense of its ban against the demonstration, the school district called the court's attention to the existence of a school group in the district which wore white armbands (in opposition to the black-armband group) and yet a third group, which wore Nazi symbols and whose program sought the re-establishment of white supremacy. The court, however, ruled that even though some students were absent from class, and even though television cameras were scheduled to be present, the showing of possible disruption of classes was insufficient to justify stoppage of the demonstration, for expectation of disruption will not justify a suspension of the constitutional rights outlined in *Tinker*. These rights have since been expanded to include distribution of leaflets by junior high school students on school property, inside school buildings, and during school hours. In enjoining interference with leaflet distribution the federal court in *Riseman* v. *School Committee of City of Quincy* saw its task as that of "securing the exercise of First Amendment rights of students against unrestricted encroachment by school authorities." [7]

In addition to demonstrations, federal courts have become preoccupied with the smallest details of school administration in order to safeguard asserted federal constitutional rights invaded by dress codes. Most often considered are regulations concerning hair length. Thus for boys, a federal court issued a preliminary injunction prohibiting school officials from denying admission to a male student whose hair reached his shoulders, and another court ruled that regulation of length of hair of male high school students was unconstitutional in that the right to wear one's hair at any length or in any desired manner is an ingredient of personal freedom protected by the Constitution.[8] Courts look after girls, too: a federal court enjoined school officials from enforcing a rule requiring that a girl's hair "be kept one finger width above the eyebrows, clear across the forehead," a rule the court found unconstitutional.[9]

Hair need not grow on top of the head to be of concern to the federal district courts. One court, on behalf of a high school student, enjoined school officials from enforcing a regulation setting a maximum length for sideburns.[10] Another court upheld the validity of a high school dress code prohibiting mustaches, but it ordered the suspended student reinstated anyway, because it concluded the dress code did not apply to plaintiff's mustache, which was barely perceptible, of natural growth, and not artificially cultivated.[11] Another court held that in the absence of a showing of a relationship to health, welfare, morals, or discipline of the students, a rule prohibiting students in a junior college from wearing beards violated the equal protection clause of the Fourteenth Amendment.[12]

Pants are another popular area of concern. A federal court held unconstitutional a school dress code prohibiting boys in grammar school from wearing dungarees to school in the absence of any showing that dungarees inhibited the educational process.[13] The right to wear clothes of one's choice, said the court, is a constitutional right protected by the Fourteenth Amendment. And in the same vein school regulations prohibiting female students from wearing slacks were invalidated by a New York state court.[14]

The courts differ among themselves on what rights they are protecting when they ponder the constitutionality of school dress codes. Some courts assume that a student's choice of hair style and dress is an expression of opinion constituting symbolic speech protected by the First Amendment.[15] Others find protection for long hair either in the penumbra of rights protected by the First Amendment's freedom of speech clause or in the "additional fundamental rights" protected by the Ninth Amendment.[16] Many courts simply find that a free choice of appearance is protected by the due process clause of the Fourteenth Amendment.[17] Others rely on the equal protection clause of the Fourteenth Amendment.[18] One court found the right to long hair protected, by *either* the equal protection clause *or* the due process clause of the Fourteenth Amendment.[19]

Federal courts presently concern themselves with all aspects of school life, even including the details of the curriculum. One federal district court held that a public school teacher's "academic freedom" under the First Amendment had been violated when her employers sought to dismiss her because she had assigned a short story by a best-selling author to an eleventh grade English class over the specific objections of her employers. The court reviewed the story, found it not legally obscene under existing Supreme Court standards, compared it with other literature offered to eleventh graders, and decreed it was an appropriate story for the teacher to assign to her class.[20]

A high school teacher in Massachusetts obtained an injunction from a federal court against a meeting of a school committee which was considering the advisability of the teacher's discharge for use in class of "a vulgar term for an incestuous son," a term which the teacher told the school committee he could not "in good conscience" consent not to use again in the classroom.[21] The court's opinion suggested that such interference with the teacher's academic freedom amounted to a violation of the First Amendment and of the federal civil rights law.

Following the lead of *Tinker,* the California Supreme Court found that teachers have a constitutional right to circulate political petitions during school hours on school property.[22] On the other hand, a federal district court sitting in Louisiana took a restrictive view of the expression of political views on school property, and it ordered school faculty and school employees to remove Confederate flags from all schools, and to refrain from their display at school functions.[23] Patently, some political views in the schoolhouse are constitutionally acceptable to the courts, while others are not.

132

Courts have also undertaken to oversee and review the grading of students. A federal court in Vermont agreed to review a student's claim that school authorities acted arbitrarily, capriciously, and in bad faith in the matter of grades and dismissals.[24] In the California state courts a medical student sought reinstatement in the university, claiming his dismissal was arbitrary and therefore a violation of due process of law.[25] The school's answer pleaded that petitioner had spent four years attempting to complete the first three years of medical school, that he remained at the bottom of a class of 122 students, and that he had been found scholastically deficient to practice medicine. The trial court's judgment of dismissal was reversed on appeal, and a hearing was ordered.

As we have seen earlier, prisoners are allowed to represent themselves in legal proceedings. In this process courts have reviewed and weighed such matters as the adequacy of typewriter facilities for a prisoner, the quantity of writing paper allowed prisoners each day, the length of writing pencils furnished prisoners, and the wattage of the light bulbs in their cells.[26]

The most minute details of state custodial care are now reviewed by the federal courts. A federal court in New York held that it was a denial of Angela Davis' right to the equal protection of the laws under the Fourteenth Amendment for New York authorities to keep her in a state jail separate from other inmates pending her extradition on state charges to California.[27] A federal district court in Connecticut ruled that the wearing of a goatee by a prisoner in a state jail awaiting trial in a state court was a federally protected right under the Fourteenth Amendment to the Constitution.[28] A federal district court in California ruled, apparently under the Fourteenth Amendment's application to the states of freedom of speech and religion, that a state prisoner must be allowed to subscribe to *Muhammad Speaks;* that each California prison library must make available a copy of *The Holy Qu-ran* by Elsef Ali; and that the state prison system must employ a Muslim minister, when available, at an hourly rate comparable to that paid to chaplains of the Catholic, Jewish, and Protestant faiths.[29]

The frivolity of court regulation of appearance and dress in schools as a matter of constitutional law was commented upon by Justice Black, who, acting as circuit justice, denied an injunction in 1971 against a school rule which prohibited schoolboys' hair from hanging over the ears or the top of the collar and from obstructing vision:

"I refuse to hold for myself that the federal courts have constitutional power to interfere in this way with the public school system operated by the States. . . . The only thing about it that borders on the serious to me is the idea that anyone should think the Federal Constitution imposes on the United States courts the burden of supervising the length of hair that public school students should wear." [30]

16

JUDICIAL AVANT-GARDISM

THE expansion of the ideal of perfectibility and its related concept that judges are the chosen instruments for the achievement of perfectibility by means of the constitutional doctrines of due process and equal protection has brought about a vast increase in the phenomenon known as judicial avant-gardism.

Judicial avant-gardism is a delusion of a judge that he has achieved a unique special insight into a public problem whose solution has theretofore eluded all other courts and judges. The problem is usually one of current social interest on which the intellectual community has taken a strong stand. The typical victim of avant-gardism is a judge of a lower court engaged in routine work of the law, who, like other judges, is periodically urged by litigants to make sweeping judicial pronouncements on problems of current fashionability. If one day he succumbs to temptation, he may find himself transformed into a temporary celebrity who is praised for the freshness and boldness of his judicial approach. After such a taste of judicial highlife, it is difficult for the judge to sink back into relative obscurity, and he may succumb to temptation a second time. Very quickly the temptation grows addictive, and the problem becomes what to do for an encore. Once well launched on his career, the avant-gardist couches his judicial opinions in the most sweeping general terms, refers frequently to the dictates of his conscience, finds constitutional issues latent in the most pedestrian problems, and decides all controversies on the broadest possible grounds. Many of his pronouncements have no visible connection with the facts of the case pending before him and are explicable only in the light of the avant-garde maxim, "Have opinion, need case."

The true avant-gardist has a special fondness for interdisciplinary studies, and he draws his greatest inspiration from those academic pastures entitled "Law and _____." These may include such fields as "Law and Social Psychology," "Law and Psychological Sociology," "Law and Mathematical Behavior," "Law and Behavioral Mathematics," "Law and Social Psychiatry," "Law and Psychiatric Sociology," perhaps even "Law and Psychoanalytical Metaphysics." The function performed by these studies is to release the avant-gardist from the confinement of statute and case law in order to enable him to follow his personal inclinations and instincts.

Judicial avant-gardism has always existed on the bench, but heretofore it has been kept under relatively firm control by the concept that a judge is the servant of the law, not its master; that his function is to speak the law, not to make it. But in recent years, Bacon's classic statement of the judge's function [1] has been challenged in some academic circles, which have theorized that a judge should become an activist, that he should adopt the boldness of an advocate in breaking new ground in the law. The theory has acquired sufficient currency to enable a handful of avant-garde judges to keep the law in a state of uproar.

It would be imprudent for the author to single out the decisions of any sitting judge as examples of judicial avant-gardism. However, the interested reader, by following the news magazines closely for a few months, can readily compile his own list. One example from the past will alert the reader what to look for.

In 1930 the Eighteenth Amendment to the Constitution, which prohibited the manufacture, sale, or transportation of intoxicating liquors, had demonstrated that it was a very unpopular law which had failed to accomplish the beneficent results for which it had been designed. However, no amendment to the Constitution had ever been repealed, and conventional wisdom prevailed at the time that repeal was a practical impossibility. It appeared that the nation was permanently saddled with an unpopular and unenforceable law. Into this impasse stepped William Clark, federal district judge in New Jersey, who in *United States* v. *Sprague* quashed an indictment against Sprague for violating the National Prohibition Act on the ground that the Eighteenth Amendment had not been properly ratified by the states and therefore had never become part of the Constitution.[2] Article V of the Constitution provides for ratification of amendments proposed by Congress "by the Legislatures of three fourths of the several States, or by Conventions in three fourths thereof." The Eighteenth Amendment, like all other amendments, had been ratified by state legislatures. Nevertheless, Judge Clark reasoned:

> "Political science can give only one answer to the question presented by the alternative methods of ratification prescribed by article 5. If

the amendment to be considered is one designed to transfer to the United States powers heretofore reserved to the states, or, if there are any such, to the people, that answer must be in favor of the convention method." (44 F.2d 967, at p. 981)

Judge Clark thus disposed of the Eighteenth Amendment to the Constitution by declaring it unconstitutional because it had not been ratified by convention. As a backup argument, he also suggested that the Eighteenth Amendment was unconstitutional because it conflicted with the due process clause of the Fifth Amendment.

With the filing of this decision Judge Clark became an instant celebrity, and in drinking circles he acquired the saintlike reputation of a folk hero. His popular status as a celebrity was only slightly diminished when the United States Supreme Court unanimously reversed his ruling, stating that:

"If the framers of the instrument had any thought that amendments differing in purpose should be ratified in differing ways, nothing would have been simpler than so to phrase Article V as to exclude implication or speculation. . . .

"This Court has repeatedly and consistently declared that the choice of mode rests solely in the discretion of Congress." [3]

Two years later Prohibition was repealed through the normal process of constitutional amendment. Those who had despaired of the democratic process took heart.

The vice of avant-gardism does not lie in the posturing of a few judges, but in the fact that it makes extraordinarily difficult the creation of a stable legal order operating under known rules and following known law. If only one judge, or one highly disciplined panel of judges, conscious of a sense of proportion and endowed with a granite sense of self-restraint, were operating under a system of personal predilection, the system of law might operate for a time. But it can never work when dozens of judges are turned loose and given carte blanche to vie with one another for leadership in judicial avant-gardism.

17

TRIAL COURTS AS CHILDREN OF ISRAEL—MAKE BRICK WITHOUT STRAW

AN early version of the speedup, the stretchout, and cost absorption is found in the Book of Exodus, where Pharaoh, doubtless wishing to increase the productivity of labor and reduce the cost of public works, ordered the children of Israel to make brick without straw—more precisely, to gather their own straw. In comparable fashion appellate courts, like Pharaoh, increasingly demand that trial judges turn out a more complicated product of higher quality, but at the same time they keep removing from the reach of the trial judges many of the tools needed to accomplish the work.

Ideally, the trial court should be a tranquil, hallowed place of calm and quiet, where legal reasoning is dispassionately applied to impartially found facts in order to reach a rational decision. To achieve this ideal of the perfect tribunal, appellate courts have decreed that the trial judge exercise firm control over the participants, including parties, counsel, witnesses, court staff, spectators, and investigative officers. In *Sheppard* v. *Maxwell* the United States Supreme Court in 1966 vacated a state judgment of conviction for murder, a judgment which had become final ten years earlier, because the trial judge had not fulfilled his duty to control disruptive influences in the courtroom and thereby protect petitioner from inherently prejudicial publicity.[1] The trial judge, said the Supreme Court, should have regulated more closely the use of the courtroom by newsmen and the con-

138

duct of newsmen in the courtroom; should have insulated witnesses from newsmen and prevented newspaper and radio interviews of prospective witnesses; should have controlled the release of information to the press by police officers, witnesses, and counsel; should have warned the newspapers to check the accuracy of their accounts of the proceedings; should have controlled statements made to the news media by counsel, witnesses, the coroner, and police officers, and might well have proscribed extrajudicial statements by any lawyer, party, witness, or court official; should have requested appropriate city and county officials to promulgate regulations with respect to dissemination of information by their employees; should have warned reporters about the impropriety of publicizing material not introduced in the proceedings; and should have taken strong measures to efface prejudicial publicity from the minds of the jurors.

This is a tall order involving tasks of herculean dimensions. What tools are available to the trial judge to control the activities of those involved in a trial in order that he may carry out his assigned function?

Regulatory Tools of the Trial Judge

CONTROL OF THE PRESS

For all practical purposes the trial judge has no control whatever over anything the news media say, write, broadcast, or publish, either before, during, or after a trial. The Supreme Court has ruled that the constitutional protection of freedom of speech and press prevents a trial judge from imposing limitations on what may be published, and this rule is close to a constitutional absolute.[2] Justice Frankfurter's recurrent attempts to sanction something resembling the contempt powers of English courts with respect to newspaper comment on pending cases never attracted any substantial backing from the public or from his colleagues.[3]

CONTROL OF IMMEDIATE COURTHOUSE AREA

The power of the trial judge to regulate and control the immediate courthouse area in order to prevent disruption of court proceedings has been recognized in the abstract by the United States Supreme Court. Yet specific support for this control has been so hesitant that circumvention rather than enforcement describes the operation of the rule. For example, in *Cox* v. *Louisiana,* the Supreme Court in 1965 invalidated the arrest of a person demonstrating opposite the courthouse steps to secure the release of jailed student protestors on the theory that the demonstrator had been enticed into a violation of the law and thus subjected to a form of entrapment.[4] Justice Black, dissenting, warned:

> "This statute, like the federal one which it closely resembles, was enacted to protect courts and court officials from the intimidation and dangers that inhere in huge gatherings at courthouse doors and jail doors to protest arrests and to influence court officials in performing their duties. . . . Justice cannot be rightly administered, nor are the lives and safety of prisoners secure, where throngs of people clamor against the processes of justice right outside the courthouse or jailhouse doors. . . . Experience demonstrates that it is not a far step from what to many seems the earnest, honest, patriotic, kind-spirited multitude of today, to the fanatical, threatening, lawless mob of tomorrow. And the crowds that press in the streets for noble goals today can be supplanted tomorrow by street mobs pressuring the courts for precisely opposite ends." (379 U.S. 559, at pp. 583, 584)

In *Cohen* v. *California,* petitioner was patrolling a courthouse corridor in the Los Angeles courthouse demonstrating against the draft by wearing a vulgar four-letter sign on his jacket.[5] The United States Supreme Court reversed his conviction for breach of the peace on the ground that the conviction interfered with petitioner's right to freedom of expression guaranteed by the First and Fourteenth Amendments. What would happen, the author wonders, if petitioner started to patrol the corridors of the United States Supreme Court building wearing a jacket expressing a similar sentiment about the Supreme Court?

CONTROL OVER DEFENDANT

Outside the courtroom the trial judge's control over the activities of a defendant is minimal. Defendants regularly issue press releases, hold press conferences, give newspaper interviews, appear on television programs, and, if their cases are celebrated, market their memoirs, often in direct violation of court orders to the contrary. Usually, this activity is designed to secure favorable publicity for defendant's side of the case and to propagandize his version of the facts and issues. As matters now stand, prosecutors and investigating officers in many instances are prohibited from replying in kind to this defense propaganda, and as a consequence only one side of a cause may become exposed to public view in advance of trial. Enforcement of an order restricting a defendant from public discussion of his case in advance of trial is sufficiently rare to be classified as a curiosity.[6]

Inside the courtroom the trial judge's control over the behavior of the defendant was strengthened by the 1970 ruling of the United States Supreme Court in *Illinois* v. *Allen* that a disruptive defendant may be removed from the courtroom and the trial continued in his absence.[7] However, the trial judge's authority to order the misbehaving defendant's removal is closely circumscribed. The defendant cannot be removed at the initial instance of disruptive behavior, since he must first be warned that his conduct is disruptive and that its repetition may result in his removal. Once removed, the defendant can reclaim his right to be present at his trial by indicating his willingness to conduct himself properly. The application of these rules to causes involving multiple defendants intent on disruption has turned certain trials into something resembling French farce: Defendant A disrupts the trial, and is warned; next, defendant B disrupts the trial, and is warned; then, defendant C disrupts and is warned. Defendant A then disrupts a second time and is removed, B disrupts a second time and is removed, and C does the same. The following day A, B, and C reclaim their right to be present by promising to conduct themselves properly. The scenario is then repeated with some different type of disruption. Soon the trial comes to resemble a hot pennant race where combative baseball managers are thrown out of the game by the umpires each day, only to reappear as lively as ever the following day. Such antics may be good for baseball, but they contribute nothing to public esteem for the courts.

Although the trial judge's control over the defendant's behavior in court has been recently strengthened, his control over the defendant's right to talk has not. A trial judge acts at his peril in prohibiting a defendant from talking when the defendant wishes to talk, for the defendant may later claim that if he had been allowed to talk he would have raised such-and-such a contention, and that the court's refusal to allow him to present that contention was erroneous. This risk is present even when a defendant is represented by counsel, for defendant may wish to speak on the subject of asserted incompetency of his counsel. In one California case defendant complained during the trial about the competency of his appointed counsel and requested the court to appoint new counsel. The trial court interrogated defendant and his counsel in chambers, determined that defendant was not competent to represent himself, concluded that appointed counsel's representation had been satisfactory, and denied the motion. Defendant then sought to bring up specific instances of inadequate representation, but the trial court rejected this request and resumed the conduct of the trial. Defendant's conviction for forgery was reversed on appeal by the California Supreme Court because the trial court had not allowed defendant to cite instances of inadequate representation and had not fully listened to defendant's specification of complaints.[8] The reviewing court's opinion in no way suggested that defendant was innocent, or that counsel's representation was inadequate, or that defendant had shown or could show instances of inadequate representation. The sole basis for reversal was the refusal of the trail court to let defendant talk at a time the reviewing court thought defendant should have been allowed to talk; the merits of whatever the defendant might have said were considered immaterial. This view was made explicit in a robbery and kidnapping case, where defendant's conviction was reversed on appeal because defendant had not been allowed to complain during the trial about the competency of his counsel, even though he had been allowed to do so at a later time and even though the reviewing court found his complaint was without merit.[9]

There has thus been made available to defendants one more game, this one entitled Opportunity to Personally Explain. If the opportunity is granted, the proceedings can quickly become chaotic; if it is denied, reversible error can later be claimed.

CONTROL OVER COUNSEL

In recent years appellate courts in passing on the qualifications of applicants for admission to the practice of law have tended to conclude as a matter of constitutional law that an applicant's prior misbehavior may not be given undue weight. In *Schware* v. *Board of Bar Examiners* the United States Supreme Court held in 1957 that a state could not exclude a person from the practice of law, or from any other occupation, in a manner or for reasons that contravene the due process or equal protection clauses of the Fourteenth Amendment.[10] The court ruled that New Mexico could not refuse to license an applicant to practice law who had used aliases for four years, who had been arrested on several occasions, who had been indicted for violation of the Neutrality Act, and who had been a member of the Communist Party for eight years. In effect, the court held that these prior activities had no rational connection with applicant's fitness or capacity to practice law.

The full flowering of this doctrine appeared in *Hallinan* v. *Committee of Bar Examiners,* where the applicant for admission to practice law in California had been arrested on seven different occasions for direct-action demonstrations that involved sit-ins, and had been convicted twice for unlawful assembly, trespass, and disturbance of the peace.[11] Applicant did not deny these acts of civil disobedience but justified his conduct on moral and political considerations. The bar examiners also produced evidence of applicant's propensity for violence, evidence of nine different fistfight incidents in which applicant had been involved. Three of these had resulted in criminal charges, and two had resulted in civil suits for battery. The California Supreme Court characterized these brawls as "youthful indiscretions" and held this evidence did not support the conclusion of the bar examiners that applicant had "a fixed and dominant propensity for lawlessness whenever [it suited] his purposes of the particular moment" or the conclusion that applicant lacked the good moral character requisite to the practice of law. The court concluded that these acts did not bear a direct relationship to applicant's fitness to practice law and ordered that he be licensed. The case thus squarely holds that a bar examining committee cannot attach any great weight to a prior history of disruptive behavior in reviewing an applicant's qualifications to practice law.

This same standard is now followed in granting permission to counsel from other jurisdictions to appear locally in a particular case.[12] It is now all but compulsory that such applicants be allowed to appear, and in at least one instance a federal appellate court issued its writ to compel the federal district court to admit unlicensed counsel to handle a particular case.[13] Generally speaking, a prior record of disruptive conduct by the applicant is disregarded. As a result there has come into prominence a traveling road show of counsel who specialize in disruption and confrontation in trial courts in which they are not permanently licensed to practice. Courts find themselves without any effective means to discipline or control such outside counsel by suspension from practice. Justice Blackmun commented on this phenomenon:

> "We have seen, of late, an overabundance of courtroom spectacle brought about by attorneys—frequently those who, being unlicensed in the particular State, are nevertheless permitted, by the court's indulgence, to appear for clients in a given case—who give indications of ignoring their responsibility to the courts and to the judicial process." [14]

The extremely limited nature of control exercisable by local courts over outside counsel may be seen in the rare instance in which discipline has actually been imposed on an outside attorney for misconduct. In one instance, counsel who had been admitted to practice in New Jersey for the purpose of trying a particular case, prior to the trial made public a statement that charged the prosecution with planning to use perjured testimony. His admittance in New Jersey was revoked, and his privilege to apply for further temporary admission in New Jersey was suspended for one year.[15] Even with respect to counsel permanently admitted to practice within the jurisdiction, control of counsel's activities by the trial judge has been viewed by appellate courts with grudging eye. In the case of *Sawyer,* petitioner, while participating as defense counsel in a highly publicized trial in the federal court in Honolulu, made a speech on the Island of Hawaii attacking the conduct of the court in the pending trial, which led to charges that she had impugned the impartiality and fairness of the trial court and had reflected upon its integrity in the conduct of the trial.[16] On the complaint of the trial judge, petitioner was suspended from the practice of law for one year by the Supreme Court of Hawaii. But on review her suspension was set aside by the United States Supreme Court, which interpreted her remarks as merely criticizing the state of the law and the rules of evidence and not as constituting an improper attack on the judge who enforced those rules and presided at the trial. For the four dissenters, Justice Frankfurter reached the following conclusion:

> "The record is thus replete with evidence to support the conclusion that virtually the entire speech constituted a direct attack on the judicial conduct of this trial during its progress by one of the lawyers for the defense. When a lawyer attacks the fairness, the evenhandedness, and the integrity of the proceedings in a trial in which he himself is actively engaged, in the inflammatory, public fashion that this record reveals, supplemented with specific attack on the presiding judge, how can the conclusion be escaped that it was not rules of law in the abstract which were assailed, but the manner in which the processes of justice in the particular case were being conducted? More particularly, such an attack inescapably impugns the integrity of the judge." (360 U.S. 622, at pp. 664, 665)

In *Smith* v. *Superior Court* a trial judge in Los Angeles removed court-appointed defense counsel in a first degree murder case on the ground that counsel was incompetent to try a death penalty case.[17] The California Supreme Court vacated the ruling and reinstated the attorney as counsel for the defendant and undertook to comment on the circumstances which led to counsel's removal. After referring to "an apparent compulsive tendency" of the attorney to interrupt the judge, the court observed that neither party was wholly blameless and then went on to say, "We do not condone intemperate behavior by counsel. . . . But . . . the wise judge will overlook or try to forgive" excesses of zeal and be guided by patience and understanding rather than punctilious insistence on courtroom etiquette. While it is the duty of the trial judge to protect defendant's right to effective counsel, said the court, the trial judge will not be permitted to compromise the independence of the bar by threat of removal.

It may thus be seen that the trial court today has virtually no power to refuse to admit outside counsel who wish to try cases before it, to suspend from practice or remove from a case counsel who misconduct themselves before the court, or to remove counsel who have demonstrated their incompetency.

CONTEMPT OF COURT

The sole remaining tool available to the trial judge to enable him to perform the multifarious duties assigned to him by *Sheppard* v. *Maxwell* [18] is the contempt power.

Why does a court need the summary power of contempt? The elder Justice Harlan put it well in *Ex parte Terry,* a case which upheld in 1888 the contempt conviction of David S. Terry for disruptive conduct in the courtroom:

> " 'The power to commit or fine for contempt is essential to the existence of every court. Business cannot be conducted unless the court can suppress disturbances and the only means of doing that is by immediate punishment. . . .' Without it, *judicial tribunals would be at the mercy of the disorderly and violent,* who respect neither the laws enacted for the vindication of public and private rights, nor the officers charged with the duty of administering them." [19] (Italics added.)

But during the past two decades the historic authority of the trial judge to maintain order in the court by the exercise of the power of summary contempt has been sharply eroded by an expanded interpretation of the due process clause. Appellate courts now tend to keep the word of contempt to the trial judge's ear and break it to his use. All too often the approach of appellate courts to controversies and disruptions in the trial court is to put trial judge and trial counsel on the same plane and then determine which one provoked the other first. Excesses and misbehavior of counsel are excused as robust advocacy in the heat of combat.

For example, in *Cooper* v. *Superior Court* counsel insisted on interrupting the court while the court was addressing the jury, and counsel was held in contempt.[20] On review the contempt order was annulled by the California Supreme Court, which concluded that counsel had been legally correct in the objection he was seeking to make. Said the court:

145

"[T]he judge is without power to foreclose that opportunity [to make an objection] by any order or admonition to sit down or to be quiet or not to address the court. The power to silence an attorney does not begin until reasonable opportunity for appropriate objection or other indicated advocacy has been afforded." (55 Cal. 2d 291, at p. 298)

Baldly stated, this means that the judge cannot tell counsel at a given time to be silent. The court observed that the trial of a criminal cause involves three principal officers of the court—the judge, the prosecutor, and defense counsel, that each of these officers has his role, and that each is "equally" essential to the fairness of the trial. "A fair trial is the product of the contributions of the judge and of all participating attorneys." What this ruling boils down to is that the authority of the judge to determine who shall speak at any given time is one that is arguable and negotiable.

Another example of the erosion of the contempt power, this time when used to protect a witness from abuse, is found in the California case of *In re Hallinan*.[21] Counsel concluded his examination of an adverse witness with the remark, "You can crawl down off the witness stand." The trial court held counsel in contempt, finding that the remark had been made in an antagonistic and insulting tone of voice in the immediate view and presence of the court. In annulling the order of contempt the California Supreme Court stated that the remark did not constitute contemptuous behavior toward the judge (only toward the witness) and did not constitute disobedience of the court, since petitioner had not been given a previous court order or warning with respect to his conduct toward witnesses. The court did state that if a similar incident had followed, the trial court could have properly cited counsel for contempt, thus applying a rule comparable to that formerly used in dog-bite cases—every dog gets one free bite.

These and other cases suggest that a trial judge is on shaky ground if he tells counsel to be quiet, tells counsel to sit down, holds counsel in contempt for announcing that he will not follow the orders of the judge, or holds counsel in contempt for insulting a witness. The statements of Justice Jackson in *Sacher* v. *United States* that "if the ruling is adverse, it is not counsel's right to resist it or to insult the judge," and that "[d]uring a trial, lawyers must speak, each in his own time and within his allowed time, and with relevance and moderation," [22] may well be obsolete.

It is probably no longer possible for a trial judge to find counsel in contempt at the conclusion of a trial for conduct that occurred during the course of the trial. Such a procedure was upheld in *Sacher* v. *United States* on the theory that to pronounce a lawyer guilty of contempt during the trial might prejudice the cause of his client. However, the current rule seems to require that a contempt charge initiated at the conclusion of a trial receive a public hearing before a different judge, a procedure which is then no longer summary.[23] Thus the power of summary contempt must be exercised by the trial court at the time of the contempt, or not at all.

Misbehavior of counsel puts the trial court in a dilemma, for if the court finds counsel in contempt but does not immediately punish him, the misbehavior is apt to become worse; and if the court commits contumacious counsel to jail, the client on trial has been deprived of the assistance of counsel, and the trial must be suspended until counsel is released or new counsel has been brought in. Since in many instances suspension of the trial is the very objective sought by counsel and his client, the latter course may not furnish the judge with any true option. In most instances the only practical choice for the judge is to relinquish summary power to punish counsel for contempt, and the real control over the conduct of the trial that summary punishment brings, and hope that a finding of contempt with sentence deferred or with punishment deferred will suffice to restore order in the courtroom. Even here the judge may be met with a contention that deferred sentence or deferred punishment can only be imposed after a public hearing by a different judge. When misbehaving counsel come from outside the jurisdiction and are not subject to permanent control by the local courts, these difficulties are compounded.

During the twenty years from 1952 to 1972 the United States Supreme Court in its published opinions did not once uphold a conviction of counsel for contempt of court. During that same period it reversed eight convictions of counsel for contempt.[24] In two opinions the court did affirm contempt convictions of persons who were lawyers, but they were lawyers appearing as witnesses and not as counsel.[25]

Litigants, witnesses, and counsel have been quick to get the message, to note this dilution of the summary contempt power and turn it to their own ends. Criminal defendants in particular have found considerable profit in a course of behavior calculated to disrupt courtroom proceedings. In today's climate and under skillful stage management, contempt can be equated with courage and insults with independence, Justice Jackson's views to the contrary notwithstanding.[26] If sufficient disruption can be provoked in the courtroom, important defense objectives may thereby be achieved. Vast publicity flows from disruptive activities, and defendants and defense counsel with a flair for publicity have become instant celebrities comparable in notoriety to star professional quarterbacks. Other defendants have become collective celebrities, often under numerical designation, such as Catonsville Nine, Chicago Seven, Seattle Six, or New York Nineteen.

This weakening of the summary contempt power, like the sowing of the dragon's teeth, has produced a ripe harvest of confrontations and disruptions in which court proceedings often more resemble slapstick theater or barroom brawl than a court of law. When this occurs, the unfortunate trial judge, often as not, is irrationally condemned for failing to keep order in the courtroom, and his efforts to cope with disruption are faulted as underreaction or overreaction.

Trial Court Experience
of Supreme Court Justices

Justice Black has written that " [t]heoretical contemplation is a highly valuable means of moving toward improved techniques in many fields, but it cannot wholly displace the knowledge that comes from the hard facts of everyday experience." [27]

Control over the trial proceedings by a trial judge necessarily involves more art than science, and the exercise of that art must be backed by authority on the occasions when authority becomes essential to preserve control. One of the sources of continuing strength in the English system of justice is found in the English practice of requiring judges, even those who belong to the highest courts, to sit regularly as trial judges in the trial courts. This was also the practice of the justices of the United States Supreme Court in the early days of the Republic, and the regular appearance in the trial courts of such justices as Marshall and Story undoubtedly contributed to the strength of the federal judicial system. Personal experience of Supreme Court justices with the difficulties and problems of the trial courts is particularly needed today when the Supreme Court has undertaken to regulate substantially all trial procedures in both federal and state courts and to establish detailed codes of criminal procedure for the states as a matter of constitutional law.

What experience as trial judges do the justices of the Supreme Court possess? As the court was constituted in June 1971, the members of the court, according to *Who's Who in America*,[28] had enjoyed the following trial court judicial experience:

> Chief Justice Burger —none
> Justice Black —part-time police court judge, 1911–1912
> Justice Douglas —none
> Justice Harlan —none

Justice Brennan —Superior Court judge, New Jersey, 1949–1950
Justice Stewart —none
Justice White —none
Justice Marshall —none
Justice Blackmun —none

On the retirement of Justices Black and Harlan two new justices joined the court. Their trial court judicial experience has been:

Justice Powell—none
Justice Rehnquist—none

A comparable situation would be that of a large metropolitan hospital whose directing board of surgeons consisted of surgeons who had never been in charge of an operation, some of whom had never been inside an operating theater in any capacity.

This situation sharply contrasts with that in Great Britain. Of thirteen persons who sat in 1971 as Lords of Appeal in Ordinary in the House of Lords, eleven had enjoyed extensive experience as trial court judges.[29]

If the United States Supreme Court is to continue to regulate in detail the conduct of causes in the trial courts, it would seem highly desirable for individual justices to look to the example of Justice Clark, who after his retirement in 1967 sat for the first time on the trial bench. The Supreme Court recesses each year from June to October. Would it not be advisable for its members to escape their paper world during recess and sit as trial judges for a month each year? Would not this experience strengthen the ability of the court to issue sound rulings governing the trial of cases in state and federal courts?

From this brief survey of the current status of powers of control exercisable by trial judges over proceedings in the courts, one conclusion emerges: perfectibility in the protection of a defendant's rights has been sought at the expense of the integrity of the proceedings in which those rights are being adjudicated. Paradoxically, appellate courts in seeking a better trial for the accused have sanctified worse conduct by the participants.

18

ONE SYSTEM OF COURTS

$\mathbb{A}$T the time of the adoption of the Constitution the establishment of lower federal courts was left to the discretion of Congress, a discretion the first Congress promptly exercised in the Judiciary Act of 1789 by creating lower federal courts of limited and defined jurisdiction. The principal motivation for the establishment of these lower federal courts was to provide an impartial tribunal for litigation between citizens of different states, for it was felt that in state courts nonresidents might not secure impartial justice when opposed to residents.[1]

The exclusive authority of Congress over the jurisdiction of lower federal courts has been frequently recognized by the Supreme Court—as long ago, for example, as 1812, when Justice Johnson declared that lower federal courts only possess the jurisdiction given them by Congress, the authority that created them.[2] Central to the establishment of a system of lower federal courts was the idea that such courts would remain courts of limited jurisdiction. Adjunct to this was the related idea that state courts are fully competent to interpret and apply federal law, a view expressed by Justice Story in 1816.[3]

These two concepts, that lower federal courts are courts of limited, defined jurisdiction and that state courts are fully qualified to interpret and apply federal law, commanded general acceptance from courts and Congress until quite recently. But during the past twenty years expansion of the scope of federal constitutional rights into all aspects of state criminal law and procedure and into the entire field of state legislative classification, has made the description of lower federal courts as courts of limited jurisdiction a species of legal fiction. The scope of this expansion need not be reviewed again, except to point out that lower federal courts are now

150

routinely involved in regulating day-to-day operations of local schools and colleges, local jails and prisons, local municipalities, local welfare agencies, local courts, and local police. The theory behind this regulation is that restraints contrary to fundamental law may be directly redressed by lower federal courts.[4] Federal jurisdiction over a controversy is now created by the mere allegation of unconstitutional restraint.

Likewise within the past two decades the idea that state courts are fully competent to interpret federal law has undergone sharp modification. As recently as 1953 Justice Reed declared on behalf of the Supreme Court that "state and federal courts have the same responsibilities to protect persons from violation of their constitutional rights." [5] But in recent years a number of justices of the Supreme Court have adopted the view that because federal law is superior to state law, lower federal courts are superior interpreters of federal law to even the highest state courts. From this premise, the conclusion is drawn that lower federal courts may overrule the highest state courts whenever a question of federal law is involved. Such was the view of Justice Frankfurter and of Chief Justice Warren.[6] This claim has been boldly advanced on several occasions by Justice Brennan, who declared in a 1971 dissent that "the federal courts [are] the primary guardians of constitutional rights." [7] Under such a conception the unanimous judgment of seven justices of the California Supreme Court affirming a state murder conviction may be later overturned by an order of a single judge of a federal district court, as in *California* v. *Imbler* [8] (discussed in Chapter 3).

These developments have brought about the current phenomenon of two systems of courts operating simultaneously on the same subject matter, and the ensuing tug of war, waste, confusion, and plain muddle are painfully evident to anyone involved in the process. Yet the mischief goes beyond inefficiency brought about by duplication of effort, this by reason of the fact that lower federal courts continue to retain the provincial outlook associated with courts of limited jurisdiction. Normally, lower federal courts assume no share of responsibility for protection of the community against disaster; for maintenance of public order; for enforcement of laws against murder, robbery, burglary, aggravated assault, theft, and rape; for continuance of municipal services; or for maintenance of local institutions. From these responsibilities lower federal courts dissociate themselves almost completely in their concentration on protection of federal constitutional rights. Lower federal courts, in areas where their jurisdiction overlaps that of state courts, suffer the weakness of being one-interest courts—courts which concern themselves exclusively with protection of personal rights and privileges and not at all with performance of personal duties and obligations. Too often, this one-sided viewpoint upsets the balance between right and duty within our dual court system and produces irresponsibility, much as though a government were to operate with duplicate legislatures, one concerned solely with spending money, the other solely with imposing taxes.

The assumption that a federal form of government requires duplicate systems of courts is one which has not been made by either Canada or Australia in establishing its judicial machinery. Canada has a unitary court system.[9] The provincial courts possess original jurisdiction over civil and criminal cases arising under most federal and all provincial law; the federal Exchequer Court has exclusive original jurisdiction in cases involving patents, copyrights, taxation, admiralty, disputes between provinces, and claims against the crown; and the Supreme Court of Canada serves as the final court of appeal from the provincial and Exchequer courts. Judges of both provincial and federal courts are appointed by the federal government.

Australia, too, has a unitary court system.[10] Each state maintains its own courts, which exercise both state and federal jurisdiction. The major federal courts are the specialized Bankruptcy and Industrial courts, and the High Court of Australia, the latter serving as a final court of appeal from all federal and state courts, and also possessing original jurisdiction in suits where the commonwealth is a party, in suits between states, and in actions against commonwealth officials. Although the Australian parliament possesses the power to create lower federal courts, with the exception of the Bankruptcy and Industrial courts it has not done so. Rather, it has clothed state courts with federal jurisdiction, even to the extent of initially placing the original jurisdiction of the High Court in the state courts. Judges of state courts are appointed by state governments, and judges of federal courts are appointed by the federal government. A significant achievement of both the Canadian and Australian court systems is their avoidance of overlap and duplication.

The goal of American court reorganization should be to eliminate overlap and duplication and create a system under which only one set of courts operates on a given subject matter. Theoretically, this might be accomplished in a number of ways. A single system of courts could be achieved by abolishing the lower federal courts and relying exclusively on state courts to handle cases arising under both state and federal law. Alternatively, the same result could be achieved by abolishing the state courts and relying exclusively on federal courts to handle cases arising under both state and federal law. The latter system has been used in the past by Congress in establishing court systems for some of the American territories. Or a combination of two systems might be evolved, as has occurred in Canada.

While such changes may sound radical in theory, in actual operation of a judicial system the effect of the changes would probably be small. Whether a revised American court system were denominated a federal system or a state system, it would be manned by roughly the same group of persons, and it would apply the same laws and follow most of the procedures that are presently used. The critical difference would be in the binding authority of the system's judgments.

But it would be highly optimistic to think that a consolidation of our judicial machinery into one court system is likely to occur in the foreseeable future. The only thing harder to abolish than a government bureau is an independent government agency, and no agency of government is more independent than the judiciary. The occasional suggestion that American courts be consolidated into one system has been greeted with the deafening silence that accompanies the launching of a lead balloon.[11] So long as patronage plays an important role in public life, systems of courts with different appointing authorities are likely to endure.

Does this mean, then, that the problem of duplicate systems of courts is insoluble, that nothing constructive can be done? By no means. Even though a wholly federal system, a wholly state system, or a consolidated system is each presently impracticable of achievement, no reason exists why the original federal system cannot be refurbished and the lower federal courts restored to their position as courts of *limited* jurisdiction. Congress retains exclusive control over the jurisdiction of the lower federal courts,[12] and by amendment to the United States Judicial Code it could reinstate the lower federal courts as courts of limited jurisdiction (bankruptcy, copyright, patents, admiralty, antitrust, federal taxation, claims against the federal government, and so on) and remove their jurisdiction over matters that duplicate the work of the state courts. Federal law and federal rights arising out of the work of the state courts could be enforced in the state courts, as they are in Canada and Australia. State court judges are sworn to uphold the Constitution and the laws of the United States, and they could be made federally accountable on their oaths. The jurisdiction of the United States Supreme Court over all courts would continue as before, and cases from the highest state courts involving federal law would be reviewable by the Supreme Court. But final judgments of state or federal courts would not be subject to further review in the lower federal courts.

All the tools needed to control the present disorder in our court system lie within the hands of Congress, as may be seen in the statement of Justice Daniel, writing for the Supreme Court in 1845:

> "[T]he judicial power of the United States . . . depend [s] . . . upon the action of Congress, who possess the sole power of creating the tribunals (inferior to the Supreme Court) . . . and of investing them with jurisdiction either limited, concurrent, or exclusive, and of withholding jurisdiction from them in the exact degrees and character which to Congress may seem proper for the public good." [13]

What is required is for Congress to act.

19

ELITISM, ABSOLUTISM, AND TERM OLIGARCHY

Elitism is a delusion suffered by appellate judges that courts are better equipped than other organs of government to devise solutions for the great public problems of the times. Fortunately, all appellate courts in the United States are subject to higher authority, and hence their tendencies toward elitism are correctible. All courts, that is, except one—the United States Supreme Court. For all practical purposes that court can issue a ruling on any legal or political question that strikes its fancy, and in so doing it becomes answerable to no one and subject to no review. Under the Constitution the judges of the Supreme Court hold their offices during good behavior (Const. Art. III, Section 1), and the one constitutional limitation on their power is that found in Article III, Section 2 (2), which, after giving the Supreme Court original jurisdiction in a few classes of cases, provides that in other cases the Supreme Court shall have appellate jurisdiction—"with such Exceptions, and under such Regulations as the Congress shall make."

In the course of this country's constitutional development, the Supreme Court has acquired absolute power to decide any case or controversy arising within the United States, absolute power to invalidate any act of the President or of Congress, and absolute power to control virtually all acts of a state government, whether legislative, executive, or judicial. This absolute power is exercisable by five of the nine members of the court, and is neither limited by precedent nor circumscribed by any requirement that the judgments of the court be accompanied by reasoned opinions. If this

155

summary appears to overstate, consider what the justices themselves have said:

Charles Evans Hughes, later Justice, still later Chief Justice:

"We are under a Constitution, but the Constitution is what the judges say it is. . . ." [1]

Harlan F. Stone, Justice, later Chief Justice:

". . . the only check upon our own exercise of power is our own sense of self-restraint." [2]

Oliver Wendell Holmes, Justice:

"As the decisions now stand, I see hardly any limit but the sky to the invalidating of those rights if they happen to strike a majority of this Court as for any reason undesirable." [3]

Robert H. Jackson, Justice:

"Rightly or wrongly, the belief is widely held by the practicing profession that this Court no longer respects impersonal rules of law but is guided in these matters by personal impressions which from time to time may be shared by a majority of Justices. Whatever has been intended, this Court also has generated an impression in much of the judiciary that regard for precedents and authorities is obsolete, that words no longer mean what they have always meant to the profession, that the law knows no fixed principles." [4]

Felix Frankfurter, Justice:

"Because the powers exercised by this Court are inherently oligarchic, Jefferson all of his life thought of the Court as 'an irresponsible body' and 'independent of the nation itself.' The Court is not saved from being oligarchic because it professes to act in the service of humane ends. As history amply proves, the judiciary is prone to misconceive the public good by confounding private notions with constitutional requirements, and such misconceptions are not subject to legitimate displacement by the will of the people except at too slow a pace." [5]

Hugo L. Black, Justice:

> ". . . use of 'privacy' as the keyword in the Fourth Amendment simply gives this Court a useful new tool, as I see it, both to usurp the policy-making power of the Congress and to hold more state and federal laws unconstitutional when the Court entertains a sufficient hostility to them." [6]

John M. Harlan, Justice:

> ". . . the federal judiciary, which by express constitutional provision is appointed for life, and therefore cannot be held responsible by the electorate, has no inherent general authority to establish the norms for the rest of society. It is limited to elaboration and application of the precepts ordained in the Constitution by the political representatives of the people. When the Court disregards the express intent and understanding of the Framers, it has invaded the realm of the political process to which the amending power was committed, and it has violated the constitutional structure which it is its highest duty to protect." [7]

Normally, justices of the Supreme Court deplore the exercise of absolute judicial power only when they find themselves in the minority on a particular issue. Yet this circumstance in no way undermines the validity of their comments, nor does it impair the accuracy of their observations on the exercise of absolute judicial power, a power which in practical operation establishes the personal views and convictions of a majority of the members of the Supreme Court as the supreme law of the land. Time and again the Supreme Court has said that it does not sit as a super-legislature, does not sit as a super-board of education, does not sit as a supreme board of censors.[8] Yet these are the precise functions the Supreme Court has undertaken in particular cases which have captured its attention.[9] A full analysis of the actions of the Supreme Court as super-legislature would involve the entire spectrum of constitutional law, but two examples from cases prieviously discussed in this book will illustrate the point.

In *Griswold* v. *Connecticut* the court invalidated a Connecticut law against contraception on the ground that the law unconstitutionally violated the right of marital privacy, a right which falls within the penumbras formed by emanations from fundamental constitutional guarantees that create zones of privacy, among them the First, Third, Fourth, Fifth, Ninth, and Fourteenth Amendments.[10] In dissent in *Griswold,* Justices Black and

Stewart, after expressing their personal opinion that the Connecticut law was an uncommonly silly law, pointed out:

". . . there is no provision of the Constitution which either expressly or impliedly vests power in this Court to sit as a supervisory agent over acts of duly constituted legislative bodies and set aside their laws because of this Court's belief that the legislative policies adopted are unreasonable, unwise, arbitrary, capricious or irrational. The adoption of such a loose, flexible, uncontrolled standard for holding laws unconstitutional, if ever it is finally achieved, will amount to a great unconstitutional shift of power to the courts which I believe and am constrained to say will be bad for the courts and worse for the country." (381 U.S. 479, at pp. 520, 521)

Quite clearly, the court in *Griswold* struck down state legislation because it found the legislation irrational, unreasonable, and offensive; in effect the court exercised a supervisory veto over legislation whose fairness and wisdom failed to pass muster with the court.

The second example of the court acting as super-legislature, this time not to invalidate a state law but to enact legislation of its own, is *Miranda v. Arizona,* where the court undertook to prescribe as a matter of constitutional law a detailed form of legal advice which it said must be given a detained suspect before he could be found to have waived his rights and agreed to questioning.[11] In doing this the court transformed the critical issue connected with such questioning from the voluntariness of the answers given to the voluntariness of the suspect's waiver of rights. Here, the court undertook to function as a legislature—which sees a problem, devises a solution, and puts its solution into effect by creating and adopting new law. But unlike statute law, which can be repealed if it doesn't work, unsatisfactory court-decreed constitutional legislation can never be repealed short of constitutional amendment or a change of heart by the court itself.

Because of its absolute authority as an oligarchy whose members serve for life, the Supreme Court has the power to impose its ideas of policy on all other branches of government. Interested parties are continually asking the court to do this, for change by court dictate is relatively easy to accomplish, it is cheap, and it avoids the arduous labors required to convince the general public and legislative committees that the proposed change is a desirable one. Here we arrive at the heart of elitism. This appeal to and reliance on elitism may be seen in an article by Professor Judith Blake of the University of California, Berkeley, writing in 1971 about public opinion and the abortion laws.[12] Professor Blake analyzed six nationally known

158

surveys of public opinion on abortion between 1962 and 1969, and then concluded that a substantial majority of persons were opposed to abortion when sought for financial reasons or to prevent the birth of an unwanted child. Professor Blake further concluded that state-by-state change in the legislatures would be slow and unproductive, that the only method of rapid change would be to persuade the Supreme Court to declare the laws against abortion unconstitutional:

"We may conclude, therefore, that changes in abortion laws, like most social changes, will not come about by agitation at the grass roots level. . . . This popular ambivalence [80 per cent of the white population disapproves elective abortion], plus the cumbersomeness of state-by-state change in abortion laws, suggest that a Supreme Court ruling concerning the constitutionality of existing state restrictions is the only road to rapid change in the grounds for abortion. Interestingly, such a ruling would be no more at variance with public opinion than some other famous judicial decisions have been."

Litigants with a passion for instant change are continually tempting the court to plunge into instant reform. And with regularity the court has been succumbing to temptation. In 1973, for example, the court yielded to the temptation to enact a complete legislative scheme on the subject of abortion, thereby abrogating years of legislative efforts to work out acceptable solutions to the abortion problem and its related issues.[13] Only rarely does the court recall the desirability of the self-restraint extolled by Justices Stone and Frankfurter, although when it does do so it sees the issue clearly enough. In *New York Times Co.* v. *United States* the court in 1971 refused to enjoin newspaper publication of government documents which had been unlawfully removed from a government department, and Justice Thurgood Marshall forcefully presented the argument for self-restraint:

"The issue is whether this Court or the Congress has the power to make law. . . . It may be more convenient for the Executive Branch if it need only convince a judge to prohibit conduct rather than ask the Congress to pass a law, and it may be more convenient to enforce a contempt order than to seek a criminal conviction in a jury trial. . . . But convenience and political considerations of the moment do not justify a basic departure from the principles of our system of government." [14]

The disadvantages of an elitist approach to the creation of law may be succinctly stated: the process doesn't work very well. First, elitism debilitates the strength of representative government. Even when the social undesirability of a law may be convincingly urged, said Justice Frankfurter,

> "it is better that its defects should be demonstrated and removed than that the law should be aborted by judicial fiat. Such an assertion of judicial power deflects responsibility from those on whom in a democratic society it ultimately rests—the people." [15]

But additionally, the process.of elitism carries the disadvantage of introducing a large element of instability into the legal system, for the child quickly and painlessly delivered by the stork can just as easily be stolen away by the vulture.[16] Conservative doctrines imposed by a Sutherland court can be overturned by a Stone court, and liberal doctrines imposed by a Warren majority can be repealed by a Burger majority. Law becomes a series of judge-made rules imposed by a temporarily dominant majority of judicial officeholders, and a new majority can decree a new norm based on no more authority than that by which the old norm was created. Hence the desirability of judicial restraint as a mean to continuity in the law.

Unfortunately, judicial restraint tends to be a counsel of perfection, to which an individual justice pays tribute only when he finds himself in the minority on a particular issue. For justices who hold office for life, who are answerable to no other authority, who may override presidential, congressional, and state action, and whose decisions are final, the temptation appears altogether irresistible to equate personal views with wisdom and sound policy and gradually arrive at the position described by Emerson— "difference from me is the measure of absurdity." [17] Even Justice Frankfurter, the most articulate spokesman for judicial restraint, was willing to lead the court in striking down laws which were offensive to his sense of fairness and justice and which shocked his conscience.[18]

Historically, it seems inescapable that reliance on judicial self-restraint is reliance on a rope of sand. Twice in the author's lifetime the Supreme Court has lost the confidence of a large segment of the public in its integrity, impartiality, and willingness to apply written, reasoned law to the causes which come before it. We have noted that this public dissatisfaction has been described elegantly and gracefully by Justices Frankfurter and Jackson. More blunt and direct is the statement of dissatisfaction by Senator Russell B. Long, who said that the Supreme Court handles the Constitution and the laws of the nation like a professional gambler handling loaded dice.[19] In the public mind sleight-of-hand remains sleight-of-hand, even when practiced in support of noble causes in the name of humanity.

It is quite apparent that the reason for this periodic loss of public confi-

dence in the Supreme Court lies in the court's willingness to use its absolute power to promote its own ideas of public policy and do this in a manner that emphasizes naked authority to the neglect of reasoned persuasion.
A court which declares that it is bound neither by custom, nor precedent,
nor statute, nor the specific language of the Constitution itself, is a court
that has asserted its right to disregard the law. A court free to disregard
the law is an instrument of absolute power, and, to the extent a court uses
that power to transform its personal views into law, to that extent does it
become a lawless court. Lord Acton's maxim that all power tends to cor-
rupt and absolute power corrupts absolutely is one that has particular application to the Supreme Court.

Is the solution, then, to abolish the Supreme Court's absolute power?
Heretofore, an elaborate pretense has been indulged, by both the Supreme
Court and others, to the effect that the court has no power of its own, that
its sole function is to apply law created by others and decide cases on the
basis of what is written in the Constitution and in acts of Congress. This
fiction was most directly articulated by Justice Roberts in 1936:

> "When an act of Congress is appropriately challenged in the courts as
> not conforming to the constitutional mandate the judicial branch of
> the Government has only one duty,—to lay the article of the Consti-
> tution which is invoked beside the statute which is challenged and to
> decide whether the latter squares with the former. All the court does,
> or can do, is to announce its considered judgment upon the question.
> The only power it has, if such it may be called, is the power of judg-
> ment. This court neither approves nor condemns any legislative pol-
> icy. Its delicate and difficult office is to ascertain and declare whether
> the legislation is in accordance with, or in contravention of, the pro-
> visions of the Constitution; and, having done that, its duty ends." [20]

So long as we entertain the Roberts view that the Supreme Court exercises
no power of its own, so long do we indulge ourselves in legal fiction which
precludes any serious consideration of the real problem.

Our first step, then, is to recognize the existence in the Supreme Court
of absolute power in oligarchical corporate form, power the court exercises
without any effective restraint. Initial recognition may prove difficult, for
we are trained to a form of government decked out with the finery and
trappings of a written constitution, and we tend to delude ourselves that
absolute power, or sovereignty, has somehow been abolished by the adoption of a written constitution. In point of fact, absolute power is lodged in
the Supreme Court, which has the power to restrain executive and legisla-

tive action and to declare the meaning of the words of the Constitution free from the fetters of law. The power of a sovereign, according to Austin, is incapable of legal limitation, for only a higher sovereign could enforce the limitation. "Supreme power limited by positive law, is a flat contradiction in terms," [21] for the power of the higher sovereign would still remain free from the legal restraints of positive law.

Once we have recognized and acknowledged the existence of absolute power in the Supreme Court, the next step is to consider whether the solution to the problem of absolute power is to abolish the court's absolute power, or in some manner restrain or hedge its exercise. Here we come face to face with the reality that any attempt to abolish or limit the absolute power of the Supreme Court would result either in the transfer of the power to some other entity, or in its retention in the Supreme Court under the guise of some new and different legal fiction; for in the words of Learned Hand, " [g]ranted that 'all power corrupts, and absolute power corrupts absolutely'; absolute power must in the end be lodged somewhere." [22] In a federal system it is apparent there must exist a final shrine wherein the sovereign Delphic oracle resides, in order that she may arbitrate and decide controversies between competing branches of the federal government, between state and federal governments, and between individuals and the community. The Supreme Court is well organized to perform this function, and it has done its work with great credit in such difficult and critical causes as *Brown* v. *Board of Education,* the case holding legally segregated education unconstitutional, and *Youngstown Sheet & Tube Co.* v. *Sawyer,* the case ruling that the President cannot seize private property without the authority of an Act of Congress.[23] All in all, it is difficult to imagine a better soothsayer than the Supreme Court, and easy to conjure up one who would prove worse. And quite obviously, the substitution of some new legal fiction for the Roberts fiction that the Supreme Court exercises no power of its own would achieve no permanent results.

If therefore we conclude that absolute power must be lodged somewhere and that the Supreme Court is the best available instrument for that purpose, the next question is what can be done to improve the exercise of this absolute power over the manner of its exercise in the past. At this point we return again to the thesis that absolute power corrupts absolutely the person exercising that power for any length of time. How, we ask, can this corruption be tempered, limited, attenuated, and ameliorated? From past experience we know that the corrosive effect of absolute power on justices is not avoided by arduous training, personal discipline, profound scholarship, impeccable theory, or the good intentions of the justices themselves.

What about a process of rigorous selection? In recent years the United States Senate has shown its keen appreciation of the absolute power of the Supreme Court by its minute scrutiny of nominees whose names have been submitted for confirmation to the court. During the period 1968 to 1970 four of the six nominees for appointment to the court failed to gain Senate confirmation.[24] This critical examination of the views of nominees for appointment to a position of absolute power is all to the good, but unfortunately the process has gotten out of hand. Too often those who oppose the basic philosophical views of a particular nominee have not been content to rest their opposition on honest difference of philosophical opinion but have sought to fortify opposition to a particular nomination by attacks on the nominee's character, honesty, temperament, and competence. Winston Churchill once said that when you kill a man, it costs nothing to be polite; opposition to a Supreme Court nominee should furnish no excuse for personal invective and reckless character assassination. If intemperance continues as the order of the day in the confirmation process, it may well restrict available nominees to those who possess the wholly negative virtues of being unknown to public life, uncommitted on public issues, and hence invulnerable to specific attack, much as rising political passions from 1840 to 1860 foreclosed the Presidency from men of genuine stature.

Yet the rigors of the selection process do not reach the heart of the problem, for the corruption of absolute power starts only after the successful nominee takes his seat on the bench. Then all too often, in a progression uncontrollable by the selection process, the youthful rationalist on the court changes with the passage of years into an aging absolutist, as happened, for example, with President Wilson's appointee, Justice McReynolds. Nor is the process of change limited to the aging of the justices themselves. Society, too, changes, and the elders on the court may find themselves ill equipped to cope with contemporary problems, as happened in the instance of Justice Van Devanter, whose Wyoming frontier background brought him little understanding of the problems of an industrial society in an economic depression.

As we reflect on the problem of the necessary exercise of absolute power, we realize the dilemma it imposes is not a new one nor is it restricted to the exercise of judicial power. In even more virulent form it is found in the exercise of military command and in the conduct of the executive branch of the government. And with recognition of similarity of danger we begin to think in terms of similarity of solution. When we examine the history of the executive branch of the government, we observe that one of the great strengths of the Republic, perhaps the principal secret of its survival for almost two centuries, has been its ability to give absolute executive power to its President and then take away that absolute power at the end of his term. Like the ancient Romans we call Cincinnatus from the plow to serve as supreme commander, and at the end of his tour of duty we return him to private life. The example was set by George Washington in 1797, and thereafter only once has the tradition of a limited term for the exercise of absolute power as President been disregarded, a disregard that occurred with the election of Franklin D. Roosevelt to a third and a fourth term of office. In the reaction that followed this lapse from the tradition of George Washington, the Twenty-second Amendment to the Constitution was adopted in 1951, under which election to the office of President more than twice is prohibited. This amendment limits the tenure of a President to eight years, except that a person who succeeds to another's term may be eligible to serve as few as six years or as many as ten. The theory behind the Twenty-second Amendment is that no person should exercise the absolute executive power of the Presidency for too long a time.

We could apply the same method for limiting the exercise of absolute judicial power to the justices of the Supreme Court. While it is true that the absolute power of the Supreme Court is collegial rather than individual, the power of the Supreme Court to create, vacate, and modify law in critical respects transcends the powers of Congress and of the President and makes the court an oligarchical body "independent of the nation itself." The Twenty-second Amendment carries the strong implication that the limitation of the term of office of President serves to combat the corruption of absolute power in the person who holds the office. Would not the same beneficent result flow from an amendment limiting the term of office of the members of the Supreme Court? A fixed term of office for sixteen years would not interfere with the exercise of absolute power by the Supreme Court on those occasions when the exercise of that power should prove necessary. But it would limit the length of time that a share of that power remained lodged in the hands of an individual justice. For the individual justice the corrupting effect of absolute power would be nullified on a date certain. And the very existence of a fixed termination date should tend to slow the growth of corruption by reminding the justice who exercised a share of absolute power that he exercised it for a limited term only.

A term of sixteen years would give a justice of the Supreme Court ample time to develop, express, and expound his legal, political, and philosophical views for the benefit and enlightenment of the country. A term of sixteen years would be sufficiently long to protect a justice from pressures of outside interests, of Presidents, of members of Congress, and to protect the court from domination by any single administration. At the conclusion of sixteen years' service a justice of the Supreme Court would be ineligible for reappointment. Provision should be made for him to serve as a judge on some other court if he wished, and payment of his salary should continue for life. A justice who had completed his term of service could write, teach, lecture, practice law, serve as judge on another court, enter politics, go into business—in short do anything except exercise absolute oligarchical power as a member of the Supreme Court. As with the Twenty-second Amendment, an amendment limiting the term of office of a Supreme Court justice to sixteen years would not apply to justices then in office.

On the adoption of such an amendment, term oligarchy would replace absolute oligarchy. The Supreme Court would continue to function as an instrument of absolute power, but its members would serve only for a term of years, and the court would be less likely to lose touch with the underlying currents of the times. The periodic crises in the Supreme Court—which took place in 1857 (Dred Scott), 1895 (income tax), 1937 (New Deal), and 1968 (*Miranda* aftermath)—would be less likely to recur, and the rule of law rather than of personal predilection would be more likely to become the norm.

IV

The Price of
Perfect Justice

20

L'ENVOI

THE ideal of perfectibility has found its practical expression in three themes: the tendency of courts in their quest for perfect justice to duplicate and triplicate the judicial process; the tendency of courts in their preoccupation with form to avoid final judgment; and the tendency of courts routinely to supersede legislatures as founts of wisdom and creators of new law. Together, these tendencies have seriously impaired the capacity of the courts to perform the function for which they were created—to keep in phase the sword and the scales. For as Hobbes has said, covenants without the sword are but words and of no strength to secure a man.[1]

During the past decade these tendencies have been fostered and encouraged by the law schools, whose faculties have generally exalted the work of the courts and downgraded the work of legislative assemblies. In this respect legal fashion in the schools has completely reversed itself from the position it took in the 1930s, when it was accustomed to glorify the work of the legislatures and deprecate the work of the courts. Unhappily, the judges have begun to believe their panegyrists in the law schools and to assume that legislative and governmental wisdom is more often found on the bench than in legislative halls and executive suites. Like Yeats and Hemingway, some judges have become their disciples. As a consequence, what should be government by law has become to some degree government by personal predilection, referred to here as elitism. The transformation of personal predilection into enforceable law is a veiled process in which, according to Learned Hand, the judges

"wrap up their veto in a protective veil of adjectives such as 'arbitrary,' 'artificial,' 'normal,' 'reasonable,' 'inherent,' 'fundamental,' or 'essential,' whose office usually, though quite innocently, is to disguise

169

what they are doing and impute to it a derivation far more impressive than their personal preferences, which are all that in fact lie behind the decision." [2]

This process has so far advanced in recent years that a direct relationship to the written Constitution is no longer considered essential to put personal predilection into effect. Thus has been repudiated Hamilton's reply in *The Federalist* to suggestions that the Supreme Court would construe laws in accordance with the *spirit* of the Constitution and thereby mold them into whatever shape the court thought proper. There is not a syllable in the plan of union, said Hamilton, which "empowers the national courts to construe the laws according to the spirit of the Constitution, or which gives them any greater latitude in this respect than may be claimed by the courts of every State." [3]

The critical problems of modern society do not readily yield themselves to judicial solution, and the consequence of attempts to make them do so has been to increase and accentuate the disruptive tendencies latent in the adversary judicial process. Additionally, lack of compliance by the judges themselves with constitutionally established principles of law has weakened the belief that ours is a government of law, and has tended to bring the judicial process into popular disrepute. Demonstration, confrontation, legal theater, are but varying manifestations of this disrepute. The discrepancy between scholastic theory and actual practice has become so great, and theory has influenced conduct in ways so different from those its originators intended, that affairs have reached the state described by T. S. Eliot:

> Between the idea
> And the reality
> Between the motion
> And the act
> Falls the Shadow [4]

For the existence of a monumental shadow of failure the courts have a number of excuses pointing the finger of responsibility in other directions and absolving themselves from a share of the responsibility for the present disorder. Yet the shadow adheres to the courts, for it is the price of perfect justice.

It is time for courts to recall the statement of Justice Stone that "[c]ourts are not the only agency of government that must be assumed to have capacity to govern," [5] and of Justice Holmes that "legislatures are ultimate guardians of the liberties and welfare of the people in quite as great a degree as [are] the courts." [6] It is time for courts to limit themselves to what they can do well and recall the warning given the Supreme Court by Justice Jackson: "This Court is forever adding new stories to the temples of constitutional law, and the temples have a way of collapsing when one story too many is added." [7]

And it is time for Congress and the legislatures to examine our judicial and legislative institutions critically and put into motion the changes needed to enable those institutions to do the work they are supposed to do. In making changes we must keep ends in view and not fall in love with means, and like St. Ambrose, Bishop of Milan, also a lawyer, learn to distinguish between basic precepts and counsels of perfection.

NOTES

PREFACE

1. Rudolph von Jhering, *The Struggle for Law* (2nd Am. ed.), Chicago, Callaghan (1915), at p. 2.

2. Benjamin N. Cardozo, *The Growth of the Law* (1924), New Haven, Yale University Press, pp. 144–45.

1 / THE IDEAL OF PERFECTIBILITY

1. Macaulay, *Critical and Historical Essays* (Trevelyan ed.), London, Longman's Green (1890), vol. II, p. 335.

2. Annual statistics of automobile deaths are found in United States Bureau of the Census, *Statistical Abstract of the United States: 1971* (92d ed.), Washington, D.C., United States Government Printing Office (1971), p. 540.

3. Comparative statistics for strip mining of coal and underground mining of coal are reported in United States Congress, House Committee on Labor and Education, *Hearings on Amendments to the Federal Coal Mine Safety Act,* Washington, D.C., United States Government Printing Office, Washington, D.C. (1964), p. 409.

4. For California statistics on highway deaths, see California Department of Finance, *California Statistical Abstract, 1971* (12th ed.), Sacramento, State of California, Table J-16, p. 115.

5. For an analysis of the relationship of drinking to fatalities see Julian A. Waller, E. M. King, George Nielson, and Henry W. Turkel, "Alcohol and Other Factors in California Highway Fatalities," *Journal of Forensic Sciences* (1969), 14:429–44.

6. For invalidity of suspension of driver's license because of failure to instruct in the words of the statute, see *Decker* v. *Dept. of Motor Vehicles* (1972), 6 Cal.3d 903.

7. For the claim that instruction in the words of the statute is misleading and therefore suspension of driver's license should be deferred until the claim had been ruled upon by appellate courts, see *Markley* v. *Dept. of Motor Vehicles* (1972), 2nd Cal.App. #39128.

8. For Scandinavian treatment of drunk driving, see David A. Scholl, "The Drinking Driver: An Approach to Solving a Problem of Underestimated Severity," *Villanova Law Review* (1968), 14:97.

9. Gibbon, *Decline and Fall of the Roman Empire* (Smith ed. 1854), London, John Murray, vol. V, p. 327.

10. William S. Holdsworth, *A History of English Law* (3d ed. 1944), London, Methuen and Co., vol. 9, p. 373.

2/PERFECTIBILITY—THE MOVING FINGER REWRITES THE PAST

1. In *Gideon* v. *Wainwright* (1963), 372 U.S. 335, the United States Supreme Court overruled its earlier decision in *Betts* v. *Brady* (1942), 316 U.S. 455.

2. Free counsel for indigents was extended to all cases where imprisonment might be imposed in *Argersinger* v. *Hamlin* (1972), 407 U.S. 25.

3. Free counsel for indigents is provided in civil cases in California for juveniles (Wel. & Inst. Code, § 700), for mentally ill persons (Wel. & Inst. Code, § 5276), for alcoholics and drug addicts (Wel. & Inst. Code, § 5226), and for conservatees (Wel. & Inst. Code, § 5365).

4. *Gideon* v. *Wainwright* (1963), 372 U.S. 335, was summarily made retroactive in *Pickelsimer* v. *Wainwright* (1963), 375 U.S. 2, and *Doughty* v. *Maxwell* (1964), 376 U.S. 202, and formally declared retroactive in *Burgett* v. *Texas* (1967), 389 U.S. 109.

5. A summary of the Florida aftermath of *Gideon* v. *Wainwright* is found in an article by Gene D. Brown, "Collateral Post-Conviction Remedies in Florida," *University of Florida Law Review* (1968), 20:306.

6. *In re Woods* (1966), 64 Cal.2d 3, 7, 8.

7. In *People* v. *Boyden,* the first affirmance of the conviction was in 1960 (181 Cal.App.2d 48). The second affirmance was in 1965 (237 Cal.App.2d 695, 696–97). The third affirmance was in 1967 (251 Cal.App.2d 798).

8. *Douglas* v. *California* (1963), 372 U.S. 353.

9. *Chapman* v. *California* (1967), 386 U.S. 18, 24.

10. *People* v. *Brunson* (1969), 1 Cal.App.3d 226, 235.

11. *Bruton* v. *United States* (1968), 391 U.S. 123.

12. *People* v. *Daniels* (1969), 71 Cal.2d 1119. It was made retroactive to 1951 in *People* v. *Mutch* (1971), 4 Cal.3d 389, 398, 399.

13. California's Indeterminate Sentence Law is found in Penal Code sections 1168, 3020 et seq., 5077.

14. The power of the Governor of California to grant reprieves, pardons, and commutations of sentence is set forth in Cal. Const., Art. V, Sec. 8.

15. The California Supreme Court's order relating to the grant of retroactive relief in *People* v. *Daniels* (1969), 71 Cal.2d 1119, appears in *Zurica on Habeas Corpus,* Crim. 13973, Supreme Court Minutes, 28 June 1971, pp. 5–6.

16. *Mackey* v. *United States* (1971), 401 U.S. 667, 677, 690, 701, concurring and dissenting opinion.

17. *Sanders* v. *United States* (1963), 373 U.S. 1, 8.

18. *Gondeck* v. *Pan American World Airways, Inc.* is reported at 382 U.S. 25 (1965), 370 U.S. 918 (1962), and 371 U.S. 856 (1962).

19. In *Weed* v. *Bilbrey* petition for hearing was denied by the Supreme Court in May 1969 (394 U.S. 1018), a petition for rehearing was denied in June 1969 (395 U.S. 971), a further petition for rehearing was denied in February 1970 (397 U.S. 930), and a third petition for rehearing was denied in December 1970 (400 U.S. 982).

20. *Nelson* v. *George* (1970), 399 U.S. 224.

21. Hand's statement appears in *Schechtman* v. *Foster* (1949), 172 F.2d 339, 341.

22. Jackson's statement is from his opinion in *Brown* v. *Allen* (1953), 344 U.S. 443, 540.

3 / PERFECTIBILITY AND PARALLEL SYSTEMS OF COURTS OPERATING ON THE SAME SUBJECT MATTER

1. Black's statement is from *Atlantic C. L. R. Co.* v. *Engineers* (1970), 398 U.S. 281, 286.

2. *Brown* v. *Allen* (1953), 344 U.S. 443, 485. Frankfurter's comments are at pp. 512 and 510.

3. *Townsend* v. *Sain* (1963), 372 U.S. 293; *Fay* v. *Noia* (1963), 372 U.S. 391.

4. The quotations from Warren's opinion in *Townsend* v. *Sain* are at pp. 312–13, and 318.

5. *Frazier* v. *Cupp* (1969), 394 U.S., 731.

6. *Chambers* v. *Maroney* (1970), 399 U.S. 42.

7. *Dutton* v. *Evans* (1970), 400 U.S. 74.

8. The leading case on pretrial review is *Dombrowski* v. *Pfister* (1965), 380 U.S. 479. Preconviction remedies in the federal courts are further discussed in Chapter 4.

9. Warren Burger, "The State of the Judiciary," *Am. Bar Assn. Journal* (1970) 56:929–30.

10. Judge Lumbard's report, made in 1970, appears in 25 Record, Assn. of Bar of City of New York, 516.

11. History of the *Bates* and *Chavez* proceedings:

Judgments of conviction were affirmed by the California Supreme Court [*People* v. *Chavez* (1958), 50 Cal.2d 778], and certiorari was denied by the United States Supreme Court [*Chavez* v. *California* (1959), 358 U.S. 946, and *Bates* v. *California* (1959), 359 U.S. 993.]

The 1959 to 1962 collateral review by federal habeas corpus is found in *Chavez* v. *Dickson* (1960), 280 F.2d 727, cert.den. (1961), 364 U.S. 934, rehearing denied (1961), 366 U.S. 922; and in *Chavez* v. *Dickson* (1962), 300 F.2d 683, cert.den. (1962), 371 U.S. 880, rehearing denied (1962), 371 U.S. 931.

The 1963 petition for writ of habeas corpus in the California Supreme Court is found *In re Chavez*, Crim. No. 7338, California Supreme Court, 13 March 1963.

The 1963 to 1971 collateral review by federal habeas corpus is reported in *Bates* v. *Wilson* (1967), 385 F.2d 771; in *Bates* v. *Nelson* (1968), 393 U.S. 16, which vacated the earlier decision of the court of appeals; in *Bates* v. *Wilson* (1969), 406 F.2d 555, which remanded the case to the federal district court for further proceedings; and in *Bates* v. *Nelson* (1971), 333 F.Supp. 896, which dismissed the petition.

12. *Whiteley* v. *Warden* (1971), 401 U.S. 560. Black's statements are found at pp. 570, 574.

13. George C. Doub, "The Case Against Modern Federal Habeas Corpus," *Am. Bar Assn. Journal* (1971), 57:323, at p. 326.

14. Henry J. Friendly, "Is Innocence Irrelevant? Collateral Attack on Criminal Judgments," *University of Chicago Law Review* (1970), 38:142, 152.

15. The only other case cited by Judge Friendly was the celebrated case of *Mooney* v. *Holohan* (1935), 294 U.S. 103. There the Supreme Court declared that a conviction secured by known use of perjured testimony would violate due process of law, but because judicial process in California adequate to correct the asserted wrong had not been fully invoked by Mooney, the Court denied his petition for habeas corpus. Subsequently, a California court appraised the evidence offered by Mooney and ruled that his allegations had not been established. [*In re Mooney* (1937), 10 Cal.2d 1, certiorari denied (1938), 305 U.S. 598.] Mooney was pardoned by Governor Olson in 1939, thus securing his release from confinement through executive clemency and not through the courts.

16. *Miller* v. *Pate* (1967), 386 U.S. 1. Miller's original judgment of conviction was affirmed by the Illinois Supreme Court in 1958 (148 N.E.2d 455); and the United States Supreme Court denied certiorari [(1958), 357 U.S. 943], and denied rehearing [(1958), 358 U.S. 859].

The dismissal of the postconviction petition under Illinois law, affirmed by the Supreme Court of Illinois, was denied certiorari by the United States Supreme Court (1960), 363 U.S. 846; rehearing denied (1960), 364 U.S. 857.

The dismissal of the second petition in the state court, affirmed by the Supreme Court of Illinois (1961), 178 N.E.2d 355, was denied certiorari by the United States Supreme Court (1962), 369 U.S. 826.

The dismissal of the petition for habeas corpus in the federal district court was affirmed by the federal court of appeals (1962), 300 F.2d 414, was denied certiorari by the United States Supreme Court (1962), 371 U.S. 898, and was denied rehearing (1962), 371 U.S. 943.

The order of the federal district court issuing the writ of habeas corpus in 1963 is found in 226 F.Supp. 541, 545; and that order was reversed in 1965, 342 F.2d 646, and certiorari was granted in 1966 in 384 U.S. 998.

17. The tender of false evidence in California is a felony (Pen. Code, § 132 ff). The same rule applies in Illinois (Ill. Crim. Code, § 32-2, perjury; § 32-3, subornation of perjury; § 33-3, official misconduct).

18. The report of the grievance committee of the Illinois State Bar Association is found in *Illinois Bar Journal* (1968) 56:955–56.

19. Miller's discharge by the federal district court appears in 299 F.Supp. 418, and the reversal of the order enjoining Illinois from retrying him is found in 429 F.2d 1001, hearing denied (1971), 401 U.S. 924.

20. *California* v. *Imbler:*

Imbler's conviction and sentence in August 1961 was unanimously affirmed by the California Supreme Court in *People* v. *Imbler* (1962), 57 Cal.2d 711.

In 1963 findings of a referee were upheld by the California Supreme Court, and a petition for habeas corpus was dismissed [*In re Imbler* (1963), 60 Cal.2d 554.] The United States Supreme Court denied certiorari [*Imbler* v. *California* (1964), 379 U.S. 908].

The judgment imposing the death penalty was reversed in 1964 (*In re Imbler,* 61 Cal.2d 556), and in January 1965 Imbler was sentenced to life imprisonment.

The opinion of the federal district court in 1969 setting aside the judgment of conviction for constitutional error and directing that Imbler be retried or released appears in *Imbler* v. *Craven* (1969), 298 F.Supp. 795, affirmed as *Imbler* v. *California* (1970), 424 F.2d 631, certiorari denied (1970), 400 U.S. 865.

4 / PRECONVICTION SHUTTLES BETWEEN PARALLEL COURT SYSTEMS

1. *Ex parte Young* (1908), 209 U.S. 123.
2. See remarks of Senator Overman, quoted in *Harv. L.R.* 47:795, at 803–5.
3. 28 U.S.C., §§ 2281, 2283.
4. *Fenner* v. *Boykin* (1926), 271 U.S. 241, 244.
5. The use of injunctive relief against the federal government is seen in *Panama Refining Co.* v. *Ryan* (1935), 293 U.S. 388; *Schechter Corp.* v. *United States* (1935), 295 U.S. 495; *United States* v. *Butler* (1936), 297 U.S. 1.
6. 28 U.S.C., §§ 2282, 2284.
7. *Stefanelli* v. *Minard* (1951), 342 U.S. 117.
8. *Dombrowski* v. *Pfister* (1965), 380 U.S. 479.
9. For injunctions against obscenity prosecutions, see *Karalexis* v. *Byrne* (1969),

306 F.Supp. 1363, vacated in *Byrne* v. *Karalexis* (1971), 401 U.S. 216; *Demich, Inc.* v. *Ferdon* (1970), 426 F.2d 643, vacated (1971), 401 U.S. 990.

10. The view that a single judge may enjoin an unconstitutional use or application of a state law is found in *Stein* v. *Batchelor* (1969), 300 F. Supp. 602, vacated in *Dyson* v. *Stein* (1971), 401 U.S. 200, and in *Metzger* v. *Pearcy* (1968), 393 F.2d 202.

11. For statutes relating to three-judge courts, see 28 U.S.C., §§ 2284, 1292, 1253.

12. *Dombrowski* v. *Pfister* (1965), 380 U.S. 479.

13. *Miller* v. *Reddin* (1968), 293 F.Supp. 216 (1970), 422 F.2d 1264.

14. *Younger* v. *Harris* (1971), 401 U.S. 37. Reference to extraordinary circumstances is found at pp. 53–54.

15. *Perez* v. *Ledesma* (1971), 401 U.S. 82 at p. 84.

16. The declaratory relief statute is found in 28 U.S.C., § 2201.

17. *Zwickler* v. *Koota* (1967), 389 U.S. 241.

18. *Babbitz* v. *McCann* (1970), 310 Fed.Supp. 293, appeal dismissed, *McCann* v. *Babbitz* (1970), 400 U.S. 1.

19. *Stein* v. *Batchelor* (1969), 300 F.Supp. 602, vacated in *Dyson* v. *Stein* (1971), 401 U.S. 200.

20. See 28 U.S.C., § 2201.

21. *Samuels* v. *Mackell* (1971), 401 U.S. 66. Brennan's separate opinion (p. 76) incorporated his statements from his opinion in *Perez* v. *Ledesma* (1971), 401 U.S. 82, 120–30.

22. For federal civil rights statutes, see 42 U.S.C. 1981–86; 28 U.S.C. § 1343.

23. *Monroe* v. *Pape* (1961), 365 U.S. 167.

24. Damage suits for false arrest were extended to federal officers in *Bivens* v. *Six Unknown Fed. Narcotics Agents* (1971), 403 U.S. 388.

25. See, for example, *Demich* v. *Ferdon* (1970), 426 F.2d 643, vacated (1971), 401 U.S. 990.

26. Federal removal statutes are found in 28 U.S.C., §§ 1441–1450.

27. Removal of actions involving federal civil rights is authorized by 28 U.S.C., § 1443.

28. *State of Maryland* v. *Brown* (1969), 295 F.Supp. 63; (1970) 396 U.S. 1029; (1970) 311 F.Supp. 1164; (1970) 426 F.2d 809.

29. For multiple use of preconviction remedies, see *Miller* v. *Reddin* (1968), 293 F.Supp. 216.

30. *State of Maryland* v. *Brown* (1970), 311 F.Supp. 1164, affirmed (1970), 426 F.2d 809.

31. *LaRue* v. *State of California* (1971), 326 F.Supp. 348. Judgment reversed in *California* v. *LaRue* (1972), 409 U.S. 109.

5 / MULTIPLE TRIALS OF THE SAME CAUSE

1. *People* v. *Terry* (1962), 57 Cal.2d 538; (1964) 61 Cal.2d 137; (1969) 70 Cal.2d 410. *People* v. *Anderson* (1972), 6 Cal.3d 628.

2. *People* v. *Seiterle* (1961), 56 Cal.2d 320; (1963) 59 Cal.2d 703; (1964) 61 Cal.2d 651; (1966) 65 Cal.2d 333; (1969) 71 Cal.2d 698.

3. *People* v. *Ketchel* (1963), 59 Cal.2d 503; (1966) 63 Cal.2d 859; (1969) 71 Cal.2d 635.

4. *People* v. *Modesto* (1963), 59 Cal.2d 722; (1965) 62 Cal.2d 436; (1967) 66 Cal.2d 695.

5. *People* v. *Arguello* (1964), 61 Cal.2d 210; (1965) 63 Cal.2d 566; (1967) 65 Cal.2d 768; (1969) 71 Cal.2d 13.

6. *People* v. *Hillery* (1965), 62 Cal.2d 692; (1967) 65 Cal.2d 795; *In re Hillery* (1969) 71 Cal.2d 857.

7. *People* v. *Sears* (1965), 62 Cal.2d 737; (1970) 2 Cal.3d 180.

8. *United States* v. *Persico* (1970), 425 F.2d 1375, certiorari denied (1970), 400 U.S. 869.

9. Sir William Blackstone, *Commentaries on the Laws of England* (1765), Book IV, pp. 335–36.

10. *United States* v. *Gibert* (1834), 25 Fed. Cas. No. 15,204. Story's comments are found at pp. 1295, 1302.

11. The propriety of a new trial after a hung jury was upheld in *United States* v. *Perez* (1824), 9 Wheat. 579.

12. The validity of a second trial was sustained in *United States* v. *Ball* (1896), 163 U.S. 662.

13. The 1911 amendment to the California Constitution was Art. VI, Sec. 4½, now found in slightly different form in Art. VI, Sec. 13.

14. The prejudicial error test was established in *People* v. *O'Bryan* (1913), 165 Cal. 55.

15. Revival of the miscarriage of justice test occurred in *People* v. *Watson* (1956), 46 Cal.2d 818.

16. *Chapman* v. *California* (1967), 386 U.S. 18.

17. *Harrison* v. *United States* (1968), 392 U.S. 219, at pp. 221–22.

6/MULTIPLE REVIEWS OF THE SAME ISSUE

1. A challenge to the validity of a search warrant is authorized by Cal. Pen. Code, §§ 1539, 1540.

2. A challenge to seizure without a warrant is authorized by *Gershenhorn* v. *Superior Court* (1964), 227 Cal.App.2d 361.

3. A civil action for damages is authorized by *Silva* v. *MacAuley* (1933), 135 Cal.App. 249.

4. A federal civil rights action is authorized by the Civil Rights Act (42 U.S.C., § 1983).

5. Procedural authorities for attacks on the validity of search and seizure in California are:

Step 1—Cal. Pen. Code, §§ 860, 871.

Step 2—Cal. Pen. Code, § 995.

Step 3—*Jennings* v. *Superior Court* (1967), 66 Cal.2d 867.

Step 4—*Jennings* v. *Superior Court, supra.*

Step 5—Cal. Pen. Code, § 1538.5.

Step 6—Cal. Pen. Code, § 1538.5(i).

Step 7—*Greven* v. *Superior Court* (1969), 71 Cal.2d 287, 290–91.

Step 8—28 U.S.C., § 1443.

Step 9—28 U.S.C., § 1447.

Step 10—*Brown* v. *Maryland* (1970), 396 U.S. 1029.

Step 11—*Demich* v. *Ferdon* (1970), 426 F.2d 643, vacated (1971), 401 U.S. 990.

Step 12—*Demich* v. *Ferdon, supra.*

Step 13—*Ferdon* v. *Demich* (1971), 401 U.S. 990.

Step 14—*People* v. *O'Brien* (1969), 71 Cal.2d 394, 403; *People* v. *Krivda* (1971), 5 Cal.3d 357; *People* v. *Superior Court* (1971), 4 Cal.3d 605, 611.

Step 15—Cal. Pen. Code, § 1181(5).

Step 16—Cal. Pen. Code, § 1237.

Step 17—Cal. Rules of Court, Rule 28.

Step 18—28 U.S.C., § 1257.

Step 19—Cal. Pen. Code, §§ 1473, 1487.

Step 20—*Gardner* v. *California* (1969), 393 U.S. 367; *In re Smiley* (1967), 66 Cal.2d 606; Cal. Pen. Code, §§ 1237(2), 1475.

Step 21—*In re Caffey* (1968), 68 Cal.2d 762; *In re Hochberg* (1970), 2 Cal.3d 870; Cal. Pen. Code, §§ 1237(2), 1506.

Step 22—*Case* v. *Nebraska* (1965), 381 U.S. 336; *Henry* v. *Mississippi* (1965), 379 U.S. 443.

Step 23—*Warden* v. *Hayden* (1967), 387 U.S. 294.

Step 24—*Warden* v. *Hayden, supra.*

Step 25—*Chambers* v. *Maroney* (1970), 399 U.S. 42.

Step 26—*People* v. *Shipman* (1965), 62 Cal.2d 226; Cal. Pen. Code, § 1265.

6. Petitions for rehearing are authorized in Rules, U.S. Supreme Court, Rule 58; Cal. Rules of Court, Rule 27; Fed. Rules of App. Proc., Rule 40.

7. The use of motions for reconsideration is illustrated by *Weed* v. *Bilbrey* (1970), 400 U.S. 982, where four petitions for hearing were filed.

8. For the absence of res judicata in habeas corpus, see *Smith* v. *Yeager* (1968), 393 U.S. 122; and *In re Bevill* (1968), 68 Cal.2d 854, 863.

9. *Sanders* v. *United States* (1963), 373 U.S. 1, 8.

10. William S. Holdsworth, *A History of English Law* (6th Rev. ed. 1938), Boston, Little, Brown, vol. 1, p. 438.

11. The *Carafas* case is reported in *Carafas* v. *LaVallee* (1968), 391 U.S. 234.

7 / THE LAW'S DELAY—SIDETRACKING AND MAINLINING OF CAUSES

1. Cal. Const., Art. I, Sec. 13; U.S. Const., VI Amend.

2. Unless good cause is shown a felony accusation must be dismissed if not brought to trial within 60 days (Cal. Pen. Code, § 1382).

3. Attacks on the indictment are authorized by Cal. Pen. Code, §§ 995, 999a.

4. *Cassell* v. *Texas* (1950), 339 U.S. 282.

5. *Hernandez* v. *Texas* (1954), 347 U.S. 475.

6. Cal. Pen. Code, §§ 893—904.

7. *Montez* v. *Superior Court* (1970), 10 Cal.App.3d 343, 351, indicates the type of questions put to the judges called as witnesses.

8. *Castro* v. *Superior Court* (1970), 9 Cal.App.3d 675, 680.

9. *People* v. *Sirhan,* Cal. Supreme Court, Crim. No. 14026, reported at 7 Cal.3d 710 (1972).

10. *People* v. *Newton* (1970), 8 Cal.App.3d 359.

11. *People* v. *Superior Court* (1970), 13 Cal.App.3d 672.

12. *Cassell* v. *Texas* (1950), 339 U.S. 282, 287.

13. *United States* v. *Zirpolo* (1971), 450 F.2d 424.

14. An attack on the trial jury panel was made in *People* v. *Sirhan,* Cal. Supreme Court, Crim. No. 14026, reported at 7 Cal.3d 710 (1972).

15. *People* v. *Newton* (1970), 8 Cal.App.3d 359, 389—90.

16. *People* v. *Powell and Smith,* Cal. Supreme Court, No. 14790, and Cal. 2nd Crim. No. 18355.

17. A judge in California may be challenged peremptorily (Cal. Code Civ. Proc., § 170.6) and also for cause (Cal. Code Civ. Proc., § 170 (5).

18. Examples of appellate challenges to unfavorable pretrial rulings of the trial court are found in *Saidi-Tabatabai* v. *Superior Court* (1967), 253 Cal.App.2d 257 (motion to suppress the defendant's own statements); and *Honore* v. *Superior Court* (1969), 70 Cal.2d 162 (motion for disclosure of the identity of an informer in advance of trial).

19. The reference to "potential for unfairness," etc., is from *Castro* v. *Superior Court* (1970), 9 Cal.App.3d 675, 691–92. The same point is made in the opinion in *Canon* v. *Justice Court* (1964), 61 Cal.2d 446, 450, in which the court declared that when a statute was attacked on First Amendment grounds the court could not limit itself to the facts of the case but would consider other possible applications of the statute.

20. *Younger* v. *Harris* (1971), 401 U.S. 37; *Samuels* v. *Mackell* (1971), 401 U.S. 66; *Boyle* v. *Landry* (1971), 401 U.S. 77, 81. Black's statement is found in the last case at p. 81.

21. *Sheppard* v. *Maxwell* (1966), 384 U.S. 333. The quotation is at p. 363.

22. For change of venue and review by the appellate courts in advance of trial, see *Maine* v. *Superior Court* (1968), 68 Cal.2d 375.

23. For multiple motions for change of venue and multiple appellate reviews, see *Jackson* v. *Superior Court* (1970), 13 Cal.App.3d 440.

24. The traditional view that a juror without fixed opinions is qualified to serve is found in *Spies* v. *Illinois* (1887), 123 U.S. 131, 170; the view that a juror who has been exposed to potentially prejudicial material is not qualified to serve is found in *Maine* v. *Superior Court* (1968), 68 Cal.2d 375, at pp. 382–383.

25. *State* v. *Seale* (1971), Conn. Superior Court, No. 15844. The selection of the original jury had taken five months.

26. *Cobbledick* v. *United States,* (1940), 309 U.S. 323, at pp. 325–26.

27. For the California practice, see *Maine* v. *Superior Court* (1968), 68 Cal.2d 375, at p. 378.

28. Sir William Blackstone, *Commentaries on the Laws of England* (1765), Book IV, pp. 340–41; Sir James Stephen, *A History of the Criminal Law of England,* London, Macmillan (1883), vol. I, 297–300.

29. *People* v. *Finch* (1963), 213 Cal.App.2d 752.

30. *People* v. *Sirhan,* Cal. Supreme Court, Crim. No. 14026, reported at 7 Cal.3d 710 (1972).

31. *People* v. *Manson* (1971), Los Angeles Superior Court, No. A 253156.

32. Delmar Karlen, *Anglo-American Criminal Justice,* Oxford, Clarendon Press (1967), pp. 180–81.

33. Dual presentation of a confession is compelled by *Jackson* v. *Denno* (1964), 378 U.S. 368.

34. *People* v. *Coffey* (1967), 67 Cal.2d 204, 217–20.

35. *People* v. *Manson* (1971), Los Angeles Superior Court, No. A 253156.

36. Karlen, *Anglo-American Criminal Justice,* p. 179.

8 / THE LAW'S DELAY—PROCRASTINATION AT HOME IN THE COURTS

1. *People* v. *Esparza* (1971), Cal.2nd Crim. No. 18326.

2. *People* v. *Maddox* (1967), 67 Cal.2d 647.

3. *Jennings* v. *Superior Court* (1967), 66 Cal.2d 867.

4. *People* v. *Crovedi* (1966), 65 Cal.2d 199.

5. *People* v. *Murphy* (1963), 59 Cal.2d 818.

6. State of California, 1970 Judicial Council Report, p. 86.

7. State of California, 1971 Judicial Council Report, p. 97.

8. Delmar Karlen, *Judicial Administration—The American Experience,* Dobbs Ferry, N.Y., Oceana (1970), pp. 76–77.

9. *People* v. *Grant* (1971), Cal.2nd Crim. No. 17095.

10. Cal. Rules of Court, Rule 37.

11. Cal. Const., Art. VI, Sec. 19.

12. *Castro* v. *Superior Court* (1970), 9 Cal.App.3d 675.

13. *Harrison* v. *United States* (1965), 359 F.2d 214. The same case also appears in (1968) 392 U.S. 219, and in (1969) 396 U.S. 974.

14. Cal. Rules of Court, Rule 31.

15. For substantial delay, see *People* v. *Jackson* (1965), 62 Cal.2d 803.

16. *People* v. *Flores* (1971), Cal.2nd Crim. No. 7851.

17. *People* v. *Dobson* (1971), Cal.2nd Crim. No. 18649.

9 / ERROR—INCOMPETENCY OF COUNSEL AND SELF-REPRESENTATION

1. *Gideon* v. *Wainwright* (1963), 372 U.S. 335.

2. Incompetent counsel makes a trial a farce and a sham. *People* v. *Ibarra* (1963), 60 Cal.2d 460.

3. *Douglas* v. *California* (1963), 372 U.S. 353.

4. *Anders* v. *California* (1967), 386 U.S. 738.

5. *In re Smith* (1970), 3 Cal.3d 192.

6. *Smith* v. *Superior Court* (1968), 68 Cal.2d 547.

7. *People* v. *Miyamoto* (1971), Cal. Court of Appeal, 2d District, No. 19117, Appellant's Opening Brief, pp. 26–27.

8. *Anders* v. *California* (1967), 386 U.S. 738.

9. *Los Angeles Times,* 13 December 1970.

10. Frankfurter's comment is found in his dissenting opinion in *Henslee* v. *Union Planters Bank* (1949), 335 U.S. 595, at p. 600.

11. For the lineage of this right of self-representation, see Sir William Blackstone, *Commentaries on the Laws of England* (1765), Book IV, p. 355.

12. *People* v. *Carter* (1967), 66 Cal.2d 666, at p. 673.

13. *People* v. *Weston* (1970), 9 Cal.App.3d 330, at p. 334.

14. For waiver of counsel involving multiple defendants see *Bogart* v. *Superior Court* (1963), 60 Cal.2d 436.

15. *People* v. *Carter* (1967), 66 Cal.2d 666.

16. "The criminal is to go free because the constable has blundered. . . . The privacy of the home has been infringed, and the murderer goes free." Cardozo in *People* v. *Defore* (N.Y. 1926), 150 N.E. 585, at pp. 587 and 588.

17. *People* v. *Addison* (1967), 256 Cal.App.2d 18.

18. *People* v. *Newton* (1970), 8 Cal.App.3d 359, at pp. 386–87.

19. References to legal materials for prisoners appear in Cal. Pen. Code, § 2600; and *In re Harrell* (1970), 2 Cal.3d 675.

20. *Gilmore* v. *Lynch* (1968), 400 F.2d 228; *Gilmore* v. *Lynch* (1970), 319 F.Supp. 105, affirmed as *Younger* v. *Gilmore* (1971), 404 U.S. 15.

10 / ERROR—OPEN SWITCHES THAT DERAIL THE CAUSE

1. Examples of disruptive conduct may be found in *Sacher* v. *United States* (1952), 343 U.S. 1; and in *Mayberry* v. *Pennsylvania* (1971), 400 U.S. 455.

2. For criticism of a trial judge's permissiveness and indulgence of counsel and his "failure of moral mastery," see dissenting opinion of Frankfurter in *Sacher* v. *United States* (1952), 343 U.S. 1, 23, 38, 41–42.

3. *People* v. *Jones* (1971), 16 Cal.App.3d 837.

4. *People* v. *Carter* (1967), 66 Cal.2d 666, 669. See also *Smith* v. *Superior Court* (1968), 68 Cal.2d 547, 556.

5. *People* v. *Chacon* (1968), 69 Cal.2d 765.

6. For defendant's right to be represented by counsel of his choice, see *Smith* v. *Superior Court* (1968), 68 Cal.2d 547.

7. In *People* v. *Keesee* (1967), 250 Cal.App.2d 794, the appellate court reversed Keesee's conviction for robbery because in final argument defense counsel who represented two defendants argued that the codefendant was less culpable than Keesee.

8. In *People* v. *Clark* (1965), 62 Cal.2d 870, a prosecution of three defendants for murder, two of the defendants fifty days after the indictment demanded a speedy trial within the sixty-day period for trial under California law. The third defendant, Clark, who had only recently been apprehended, moved for a twenty-day continuance of the trial in order to give his attorney time to prepare. The court granted the continuance. On appeal this was found to be reversible error, the convictions of the first two defendants were reversed, and their indictments were dismissed.

9. The dilemma presented by the self-incriminating witness appears in *People* v. *Hairgrove* (1971), 18 Cal.App.3d 606.

10. *People* v. *Newton* (1970), 8 Cal.App.3d 359. To same effect is *People* v. *Graham* (1969), 71 Cal.2d 303.

11. *People* v. *Hood* (1969), 1 Cal.3d 444.

12. *In re Tahl* (1969), 1 Cal.3d 122; *Boykin* v. *Alabama* (1969), 395 U.S. 238; and *In re Mosley* (1970), 1 Cal.3d 913.

13. *People* v. *Williams* (1969), 269 Cal.App.2d 879.

14. *People* v. *Gallow* (1970), 14 Cal.App.3d 83, 91 Cal.Rptr. 920.

11/DUE PROCESS, SHOCKED CONSCIENCE, AND EMANATIONS INTO THE PENUMBRA

1. Joseph Story, *Commentaries on the Constitution of the United States,* Boston, Hilliard, Gray and Co. (1833), Vol. III, § 1789.

2. *Scott* v. *Sandford* (1857), 19 How. 393, at p. 450.

3. *Slaughter-House Cases* (1873) 16 Wall. 36.

4. *Allgeyer* v. *Louisiana* (1897), 165 U.S. 578.

5. *Lochner* v. *New York* (1905), 198 U.S. 45.

6. *Coppage* v. *Kansas* (1915), 236 U.S. 1.

7. *Adkins* v. *Children's Hospital* (1923), 261 U.S. 525.

8. Holmes' statements are found in his dissent in *Lochner* v. *New York* (1905), 198 U.S. 45, at pp. 75, 76.

9. Representative decisions of the United States Supreme Court holding state and federal laws unconstitutional were: *Morehead* v. *N.Y. ex rel. Tipaldo* (1936), 298 U.S. 587 [New York minimum wage law for women and children held unconstitutional]; *Railroad Board* v. *Alton R. Co.* (1935), 295 U.S. 330 [compulsory pension plan for railroad employees held unconstitutional]; *Carter* v. *Carter Coal Co.* (1936), 298 U.S. 238 [regulation of commerce in coal held unconstitutional].

10. *Adkins* was overruled in *West Coast Hotel Co.* v. *Parrish* (1937), 300 U.S. 379 [minimum-wage laws for women upheld]; the constitutionality of the National Labor Relations Act was upheld in *Labor Board* v. *Jones & Laughlin* (1937), 301 U.S. 1; the decision in *Truax* v. *Corrigan* (1921), 257 U.S. 312, was overruled in *Senn* v. *Tile Layers Union* (1937), 301 U.S. 468 [Wisconsin statute restricting the use of injunctive relief to prohibit peaceful picketing upheld].

11. From Frankfurter's concurring opinion in *A. F. of L.* v. *American Sash Co.* (1949), 335 U.S. 538, at p. 555.

12. *Adamson* v. *California* (1947), 332 U.S. 46, at p. 68.

13. *Mapp* v. *Ohio* (1961), 367 U.S. 643; *Gideon* v. *Wainwright* (1963), 372 U.S. 335; *Douglas* v. *California* (1963), 372 U.S. 353; *Malloy* v. *Hogan* (1964), 378 U.S. 1;

Griffin v. *California* (1965), 380 U.S. 609; *Miranda* v. *Arizona* (1966), 384 U.S. 436; *Pointer* v. *Texas* (1965), 380 U.S. 400; *Ker* v. *California* (1963), 374 U.S. 23; *Benton* v. *Maryland* (1969), 395 U.S. 784; *Duncan* v. *Louisiana* (1968), 391 U.S. 145.

14. *Rochin* v. *California* (1952), 342 U.S. 165.

15. *Jackson* v. *Denno* (1964), 378 U.S. 368.

16. *Estes* v. *Texas* (1965), 381 U.S. 532.

17. *United States* v. *Wade* (1967), 388 U.S. 218.

18. *Schware* v. *Board of Bar Examiners* (1957), 353 U.S. 232, at p. 249.

19. Justice Harlan's comment is in *Baird* v. *State Bar of Arizona* (1971), 401 U.S. 1, 35.

20. *NAACP* v. *Alabama* (1958), 357 U.S. 449.

21. *Bryant* v. *Zimmerman* (1928), 278 U.S. 63.

22. *Shelton* v. *Tucker* (1960), 364 U.S. 479.

23. *Morey* v. *Doud* (1957), 354 U.S. 457.

24. *NAACP* v. *Button* (1963), 371 U.S. 415.

25. Supreme Court disclaimers on revival of substantive due process are found in *Day-Brite Lighting, Inc.* v. *Missouri* (1952), 342 U.S. 421; *Williamson* v. *Lee Optical Co.* (1955), 348 U.S. 483, at p. 488; and *Ferguson* v. *Skrupa* (1963), 372 U.S. 726, at p. 730.

26. The California Supreme Court in *Department of Mental Hygiene* v. *Hawley* (1963), 59 Cal.2d 247, held that the parent of a person convicted of a crime and committed to a state mental institution could not be required to pay the costs of care, support, and maintenance of that person in the institution. "The Fourteenth Amendment, 'in declaring that a State shall not "deprive any person of life, liberty or property without due process of law," gives to each of these an equal sanction; it recognizes "liberty" and "property" as coexistent human rights, and debars the States from any unwarranted interference with either.' [*Coppage* v. *Kansas* (1915), 236 U.S. 1, 17 . . .]" (59 Cal.2d, at p. 256). And in *Endler* v. *Schutzbank* (1968), 68 Cal.2d 162, the same court granted relief to plaintiff, a personal property broker, against the commissioner of corporations who was threatening disciplinary action against anyone who might employ plaintiff. "It has long been recognized that the 'right to follow any of the common occupations . . . is . . . a large ingredient in the civil liberty of the citizen.' [*Allgeyer* v. *Louisiana* (1897), 165 U.S. 578 . . .]" (68 Cal.2d, at p. 169).

27. *Griswold* v. *Connecticut* (1965), 381 U.S. 479.

28. Ibid. at pp. 486, 500, and 502.

29. The quotations from Black's dissenting opinion in *Griswold* v. *Connecticut* (1965), 381 U.S. 479, are at pp. 511 and 521. Holmes' dissenting opinion is *Baldwin* v. *Missouri* (1930), 281 U.S. 586, at p. 595. Stewart's dissenting opinion in *Griswold* v. *Connecticut, supra,* is at p. 527.

30. *Shapiro* v. *Thompson* (1969), 394 U.S. 618.

31. *Baird* v. *Eisenstadt* (1970), 429 F.2d 1398, affirmed as *Eisenstadt* v. *Baird* (1972), 405 U.S. 438.

32. *Miranda* v. *Arizona* (1966), 384 U.S. 436.

33. *Katz* v. *United States* (1967), 389 U.S. 347. The two earlier cases overruled by *Katz* were *Olmstead* v. *United States* (1928), 277 U.S. 438; and *Goldman* v. *United States* (1942), 316 U.S. 129.

34. McReynolds' opinions were cited with approval in *Tinker* v. *Des Moines School Dist.* (1969), 393 U.S. 503; and *Griswold* v. *Connecticut* (1965), 381 U.S. 479, at pp. 495, 502.

35. For the recommendation that courts use substantive due process in the field of abortion, etc., see, Herbert L. Packer, "The Aims of the Criminal Law," *So.Cal.L.R.* (1971), 44:490.

12/EQUAL PROTECTION OF THE LAWS AND EQUALITY

1. *Yick Wo* v. *Hopkins* (1886), 118 U.S. 356.
2. *Plessy* v. *Ferguson* (1896), 163 U.S. 537.
3. *Skinner* v. *Oklahoma* (1942), 316 U.S. 535.
4. *Shelley* v. *Kraemer* (1948), 334 U.S. 1.
5. *Takahashi* v. *Fish & Game Commission* (1948), 334 U.S. 410.
6. *Brown* v. *Board of Education* (1954), 347 U.S. 483.
7. For invalidation of racially segregated public facilities see *Burton* v. *Wilmington Parking Authority* (1961), 365 U.S. 715 [restaurant]; *Watson* v. *City of Memphis* (1963), 373 U.S. 526 [public parks and recreational facilities]; *Griffin* v. *Maryland* (1964), 378 U.S. 130 [amusement park]; see also *Brown* v. *Allen* (1953), 344 U.S. 443, 471.
8. 347 U.S. 483, at p. 493.
9. Aristotle, *Politics* (Modern Library ed.), New York, Random House (1943). Bk. V, ch. 1, at p. 211.
10. *Street* v. *New York* (1969), 394 U.S. 576.
11. For sexual discrimination as a suspect category, see *Sail'er Inn, Inc.* v. *Kirby* (1971), 5 Cal.3d 1; *Rosenfeld* v. *Southern Pacific Company* (1968), 293 F.Supp. 1219.
12. Statement of Horace D. Taft to author.
13. Holmes' statement is from *Buck* v. *Bell* (1927), 274 U.S. 200, at p. 208.
14. *Reynolds* v. *Sims* (1964), 377 U.S. 533.
15. *Lucas* v. *Colorado General Assembly* (1964), 377 U.S. 713.
16. Brandeis' statement is found in *New State Ice Co.* v. *Liebmann* (1932), 285 U.S. 262, dissenting opinion at p. 311.
17. *Harper* v. *Virginia Board of Elections* (1966), 383 U.S. 663.
18. *Griffin* v. *Illinois* (1956), 351 U.S. 12.
19. *Douglas* v. *California* (1963), 372 U.S. 353.
20. *Sail'er Inn, Inc.* v. *Kirby* (1971), 5 Cal.3d 1.
21. *Rosenfeld* v. *Southern Pacific Company* (1968), 293 F.Supp. 1219.
22. *Adkins* v. *Children's Hospital* (1923), 261 U.S. 525.
23. *Muller* v. *Oregon* (1908), 208 U.S. 412.
24. *Dept. of Mental Hygiene* v. *Kirchner* (1964), 60 Cal.2d 716, 720; reiterated in 62 Cal.2d 586.
25. *County of San Mateo* v. *Boss* (1971), 3 Cal.3d 962.
26. *Parr* v. *Municipal Court* (1971), 3 Cal.3d 861.
27. *Brown* v. *Board of Education* (1954), 347 U.S. 483, at p. 493.
28. Aristotle, *Politics* (Modern Library ed.), New York, Random House (1943), Bk. III, Ch. 12, at p. 150. Plato, *Republic* (Bollingen Series), Princeton, N.J., Princeton University Press (1971), Bk. VII, including pp. 768–69.
29. The ban against proportional racial selection is found in *Cassell* v. *Texas* (1950), 339 U.S. 282, at p. 287; see also *Swain* v. *Alabama* (1965), 380 U.S. 202, at p. 208.
30. *Swann* v. *Charlotte-Mecklenburg Board* (1971), 402 U.S. 1; *United States* v. *Montgomery Bd. of Educ.* (1969), 395 U.S. 225.
31. *Anderson* v. *San Francisco Unified School District* (N.D. Cal. 1972), 357 F. Supp. 248. Civil Rights Act of 1964, 42 U.S.C. 2000e–2000e(2)(a).
32. *Los Angeles Times*, 29 April 1973. Statement of Samuel H. Solomon, Office of Civil Rights, Department of Health, Education and Welfare.
33. *Guinn* v. *United States* (1915), 238 U.S. 347.

34. *Carter* v. *Jury Commission* (1970), 396 U.S. 320. Douglas' views appear at pp. 344, 345.

35. The order of the Los Angeles EYOA is reported in *Los Angeles Times,* 30 October 1971.

36. For example, see *Colgate* v. *Harvey* (1935), 296 U.S. 404, at p. 441, dissenting opinion.

37. *Shapiro* v. *Thompson* (1969), 394 U.S. 618.

38. *In re King* (1970), 3 Cal.3d 226.

39. Harlan's comment is from his concurring opinion in *Williams* v. *Illinois* (1970), 399 U.S. 235, at p. 259.

13 / THE RETREAT FROM WRITTEN LAW AND THE DECLINE OF LEGISLATIVE AUTHORITY

1. *Griswold* v. *Connecticut* (1965), 381 U.S. 479. Black's comments are at p. 509.

2. *Shapiro* v. *Thompson* (1969), 394 U.S. 618.

3. *Harper* v. *Virginia Bd. of Elections* (1966), 383 U.S. 663. Black's comments are at p. 678.

4. *Oregon* v. *Mitchell* (1970), 400 U.S. 112. References to interpretation of the Fourteenth Amendment in accordance with visions and needs of future generations are at pp. 139, 140, 278. Douglas' statement is at p. 140; Harlan's statement is at p. 201. The statement of Holmes is found in *Eisner* v. *Macomber* (1920), 252 U.S. 189, at p. 220.

5. *Baird* v. *Eisenstadt* (1970), 429 F.2d 1398, 1402, affirmed as *Eisenstadt* v. *Baird* (1972), 405 U.S. 438.

6. *The Federalist* (Modern Library ed.), New York, Random House (1937), No. 78, p. 510.

7. *Miranda* v. *Arizona* (1966), 384 U.S. 436.

8. *Levy* v. *Louisiana* (1968), 391 U.S. 68.

9. *Griswold* v. *Connecticut* (1965), 381 U.S. 479.

10. *Reynolds* v. *Sims* (1964), 377 U.S. 533.

11. *Morrissey* v. *Brewer* (1972), 408 U.S. 471.

12. *Roe* v. *Wade* (1973), 410 U.S. 113.

13. *Harper* v. *Virginia Bd. of Elections* (1966), 383 U.S. 663, at p. 686.

14. *Boddie* v. *Connecticut* (1971), 401 U.S. 371.

15. For wealth as a suspect classification, see *Boddie* v. *Connecticut* (1971), 401 U.S. 371, pp. 386, 388, concurring opinions; *Simmons* v. *West Haven Housing* (1970), 399 U.S. 510, 514, dissenting opinion: "Whether the case is criminal or civil, wealth, like race, is a suspect criterion for classification of those who have rights and those who do not."

16. Black's statements are in *Boddie* v. *Connecticut* (1971), 401 U.S. 371, at pp. 392, 393, 394.

17. *Townsend* v. *Sain* (1963), 372 U.S. 293.

18. Title 28, United States Code, Judiciary and Judicial Procedure, section 2254.

19. *Roth* v. *United States* (1957), 354 U.S. 476.

20. California's obscenity laws are found in Cal. Pen. Code, § 311 ff.

21. The first California death penalty case is *In re Anderson* (Nov. 1968), 69 Cal.2d 613, and the quotations are at pp. 630, 634–35.

22. The second California death penalty case is *People* v. *Anderson* (Feb. 1972), 6 Cal.3d 628, and the quotation is at p. 640.

23. Harlan's phrase is from his dissent in *Harper* v. *Virginia Bd. of Elections* (1966), 383 U.S. 663, at p. 686.

14 / THE IRRELEVANCE OF GUILT

1. The federal rule was adopted in *Weeks* v. *United States* (1914), 232 U.S. 383.
2. The California rule was adopted in *People* v. *Cahan* (1955), 44 Cal.2d 434.
3. *Mapp* v. *Ohio* (1961), 367 U.S. 643.
4. *Miranda* v. *Arizona* (1966), 384 U.S. 436, 479.
5. *Coolidge* v. *New Hampshire* (1971), 403 U.S. 443.
6. For suppression of murder weapon, see *People* v. *Buchanan* (1966), 63 Cal.2d 880.
7. *People* v. *Blakeslee* (1969), 2 Cal.App.3d 831.
8. *Wong Sun* v. *United States* (1963), 371 U.S. 471.
9. *People* v. *Johnson* (1969), 70 Cal.2d 541, at p. 558.
10. *United States* v. *Wade* (1967), 388 U.S. 218, 248.
11. *Whiteley* v. *Warden* (1971), 401 U.S. 560; *Foster* v. *California* (1969), 394 U.S. 440; *Orozco* v. *Texas* (1969), 394 U.S. 324.
12. For postconviction collateral attacks on the admission of illegally seized evidence, see *Mancusi* v. *DeForte* (1968), 392 U.S. 364 [state conviction]; and *Kaufman* v. *United States* (1969), 394 U.S. 217 [federal conviction].
13. Great Britain—Home Office Circular No. 31 / 1964 (Judges' Rules).
14. For the practice of English courts in dealing with illegally obtained evidence, see Halsbury, *The Laws of England* (3d ed. 1956), London, Butterworth and Co., Vol. 15, pp. 266–67; *King* v. *The Queen* [1969] 1 A.C. 304; and *Kuruma* v. *The Queen* [1955] A.C. 197.
15. For an evaluation of the effect of Judges' Rules on police conduct, see Lord Patrick Devlin, *The Criminal Prosecution in England* (1958), New Haven, Yale University Press; Delmar Karlen, *Anglo-American Criminal Justice* (1967), Oxford, Clarendon Press, pp. 104–7, 121–23.
16. 18 U.S.C., § 3501.
17. *Adkins* v. *Children's Hospital* (1923), 261 U.S. 525; *Plessy* v. *Ferguson* (1896), 163 U.S. 537.
18. *Miranda* v. *Arizona* (1966), 384 U.S. 436.
19. Chief Justice Burger's views are found in *Bivens* v. *Six Unknown Fed. Narcotics Agents* (1971), 403 U.S. 388, 411, dissenting opinion.
20. Black's and Blackmun's views appear in *Coolidge* v. *New Hampshire* (1971), 403 U.S. 443, 493, 498–99, 510, concurring and dissenting opinion.
21. Harlan's views appear in *Coolidge* v. *New Hampshire* (1971), 403 U.S. 443, at p. 490, concurring opinion.

15 / TRIVIALIZATION OF THE CONSTITUTION

1. *Hudson Water Co.* v. *McCarter* (1908), 209 U.S. 349, at p. 355.
2. Frankfurter's reference to trivialization is in *Adamson* v. *California* (1947), 332 U.S. 46, at p. 60, concurring opinion; Jackson's reference is in *Brown* v. *Allen* (1953), 344 U.S. 443, at p. 536, concurring opinion.
3. *Tinker* v. *Des Moines School Dist.* (1969), 393 U.S. 503. The court's reference to totalitarianism is at p. 511. Black's dissent is at pp. 515–26.
4. *McCollum* v. *Board of Education* (1948), 333 U.S. 203, at p. 237.
5. *Waugh* v. *Mississippi University* (1915), 237 U.S. 589.
6. *Butts* v. *Dallas Independent School District* (1971), 436 F.2d 728.
7. *Riseman* v. *School Committee of City of Quincy* (1971), 439 F.2d 148, at p. 149.
8. *Lansdale* v. *Tyler Junior College* (1970), 318 F.Supp. 529, affirmed (1972), 470

F.2d 659, cert. den. 41 U.S.L.W. 3608; *Breen* v. *Kahl* (1969), 419 F.2d 1034, 1036, cert. den. 398 U.S. 937.

9. *Sims* v. *Colfax Community School District* (1970), 307 F.Supp. 485.

10. *Alexander* v. *Thompson* (1970), 313 F.Supp. 1389.

11. *Lovelace* v. *Leechburg Area School District* (1970), 310 F.Supp. 579.

12. *Calbillo* v. *San Jacinto Junior College* (1969), 305 F.Supp. 857.

13. *Bannister* v. *Paradis* (1970), 316 F.Supp. 185.

14. *Scott* v. *Board of Ed., U.F. Sch. Dist. #17, Hicksville* (1969), 305 N.Y.S.2d 601.

15. *Crews* v. *Cloncs* (1969), 303 F.Supp. 1370, reversed (1970), 432 F.2d 1259.

16. *Breen* v. *Kahl* (1969), 419 F.2d 1034.

17. *Sims* v. *Colfax Community School District* (1970), 307 F.Supp. 485; *Richards* v. *Thurston* (1970), 424 F.2d 1281.

18. *Dunham* v. *Pulsifer* (1970), 312 F.Supp. 411.

19. *Westley* v. *Rossi* (1969), 305 F.Supp. 706.

20. *Parducci* v. *Rutland* (1970), 316 F.Supp. 352.

21. *Keefe* v. *Geanakos* (1969), 418 F.2d 359.

22. *L. A. Teachers Union* v. *L. A. City Bd. of Ed.* (1969), 71 Cal.2d 551.

23. *Smith* v. *St. Tammany Parish School Board* (1970), 316 F.Supp. 1174, affirmed (1971), 448 F.2d 414.

24. *Connelly* v. *University of Vermont* and *State Agr. Col.* (1965), 244 F.Supp. 156.

25. *Wong* v. *Regents of University of California* (1971), 15 Cal.App.3d 823.

26. *Williams* v. *U.S. Dept. of Justice, Bureau of Prison* (1970), 433 F.2d 958; *Conklin* v. *Wainwright* (1970), 424 F.2d 516; *California Dept. of Corrections* v. *Superior Court* (*Timothy F. Leary*), Cal.2d Civ. #41855 (1973).

27. *Davis* v. *Lindsay* (1970), 321 F.Supp. 1134.

28. *Seale* v. *Manson* (1971), 326 F.Supp. 1375.

29. *Northern* v. *Nelson* (1970), 315 F.Supp. 687, affirmed (1971), 448 F.2d 1266.

30. *Karr* v. *Schmidt* (1971), 401 U.S. 1201, at pp. 1202–3.

16/JUDICIAL AVANT-GARDISM

1. Bacon's *Essays,* "Of Judicature," Mount Vernon, N.Y., Peter Pauper Press, p. 210.

2. *United States* v. *Sprague* (1930), 44 F.2d 967.

3. *United States* v. *Sprague* (1931), 282 U.S. 716, at p. 732.

17/TRIAL COURTS AS CHILDREN OF ISRAEL— MAKE BRICK WITHOUT STRAW

1. *Sheppard* v. *Maxwell* (1966), 384 U.S. 333.

2. *Bridges* v. *California* (1941), 314 U.S. 252; *Craig* v. *Harney* (1947), 331 U.S. 367.

3. Frankfurter's views may be found in his dissenting opinion in *Craig* v. *Harney* (1947), 331 U.S. 367, at p. 384; and in his separate opinion in *Maryland* v. *Baltimore Radio Show* (1950), 338 U.S. 912.

4. *Cox* v. *Louisiana* (1965), 379 U.S. 559.

5. *Cohen* v. *California* (1971), 403 U.S. 15.

6. Prosecution for criminal contempt of court was upheld in *Hamilton* v. *Municipal Court* (1969), 270 Cal.App.2d 797, where defendants, about to go on trial on charges arising out of sit-ins on the campus of the University of California at Berkeley and subject to a court pretrial order prohibiting public statements in advance of

trial, held a press conference in front of the courthouse to denounce both the prosecution and the court's pretrial order. Certiorari was denied by the United States Supreme Court (396 U.S. 985).

7. *Illinois* v. *Allen* (1970), 397 U.S. 337.

8. *People* v. *Marsden* (1970), 2 Cal.3d 118.

9. *People* v. *Johnson* (1966), 241 Cal.App.2d 423.

10. *Schware* v. *Board of Bar Examiners* (1957), 353 U.S. 232.

11. *Hallinan* v. *Committee of Bar Examiners* (1966), 65 Cal.2d 447.

12. *Munoz* v. *U.S. District Court for C.D. of Cal.* (1971), 439 F.2d 1176, 446 F.2d 434, certiorari denied (1972), 404 U.S. 1059.

13. In *Sanders* v. *Russell* (1968), 401 F.2d 241, the court found a federal right to retain nonresident counsel in federal civil rights cases.

14. *Baird* v. *State Bar of Arizona* (1971), 401 U.S. 1, at p. 21, dissenting opinion.

15. Reported in 273 A2d 563 (1971).

16. *In re Sawyer* (1959), 360 U.S. 622.

17. *Smith* v. *Superior Court* (1968), 68 Cal.2d 547, 557–61.

18. *Sheppard* v. *Maxwell* (1966), 384 U.S. 333.

19. *Ex parte Terry* (1888), 128 U.S. 289, at pp. 308, 313.

20. *Cooper* v. *Superior Court* (1961), 55 Cal.2d 291. The quotations that follow are from pp. 298, 301.

21. *In re Hallinan* (1969), 71 Cal.2d 1179.

22. *Sacher* v. *United States* (1952), 343 U.S. 1, at p. 9.

23. Summary contempt at the conclusion of the trial was not appropriately exercisable in *Mayberry* v. *Pennsylvania* (1971), 400 U.S. 455.

24. *Offutt* v. *United States* (1954), 348 U.S. 11; *Cammer* v. *United States* (1956), 350 U.S. 399; *In re Sawyer* (1959), 360 U.S. 622; *In re Green* (1962), 369 U.S. 689; *In re McConnell* (1962), 370 U.S. 230; *Donovan* v. *City of Dallas* (1964), 377 U.S. 408; *Holt* v. *Virginia* (1965), 381 U.S. 131; *Bloom* v. *Illinois* (1968), 391 U.S. 194.

25. *Ungar* v. *Sarafite* (1964), 376 U.S. 575; *Nilva* v. *United States* (1957), 352 U.S. 385.

26. Jackson's views from *Sacher* v. *United States* (1952), 343 U.S. 1, 14.

27. *Jackson* v. *Denno* (1964), 378 U.S. 368, at p. 403.

28. Biographies of the United States Supreme Court Justices appear in *Who's Who in America* (37th ed.), Chicago, Marquis Who's Who (1972).

29. Biographies of the Lords of Appeal in Ordinary appear in *Who's Who, 1971–1972* (123rd ed.), St. Martin's Press (1971).

18/ONE SYSTEM OF COURTS

1. For debate in 1787 on the establishment of inferior federal courts, see Max Farrand, ed., *The Records of the Federal Convention of 1787,* New Haven, Yale University Press (1911), vol. I, pp. 21, 124–27; *The Federalist* (Modern Library ed.), New York, Random House (1937), No. 82, at pp. 534 ff.

2. *United States* v. *Hudson and Goodwin* (1812), 11 U.S. 32.

3. *Martin* v. *Hunter's Lessee* (1816), 14 U.S. 304, at p. 341–2.

4. A summary of the theory behind federal court regulation may be found in *Fay* v. *Noia* (1963), 372 U.S. 391, at pp. 408–412.

5. *Brown* v. *Allen* (1953), 344 U.S. 443, at p. 465.

6. Frankfurter's view appears in *Brown* v. *Allen* (1953), 344 U.S. 443, at p. 510; Warren's view appears in *Townsend* v. *Sain* (1963), 372 U.S. 293, at p. 318.

7. Brennan's views appear in *Kaufman* v. *United States* (1969), 394 U.S. 217, at

pp. 225–26; and in *Perez* v. *Ledesma* (1971), 401 U.S. 82, at p. 104, dissenting opinion.

8. *Imbler* v. *Craven* (1969), 298 F.Supp. 795.

9. The Canadian legal system is described in Frederick A. R. Chapman, *Fundamentals of Canadian Law,* Toronto, McGraw-Hill of Canada (1965), pp. 19–24.

10. The Australian legal system is described in Zelman Cowen, *Federal Jurisdiction in Australia,* Melbourne, Oxford University Press (1959); and Geoffrey Sawer, *Australian Federalism in the Courts,* Melbourne, Melbourne University Press (1967), pp. 15, 27–32.

11. For a proposal that state and federal courts be consolidated into one system, see Leslie L. Anderson, "The Line Between Federal and State Court Jurisdiction," *Mich. L.R.* (1965), 63:1203.

12. Jurisdiction of the lower federal courts is generally defined in 28 U.S.C., §§ 1331–1363, 2241–2255.

13. *Cary* v. *Curtis* (1845), 44 U.S. 236, at p. 245.

19 / ELITISM, ABSOLUTISM, AND TERM OLIGARCHY

1. Charles Evans Hughes, *Addresses* (2d ed. 1916), New York, G. P. Putnam's Sons, p. 185.

2. *United States* v. *Butler* (1936), 297 U.S. 1, at p. 79, dissenting opinion.

3. *Baldwin* v. *Missouri* (1930), 281 U.S. 586, at p. 595, dissenting opinion.

4. *Brown* v. *Allen* (1953), 344 U.S. 443, at p. 535, concurring opinion.

5. *A. F. of L.* v. *American Sash Co.* (1949), 335 U.S. 538, at pp. 555–56, concurring opinion.

6. *Berger* v. *New York* (1967), 388 U.S. 41, at p. 77, dissenting opinion.

7. *Oregon* v. *Mitchell* (1970), 400 U.S. 112, at p. 203, concurring and dissenting opinion.

8. The Supreme Court declared that it did not sit as a super-legislature in *Day-Brite Lighting, Inc.* v. *Missouri* (1952), 342 U.S. 421; did not sit as a super-board of education in *McCollum* v. *Board of Education* (1948), 333 U.S. 203, at p. 237, concurring opinion; and did not sit as a super-board of censors in *Kingsley Pictures Corp.* v. *Regents* (1959), 360 U.S. 684, at p. 690, concurring opinion.

9. *Shapiro* v. *Thompson* (1969), 394 U.S. 618 [legislation]; *Tinker* v. *Des Moines School Dist.* (1969), 393 U.S. 503 [school regulation]; *Jacobellis* v. *Ohio* (1964), 378 U.S. 184 [censorship].

10. *Griswold* v. *Connecticut* (1965), 381 U.S. 479.

11. *Miranda* v. *Arizona* (1966), 384 U.S. 436.

12. Judith Blake, "Abortion and Public Opinion: The 1960–1970 Decade," *Science* (1971), 171:540, at p. 548.

13. *Roe* v. *Wade* (1973), 410 U.S. 113.

14. *New York Times Co.* v. *United States* (1971), 403 U.S. 713, at pp. 741, 742–43.

15. *A. F. of L.* v. *American Sash Co.* (1949), 335 U.S. 538, at p. 553, concurring opinion.

16. The metaphor of the stork and the vulture is from Rudolph von Jhering, *The Struggle for Law* (2d Am. ed.), Chicago, Callaghan (1915), at p. 19.

17. Ralph Waldo Emerson, *Representative Men* (Rev. ed. 1889), Boston, Houghton Mifflin, p. 29.

18. Frankfurter's shock-to-conscience case is *Rochin* v. *California* (1952), 342 U.S. 165.

19. Senator Long's comment is found in Eugene C. Gerhart, ed., *Quote It,* (3rd ed. 1969), New York, Clark Broadman Co., at p. 614.

20. Roberts' statement is from the majority opinion in *United States* v. *Butler* (1936), 297 U.S. 1, at pp. 62–63.

21. John Austin, *The Province of Jurisprudence Determined* (2nd ed.), London, John Murrray (1861), p. 225.

22. Learned Hand, *The Spirit of Liberty* (3d ed. 1960), New York, Knopf, p. 260.

23. *Brown* v. *Board of Education* (1954), 347 U.S. 483; *Youngstown Sheet & Tube Co.* v. *Sawyer* (1952), 343 U.S. 579.

24. The four Supreme Court nominees who failed to secure Senate confirmation were Abe Fortas, Homer Thornberry, Clement F. Haynsworth, Jr., and G. Harrold Carswell.

20 / L'ENVOI

1. Hobbes, *Leviathan* (Oakeshott ed. 1946), Oxford, B. Blackwell, p. 94.

2. Learned Hand, *The Bill of Rights,* Cambridge, Harvard University Press, (1958), p. 70.

3. *The Federalist* (Modern Library ed.), New York, Random House (1937), No. 81, at pp. 523–24.

4. From T. S. Eliot, "The Hollow Men," in *The Complete Poems and Plays 1909–1950,* New York, Harcourt Brace Jovanovich (1962), p. 58.

5. *United States* v. *Butler* (1936), 297 U.S. 1, at p. 87.

6. *Missouri, Kansas & Texas Ry. Co.* v. *May* (1904), 194 U.S. 267, at p. 270.

7. *Douglas* v. *Jeannette* (1943), 319 U.S. 157, at p. 181.

INDEX